THE ECONOMY OF
TEXAS

TEXAS COUNCIL ON ECONOMIC EDUCATION

Editor
Calvin A. Kent, Ph.D.
Baylor University, Waco

Editorial Board
William A. Luker, Ed.D.
University of North Texas, Denton

Jay N. Welch
Texas Council on Economic Education, Houston

Clinton Daniels, Ph.D.
West Texas State University, Canyon

John B. McCall, Ph.D.
University of Texas at Arlington

Ruth Ellinger
Texas AFL-CIO, Austin

Gary Wood, Ph.D.
Texas Research League, Austin

Howard R. Yeargan
Southwest Texas State University, San Marcos

Jo Ann Sweeney, Ph.D.
University of Texas at Austin

Martha Schroeder
Baylor University, Waco

HB10AB
PUBLISHED BY
SOUTH-WESTERN PUBLISHING CO.
CINCINNATI, OH   WEST CHICAGO, IL   DALLAS, TX   LIVERMORE, CA

PREFACE

★

To most people, economics is a great mystery. The word itself creates fear among students: fear that a class in economics will be dull and fear that the subject itself is just too hard to be understood. Yet, at the same time, most of us recognize that nothing affects us more than does the economy of the nation, state, and community in which we live. Understanding economics is a survival skill. We need to comprehend the economic environment in which we live and make our living. By understanding the economy we will be able to make better choices as consumers, producers, and voters.

It is the purpose of this book to provide that economic understanding for those of you in Texas high schools. It is hoped that by the time you have finished this book you will be better informed as to why economic events happen and what the challenges and opportunities will be that will face you in the future.

Economics can be very abstract and confusing. This book hopes to remove that confusion by giving concrete examples from the Texas economy which illustrate the theories and ideas of economics.

A glance at the table of contents should stimulate the reader's interest. This book begins with the basics. There are certain terms and ideas that all of us need to understand before we can go forward with an inquiry into the economy of our state. The chapters in Part I provide a foundation for economic analysis that you will be able to use and apply as you tackle the other chapters. What these chapters stress is that economics is the science of decision making. All of us have to make decisions. Sometimes we have to select the

best from many desirable alternatives. Sometimes we have to select the least bad from a list of bad options. In either case, economic principles will help us to make the right choices.

Part II deals with the economic regions of Texas. It has often been suggested that Texas could be split into several states each with its own distinct personality and economy. This section looks at how an economist might divide Texas. No one is seriously suggesting that this be done because each region supports and sustains the others. There is no reason why this state should be split, but each of these regions has a distinct economy that distinguishes it from the economies of the other regions of the state.

While there are some economic problems that are common to all regions, each region has its own set of challenges which it must meet in the future. Many Texans assume that what is going on in their part of the state is the same as what is going on in other parts of the state. These people will be surprised to find that the economy of West Texas is very different from that of the Houston bay area, the border, or the piney woods of eastern Texas.

Part III looks at what economists call "the economic base." The term refers to the foundations of the Texas economy. What industries and economic activities are generating the jobs and income for us Texans? When students leave school, where are they likely to find employment opportunities and the best chances of making a high enough income to support themselves and their families?

Eleven major industries in Texas are featured. The purpose of these chapters is to introduce the student to the importance of each industry in the Texas economy and to that industry's outlook and problems. Oftentimes people living in Houston recognize the importance of oil and gas, but fail to understand the problems of Texas' second most important industry, which is agriculture. By the same token, people who are not directly involved in tourism do not often recognize that this is one of the fastest growing industries in the state and a major contributor to our economy.

Some parts of the Texas economy are not prospering. Oil and gas are suffering, as are Texas financial institutions which lent large amounts of money to oil and gas firms and real estate developers. Other industries are prospering. Research and development has propelled Texas to the forefront of the nation. Recreation and entertainment is a growth industry. Health care has experienced a spectacular growth in the United States, and Texas is becoming a health care center.

Nothing happens in an economy unless people cause it to happen. Part IV examines the role of people in the Texas economy. There is a very special type of person called the "entrepreneur" who is responsible for economic progress. Entrepreneurs take the risks to bring new ideas and technology to the marketplace. Texas has always provided a fertile environment for entrepreneurship. Will it continue to do so?

Will the Texas labor force be able to meet the demands of the state's rapidly changing economy? As Texas moves into the high tech era, most of the jobs being generated will require a high level of skills and sophistication. Will Texas students be prepared? What about labor unions? Can they contribute to the growth and the development of the state?

It is unfortunate, but true, that some groups of people have been left behind by the growth and development of the Texas economy. What can we do about the migrants, the unskilled and the aged? How can they be included in the prosperity of the state?

Part V is concerned with government in the Texas economy. Government is a true growth industry for the state. More and more the people of Texas have asked their state government to provide them with new and higher quality services. But these services must be paid for, and Texans have been reluctant to foot the bill. These chapters raise several questions. Where does the state get its revenue? Are there better sources than those currently used? How does the state spend its money? What are the priorities of the state as reflected in the state's budget?

What about the crisis in financing the state's schools? Should we revise the way that we pay for elementary and secondary education?

Money is certainly important and the money supply in the country is controlled by the Federal Reserve System. One of the federal reserve banks is located in Dallas. How it operates and affects the economy of our state and the southwest is investigated.

Texans pay taxes to Washington and Washington spends money in Texas. Do we break even? If we don't, should we? All these questions can be answered after a review of these chapters.

There are certain issues facing the Texas economy. These issues, discussed in Part VI, pose questions which must be answered if the state is going to continue to prosper and grow. How can we sufficiently upgrade our educational offerings so that we can provide the wide variety of educational experiences that our students and economy demand? What is the responsibility of the schools in providing quality education and how much is the responsibility of the home?

The one continuing thought throughout this book has been that the Texas economy needs to diversify. In the past it has been too reliant, first on farming and now on oil and gas, for our prosperity. How can the state branch into new and different industries? What can be done to decrease the reliance of Texas on just one or two major industries in the future? What new types of business should we try to attract?

Texas is becoming more and more a part of the world. It used to be that Texans did not need to worry about what went on outside our borders. This is no longer true. World economic developments are becoming crucial to the prosperity and growth of Texas. What must Texas industry do to adapt? Can we compete, not only with other American firms, but with those located in Japan, Europe, and elsewhere?

Part VII provides a brief economic history of Texas. Where we are today is the result of where we have been in the past. The character of Texas has been molded, not so much by current events, but by what happened in the past. Until recent years, Texas has not been a rich state. What caused our transformation? Why are we now among the world's most prosperous people? What were the problems that Texans faced when the state was first settled, and when the state was an independent nation? How well did we survive the Civil War, Reconstruction, and the Great Depression? After the great prosperity of the 1970s, how are we dealing with the bust of the 1980s? Where will we be in the future?

There is a Teacher's Manual which accompanies this book. It contains teaching objectives and an overview of the major points in each chapter. Key concepts and terms are highlighted. Answers are provided for the questions at the end of each chapter in the text. The purpose of the manual is to assist the teacher in using the text in a variety of classes such as economics, government, U.S. history, Texas history, business, or Texas problems.

This book contains 45 chapters written by people who are experts in the area in which they write. Some of them are academicians located at the finest colleges and universities in the state. Some are government officials responsible for developing and executing the economic policies that will guide our state. Others are involved in business, actually making the hard decisions. These writers represent many diverse points of view. Like most individuals, they have opinions, and they have not been reluctant in expressing their views in these chapters. None of them pretends to have the final word, but all of them convey valuable insights to the readers. It is their hope that Texans will gain a better understanding and appreciation of Texas and of the role that they will play in the continued growth of the state into the future.

CONTENTS

3
THE ECONOMIC BASE

4
PEOPLE IN THE TEXAS ECONOMY

5
GOVERNMENT IN THE TEXAS ECONOMY

6
ISSUES IN THE TEXAS ECONOMY

7
THE ECONOMIC HISTORY OF TEXAS

1

BASIC ECONOMIC CONCEPTS

In this book, you will learn about the economy of our state. Maybe you have asked yourself, "Where will I find a job when I have completed my education?" Perhaps you have wondered about the news stories you read and hear, how the price of oil affects the number of jobs in Texas and what wages those jobs pay. You may have been told about Texas becoming one of the world centers for high technology and research and asked how that might impact your future. This book will answer those questions and most others you will have about Texas' and your economic future.

This first part of the book deals with basic economic concepts. It lets you know how economists think and look at the world. You will gain a new vocabulary and new insights about the world of work.

In the first chapter you will learn the economic facts of life. Simply put, we have to make choices. We won't be able to earn enough income to buy everything we want so we will have to choose. The same choices face our nation and our state. Some things must be given up so we can have others. This is called the problem of scarcity.

The problem of scarcity is universal. How it is solved depends on what type of economic system a society chooses. The types of economic systems are discussed in Chapter 2. There are three choices for an economic system: traditional, command, and market. What are the characteristics, strengths, and weaknesses of each? You will find the answers in Chapter 2.

Chapter 3 is concerned with statistics. To understand economics, you need to know how economists measure. There is no way to avoid statistics. You are constantly hearing words and phrases like price indexes, unemployment rates, changes in the gross national product. What these mean will be explained in this chapter. If you find statistics confusing now, don't worry, this chapter will clear the mystery.

Our economy is organized according to the principles of the free enterprise or market system. Most of us are enthusiastic supporters of that system but we do not fully understand what it involves. How does a market economy work? Why has it worked so well for all Texans and all Americans? In this chapter, you will also find out something about the key person in a market economy, the entrepreneur.

1

Making decisions is hard work. We often would rather not choose, but we must. Economics has a lot to say about how we make choices. The economic way of choice making can be used to make decisions that do not necessarily involve economic issues. Chapter 5 concerns decision making. When you have learned its lessons, making decisions will not be any easier, but you will be able to make better ones.

1

THE ECONOMIC PROBLEM: SCARCITY

William A. Luker, Ed.D.[1]
and
Geneva Jo Luker[2]

Life is so much more interesting—and uncertain—because we have to make choices. The choosing process often includes such perplexing questions as how to use money, time, energy—or any of the wide variety of resources available to us. Whatever the choices, one thing is certain: We cannot escape life's choosing dilemma. But then, who would want to? The element of choice adds excitement and intrigue to our lives. But did you know that choosing lies at the heart of economics? Let's examine some fundamental economic ideas to see how our choices relate to the basic economic problem.

OPPORTUNITY COSTS OF CHOICES

Everyone agrees that every day we make a multitude of choices. Not so well understood, however, is that we cannot separate choosing from the *costs* of choices. In economics, we call the consequences of choices, **opportunity costs**. Multiple alternatives create choice; otherwise, no choosing is necessary. When you select from several possible alternatives, you must discard or give up some options. If you choose to do or to have one thing, you lose the "opportunity" to do or to have other things. So with every choice, something is given up. Whatever we lose or give up defines the *opportunity cost* of our choice.

For instance, what activity did you give up in order to spend your time reading this chapter? Whatever activity you put aside to allow time for study was the opportunity cost of your decision. Choosing one activity meant losing an opportunity to experience another.

Two examples will help you understand the importance of opportunity costs. Imagine that your summer earnings afford you the "opportunity" to buy either an expensive automobile or a trip to Europe. If you pick the car, you gain the ride at the "cost" of not having the new adventure. Or pretend that you have the choice on election day of voting for a bond issue. If passed, the bond issue will increase your taxes, allowing the city to buy land and equipment for flood control. Voting "no" on the tax increase means losing the opportunity to have the peace of mind related to controlling the force of a potentially wide river. On the the other hand, a voter decision to control the river would result in the loss of individual choice in spending one's money as desired.

ECONOMIZING AND MAXIMIZING

Every choice has effects (opportunity costs) that force us to **economize**. In the process of choosing

[1]Dean, School of Community Service, University of North Texas.
[2]Consultant.

the greatest welfare and happiness we *economize* when we focus on what we lose when we choose. In economics, we call the process of choosing to gain the greatest benefit, **maximizing**.

RELATIVE SCARCITY

Why must we constantly choose and economize? We find the answer in the idea of **relative scarcity**. Without scarcity, there would be no need to choose, no opportunity costs, no need to economize, no **economic problem** to solve. But relative scarcity, a perpetual reality of life, forces us to choose.

The discipline of economics defines scarcity in a special way. To be scarce, goods and services must satisfy two particulars. First, a scarce good or service is *useful* or *valued* by someone. Second, a scarce good or service is in *limited quantity* compared to the degree to which people want it.

For example, suppose that a limited number of broken guitars lie as discards in the closets of America. Although limited in number, these guitars are not scarce. Who wants to play a song with a broken guitar? Practically no one; and the limited supply of broken guitars doesn't change their status. In economic terms, they are not scarce since no one values or wants them. These objects of fun, once prized, lie unwanted and ignored. Although these few broken guitars are *rare*, they are not *scarce* because nobody wants them. A good or service can be scarce while also being abundant. The bicycle industry produces millions of bicycles each year. Although plentiful, they are still relatively scarce because the supply of bicycles is not sufficient to satisfy the needs of all the people who want them.

Thus, the economic use of the expression *scarcity* is modified by the term *relative*. The term *relative scarcity* applies to goods and services that are scarce relative to the degree to which users want them.

An additional example clarifies this idea. Consider the problem of space exploration. In this environment, oxygen, limited in supply and urgently needed by all living organisms, is all that stands between you and catastrophe. In this setting, oxygen is scarce. Because of oxygen's scarcity, careful choices must be made about its use. Survival may depend on whether you conserve it.

Contrast that scene with a picnic by a beautiful lake. Its cool, clear air is abundant. The air is not economically scarce. Picnickers frolic about with no thought of choosing or economizing.

SHIFTING GEARS: FROM INDIVIDUALS TO SOCIETIES

So far, we have treated scarcity (the *economic problem*) from the point of view of the individual. By shifting gears to a broader scene, we find that the economic problem of relative scarcity also applies to societies. All societies have in common the problem of how to satisfy the needs and desires for a whole range of goods and services such as food, housing, medical care, education, transportation, and recreation. But we must *produce* these goods and services. In order to produce goods and services, we must bring together resources in the form of human effort (*labor*), human-made tools of production like machines and factories (*capital*), and raw materials like soil, timber, water, oil, and minerals (*land*). At any given time or place, however, productive resources are always scarce relative to the collective "I wants" of societies. In other words, people cannot have everything they want. This scarcity of productive resources, relative to the collective "I wants" of society, defines the *economic problem* and makes it necessary for the society to economize.

Unlimited "I wants," then, go hand in hand with limited productive capacity. The limited resources of land, labor and capital, compared with the almost infinite "I wants" of the people, define the economic problem. Therefore, all societies face the problem of relative scarcity.

WHAT TO PRODUCE?

Relative scarcity defines the economic problem. This scarcity forces every society to deal with a set of sub-problems. The first, and most important, is: *What* should a society produce? First consideration must be given to providing the basic needs of people—food, shelter, and clothing. In economically underdeveloped societies, few resources are left for producing anything else. The case is different in our country because we have developed, expanded, and improved our productive resources. This expanded resource base confronts us with a mind-staggering number of choices. For instance, should we use the scarce resource of *land* for office buildings, homes, or baseball parks? Should we develop more and better highways, or mass transit? Remembering that every choice has opportunity costs, can you see the difficulty every economic system has in answering the question, What to produce?

HOW TO PRODUCE?

Besides deciding what to produce, every society must have a method of deciding *how* to produce. The scarce resources of land, labor, and capital must be brought together as productive units to satisfy the needs and wants of society.

FOR WHOM TO PRODUCE?

Every society also has to solve the problem of who is to get the economic output of the system. In other words, how does society determine the division of the supply of goods and services among the members of the society? For example, should we distribute society's output equally, or should the division depend upon how much each person contributes to the total output?

ECONOMIC GROWTH

Another related problem in dealing with scarcity is **economic growth**. Whether you and your school friends are able to have satisfying careers depends largely on economic growth. To create growth, economies throughout the world must insure that the amount of goods and services produced increases at a faster rate than the population. Comparing an economy to your family enables you to see the truth of this statement. Assume that your parents have a comfortable house with enough food and other goods to insure that each member has a pleasant life. Ask yourself what changes would occur if one hundred people came to live permanently with you. That would be quite an impressive crowd to make beds and biscuits for. Similarly, a nation's total output of goods and services must run well ahead of population growth in order to produce enough basic goods, and perhaps some luxuries, for everyone. So all modern economic systems strive

for constant growth of the economic "pie." Without growth, the general well-being suffers.

The growth of an economy depends upon the use of its base of knowledge and skills to produce all the **capital goods**—machines, tractors, computers, power lines, etc.—needed to keep production increasing. As people in a society invent and put to use new and better capital goods, the economy grows faster.

SUMMARY

Choice making and economics go hand in hand. With every choice something must be given up. The options given up when a choice is made are the opportunity costs of the choice. The opportunity costs of choosing force us to economize. Economizing means gaining from our choices the maximum amount of happiness and well-being. The universal condition that forces us to choose and to economize is relative scarcity, the economic problem.

Like individuals, societies also face the problem of relative scarcity. As with individuals, the need for choice and economizing arises because the resources of land, labor, and capital are scarce relative to their capacity to produce what we want. For a society, the economic problem takes the form of What to produce? How to produce? For whom to produce? and how to achieve economic growth. Chapter 2 addresses the question of how different societies solve the economic problem.

CONTENT QUESTIONS

1. What are the limited resources of society (i.e., what are the resources of production)?
2. What are the basic needs of people?
3. What questions must a society answer in order to solve the economic problem?

DISCUSSION QUESTIONS

1. Have students, as a class, cite opportunity cost decisions they have made in the last

week. List these decisions on the board to illustrate how many opportunity cost decisions are made by all of us.

2. As a class discuss items of relative scarcity for students. List these items on the board.

COMPARING ECONOMIC SYSTEMS

William D. Witter, Ph.D[1]
and
William McKee, Ph.D.[2]

We have seen that society has to find answers to some basic questions: What to produce? How to produce? Who will receive the output? Every society must choose a method for organizing its resources to find solutions to these problems. The method by which a society organizes its resources to solve economic problems is called its economic *system*. A computer and the human body are systems, with many parts working together as a whole. An economic system consists of producing units, distributing units, and consuming units working together. Economists have identified three basic types of economic systems: *tradition*, *command*, and *the market*.

TRADITION

Rules and beliefs handed down from the past form the basis for **traditional economic systems.** No young person in a traditional society asks why something is done, or suggests change! Each new generation accepts the customs without question and passes them on to the next. In traditional societies custom solves the problem of scarcity by *eliminating* choice. Primitive agricultural societies exist in which people have learned from their ancestors what to plant, the method of planting, and how to harvest crops. They answer the economic questions of What? How? and For whom? by following the rules set down by tradition. Since traditional societies resist the introduction of new tools or production methods, they neither face the problems of change nor experience the benefits of economic growth.

Traditional economies have some unquestionable advantages. For instance, those who live in traditional societies tend to feel more secure than people living in other economic systems. They do not have to acquire the education and skills needed to compete and survive in a modern society. No choices on complex issues are necessary. They are not asked to answer the kind of questions which perplex young people in our society. What do I want to be when I grow up? What do people expect of me? Whom shall I marry? The questions go on and on, but the point is that traditional societies provide a support and control system which excludes most personal and social decision making.

For some, such an environment has an appeal because it eliminates the uncertainty of choosing. For those who are uncomfortable with choice and risk, the security of traditional systems justifies its disadvantages. From another perspective, the security of tradition is not worth its cost — the giving up of personal freedom, cultural variation, economic growth, the stimulus of change, and, often, economic well-being.

[1]Assistant Professor, Institute of Applied Economics; Director, Center for Economic Education, University of North Texas.
[2]Associate Professor, Labor and Industrial Relations, University of North Texas.

COMMAND

The dictionary defines *command* as "to have control over or direct with authority." A **command economic system** places the authority to direct and control economic activity in the hands of a central group. Government leaders command economic activities after deciding the needs of the people and the country. Two examples of command economies are the Soviet Union and mainland China.

Here is an example of the way a command economy works. Suppose central planners decide that they need more tractors to increase food production. They direct factories to switch from the production of automobiles to tractors. Since resources are scarce, this decision involves both getting something and giving up something. The opportunity cost of the planners' choice is fewer private automobiles; the gain is more tractors to increase food production.

The distribution of output, also determined by central authority, focuses first on meeting the basic needs of the people. In return, the planners expect all people to contribute their efforts to making the system function smoothly. After the basic needs are met, the "I wants" of people have little influence on what else is available for consumption or investment or on how it is distributed.

The economic planners realize the importance of growth in a modern command system. Their authority enables them to direct productive resources in directions they believe will achieve economic growth.

Command economies have both strengths and weaknesses. The principal strength of command economies lies in the ability of central planners to carry out crash programs involving large flows of productive resources. The Russian Sputnik is an example of a successful allocation of large amounts of available resources to a single project.

One of the principal weaknesses of a command system is the inability of planners to make fully rational economic decisions (to calculate opportunity costs). This is an inevitable consequence of the complexities of the modern world.

Another problem of command economies is their reliance on large organizations, or bureaucracies. While essential to making a command economy work, these organizations tend to be unmanageable because of coordination and communication problems. Forecasts of resource needs and output tend to be highly unreliable. Information "overload" is common. Problems of internal control, irresponsibility, and motivation are also common to command bureaucracies. Too often, bureaucrats are insensitive and unresponsive to the needs of their clients.

Command economies also sacrifice personal freedom. Because central planners have the power to allocate resources, the people must accept their decisions even if they desire something else.

THE MARKET

The third system for solving the economic problem is the **market economic system**. Our country uses a form of the market, called free enterprise. The market system is also called *private enterprise* or *capitalism*. In a market system many persons take part in making choices. Consumers, producers, savers, investors, workers, managers, and owners all play active roles. Market systems have two major goals:

1. to satisfy efficiently the "I wants" of the people, and
2. to allow as much freedom of choice as possible.

The market has many sellers competing for a chance to supply the goods and services demanded by consumers. As a result, the market constantly increases the number and type of goods and services and provides more freedom of choice. The competition prevents monopolies and eliminates inefficient producers. Thus, competition keeps the cost of production and prices low, allowing more people to buy the output.

In the **free enterprise system**, the individual consumer decides what is produced. Market economies use the purchases of consumers as signals to tell it what to produce. These purchases become consumer votes for these products. Therefore, the economic system's productive ear is always finely tuned to the collective cries of "I want!" and "I'll buy!" These voices provide the chorus from which the system takes its direction on what and how to produce.

How does the free enterprise system respond to these signals? Special persons called **entrepreneurs** are the key. They carefully monitor how the public spends (or expects to spend) its money. Using the insights gained from taking the buying pulse, entrepreneurs organize the economic resources of land, labor, and capital into business enterprises to produce the goods and services the people want.

Modern economic systems use money (not barter) as a medium of exchange. In such economies, the more money income one has, the more one is able to consume the goods and services produced by that system. Therefore, the question of who gets the output becomes one of income distribution. Remember that economists have identified three resources involved in production: land, labor, and capital.

In a market economy a fourth resource is **entrepreneurship**. The market distributes income according to the contribution of resources to producing goods and services. The four categories of income are:

1. *Rent.* Landlords receive *rent* for making available the land resource.
2. *Wage.* Human contributions such as manual work, managerial skills, engineering knowledge, creative intelligence, and physical strength represent labor's contribution to the productive process and, in exchange for these contributions, the workers earn a *wage*.
3. *Interest.* For providing money to purchase new capital equipment the capitalist receives *interest*.
4. *Profit.* To create and operate business enterprises requires the taking of economic risks, organizing skills and the talent to control the operation and direction of the enterprise. For fulfilling these economic roles in the productive process, the entrepreneur obtains an income called *profit*.

How does the free enterprise system achieve economic growth? The market economy uses the profit motive. As entrepreneurs strive to increase profits by reducing costs, they constantly search for improved methods of production. This leads to the use of more efficient tools of production and to economic growth and development.

In summary, the market solves the problems of What? How? and For whom? and the problem of economic growth by using individual self-interest. Market systems assume that everyone wants to live better, and use that common spark to motivate people to produce more and better goods and services. Workers exchange their labor for a *wage* to buy the things they want. Owners gain a *profit* for the risks they take in starting and controlling businesses. Owners use their income for consumption and *investing* in new equipment to expand production.

MIXED ECONOMIES

We have looked at the workings of three economic systems. Few societies today, however, use any system in its pure form. Instead, modern economies adopt elements of all three, resulting in mixed economic systems. In dealing with the problem of scarcity in an ever-changing world, nations adopt methods that show promise for them at any given time. Most modern societies have mixed economies with one major theme that gives each a personality of its own.

For example, economists call the Soviet Union a command system. Yet it uses many methods borrowed from the market. For example, wages are often used as motivators, a device taken from market systems. Threads of tradition and custom, tightly woven into the fabric of every society, unravel slowly. In many modern market economies, women are "traditionally" paid lower wages for doing the same tasks as their male counterparts. Methods borrowed from command theory are also used by all economies, including free enterprise. Many laws and regulations exist which place controls on individual freedom and entrepreneurial efforts. Also, education is an economic activity primarily produced by some level of government. So, for these and many other reasons, our economy is not a pure market system.

The economic organization of Japan is an example of an evenly balanced mixture. The Japanese mixture calls for large helpings of tradition, command, and market methods. This mixture is unlike either the Soviet or American system, and has a special flavor of its own.

SUMMARY

Three types of economic systems, tradition, command, and the market, represent prototypes. But no society adheres to a pure form of economic organization. In dealing with scarcity in a dynamic world, nations adopt methods that show promise for them at any given time. In Chapter 3, we examine some procedures for measuring the performance of our economy.

CONTENT QUESTIONS

1. List the resources of production and the income associated with each one for a market economy.

2. What are the three basic types of economic systems?
3. What are the three working units that make up an economic system?

DISCUSSION QUESTIONS

1. As a class cite portions of our economy that represent the three types of economic systems: tradition, command, and market.
2. List the advantages and disadvantages of using the market system as far as your own personal decisions are concerned.

3
STATISTICAL CONCEPTS

Jill A. Trask[1]
and
Walton Sharp, Ph.D.[2]

Wages, prices, unemployment rates and gross national product are examples of statistical measurements one meets in the study of the American free enterprise system. These quantitative measurements are essential to explaining economic ideas and evaluating the performance of the economy. This chapter will introduce you to some basic statistical concepts. This will enhance your understanding and interpretation of economic data, as well as prevent you from being misled by data.

ARITHMETIC MEAN

A number which represents information about a group of numbers is called a measure of central tendency. One such number which we frequently use is a type of average called the **arithmetic mean**. It is derived by adding all the observations on a phenomenon of interest and dividing by the total number of observations.

In Table 3-1, our phenomenon of interest is income, labelled a variable since its values may vary. To compute the arithmetic mean, we add the income of the ten persons and divide by ten ($200,000 / 10 = $20,000). This is the average income of the ten individuals. Stated in statistical terms, this is the arithmetic mean (average) of

[1]Associate Director, Center for Economic Education, University of North Texas.
[2]Assistant Professor, Labor and Industrial Relations, University of North Texas.

TABLE 3-1
Illustration of Arithmetic Mean, Median and Mode

Person Number	Income	
1	$99,000	
2	29,000	Arithmetic mean:
3	15,000	$20,000
4	12,000	
5	10,000	Median: $9,500 (five
6	9,000	observations are above
7	9,000	it and five below it)
8	8,000	
9	5,000	Mode: $9,000 (occurs
10	4,000	most frequently)

the ten observations (persons) on the variable (income).

MEDIAN

A second measure of central tendency is the **median**. It is the value which has half the observations above it and half the observations below it. In Table 3-1, there is no middle observation. Rather, the middle point lies between two observations. That point is between persons 5 and 6. Half the observations are above this point and half the observations are below it. When the number of observations is an even number, in this case ten, we add the two observations together and divide by two to obtain the median. Thus,

11

$$\text{Median} = \frac{\$10,000 + \$9,000}{2} = \$9,500$$

Five observations occur below this value, and five observations occur above it.

MODE

A third measure of central tendency is the **mode**. It is the value which occurs most often. In Table 3-1, $9,000 occurs twice, and all other values occur only once. Therefore, $9,000 is the mode.

RELATIONSHIP BETWEEN MEAN, MEDIAN, AND MODE

Table 3-1 shows the relative positions of these three measures of central tendency. Note that the extreme value of one of the observations (Person #1) pulls the mean away from the median and the mode. Another way of demonstrating the influence of extreme values in the observations is to replace $99,000 with $30,000 and calculate the mean. The mean is now $13,100. The median and the mode do not change.

Now consider the relationship between the mean, the median and the mode when the distribution of the observations is perfectly symmetrical, as in Table 3-2. In this instance, they are all the same: $6,000.

If central tendency is a number which represents a group of observations, the distribution of the observations may determine which is the more representative: the mean, the median or the mode. With a distribution that is perfectly symmetrical or nearly so, as in Table 3-2, it may not matter. However, when the observations are characterized by extreme values, as in Table 3-1, the median or the mode may be more representative than the mean. Which measure would you use as an indicator of general economic well-being for the observations in Table 3-1? The median or the mode is probably more representative since extreme values do not affect them.

RELATIONSHIP BETWEEN MEAN AND TOTAL

One must also be careful in making comparisons between a mean and a total. The use of totals might be misleading. Consider the information in Table 3-3 comparing total personal income for four states for the year 1984. It looks as though Texas fares much better than the other states based upon total or aggregate personal income. However, when we take into account the size of the population responsible for producing the total personal income and calculate the **per capita** personal income, a different picture emerges. Note that total personal income in Texas was more than double that of Massachusetts, whereas per capita personal income in Texas was about 85 percent of that of Massachusetts; and that total personal income in Mississippi was almost four times as large as that of Vermont, whereas per capita personal income in Mississippi was about 81 percent of that of Vermont.

Per capita personal income is an average, total personal income divided by the population. It does not tell us anything about the distribution of income. Table 3-3 also contains the median per capita income for each state. Note that in all instances, the median is below the mean. Extremely large incomes have the effect of inflating the average above the median. We can conclude that the distribution of income is not symmetrical, nor would we expect it to be.

CONSUMER PRICE INDEX

Another useful tool for examining aspects of the economy is index numbers. One commonly used index is the **Consumer Price Index** as a measure of inflation. It measures the general rise in

TABLE 3-2
Illustration of the Mean, Median and Mode in a Symmetrical Series

Person Number	Income
1	$8,000
2	7,000
3	7,000
4	6,000
5	6,000
6	6,000
7	6,000
8	5,000
9	5,000
10	4,000

TABLE 3-3
Incomes in Four States in 1984

State	Total Personal Income (mil. dol.)	Per Capita Personal Income	Per Capita Median Income
Texas	$201,013	$12,572	$ 9,443
Massachusetts	85,709	14,784	10,517
Mississippi	22,802	8,777	6,801
Vermont	5,723	10,802	8,319

Source: U.S. Bureau of the Census, *State and Metropolitan Area Data Book, 1986* (Washington, D.C.: U.S. Government Printing Office, 1986), p. 128.

the prices of goods and services. A monthly sample of the prices of a representative market basket of goods and services purchased by consumers forms the basis of the Consumer Price Index. The official CPI contains over 400 items, and the statistical procedures used in its construction are very sophisticated.

A hypothetical example will demonstrate its construction as well as another statistical measurement, *the weighted average.* Table 3-4 lists three items: bread, sweaters and gasoline, with

TABLE 3-4
Price and Quantity Consumed of Three Items in 1973–74

Item	1973 Price	1974 Price	Quantity
Bread	$ .40	$ .45	70 loaves
Sweaters	$12.00	$12.50	2 sweaters
Gasoline	$ .30	$ .60	400 gallons

the prices and quantities consumed in two different years. One might compute the arithmetic mean; that is, one might add the three prices for the first year and divide by three, yielding $4.23. For the second year, the average price calculated in this manner would be $4.52. One might erroneously conclude that prices have risen by 6.8 percent ($4.52/$4.23). However, consumers purchase different quantities of the items. The proper way to build the index is to weight each

year's prices by the quantities purchased, as in Table 3-5.

The calculations in Table 3-5 show that the same "market basket" of goods which cost $172.00 in 1973 cost $296.50 in 1974. To find the rate of inflation, divide the increase of $124.50 ($296.50 - $172.00) by $172.00, the base from which we started. The quotient is .72. Thus, the price of our "market basket" has risen by 72 percent, due mainly to a doubling of gasoline prices.

Table 3-6 contains actual values of the Consumer Price Index and selected components for several years, using the base year of 1967. So in 1967 the index was 100.0. Between 1967 and 1973, the price increases of motor fuels and energy were below that of the CPI for all items. By 1980, both were above the CPI for all items. Another way of looking at the table is to look at what happened to prices between 1967 and 1980. The CPI for all items increased almost two and one-half times; the CPI for motor fuels increased over three and one-half times; and the CPI for energy increased slightly over three times.

The importance of this information is the effect it has on the purchasing power of the consumer. Thus, if the consumer had the same number of dollars to spend, the consumer could buy only about 40 percent of the goods formerly purchased (100.0/246.8 = .407). Another way of

TABLE 3-5
Calculation of Weighted Average Prices

Item	1973: P × Q	1974: P × Q
Bread	$ .40 × 70 = $ 28.00	$ .45 × 70 = $ 31.50
Sweaters	12.00 × 2 = 24.00	12.50 × 2 = 25.00
Gasoline	.30 × 400 = 120.00	.60 × 400 = 240.00
TOTALS	$172.00	$296.50

TABLE 3-6
Consumer Price Index

Year	CPI (all items)	Motor Fuels	Energy
1967	100.0	100.0	100.0
1973	133.1	118.1	126.4
1974	147.7	159.9	145.8
1979	217.4	265.6	257.8
1980	246.8	369.1	301.8

Source: Economic Report of the President, 1988.

viewing this is that a consumer would have to have wage increases of 40 percent to be able to purchase the same level of goods and services.

REAL AND NOMINAL

This background in the measure of a rise in the general level of prices, inflation, helps in the understanding of two other important statistical concepts encountered in economics, *real* and *nominal*. Real and Nominal are used in the measurement of wage increases and in the measurement of economic growth, **gross national product**.

Suppose that wages in 1973 average $10,000 and $12,500 in 1974. The increase in nominal wages is $2,500 or 25 percent. This does not consider the increased cost of goods and services. Assume that the CPI was 100 in 1973 and was 110 in 1974; then $10,000 is worth that amount in 1973 purchasing power ($10,000 / 1.00). How much is $12,500 worth in 1974? Dividing the level of nominal wages in 1974 by the CPI in 1974

($12,500 / 1.10) results in a quotient of $11,363. This is the real wage; that is, it is the wage increase adjusted for inflation. The increase in real wages is $1363 or an increase of 13.63 percent.

Inflation also affects gross national product, the annual increase in the dollar value of goods and services produced in a given year. One must distinguish between **nominal growth** in GNP and **real growth** in GNP. Table 3-7 shows nominal and real growth in GNP for selected years measured in 1982 dollars. Thus, 1982 equals 100.0.

Nominal GNP increased by 3.7 percent from 1982 to 1983. Adjusting for inflation, real GNP actually declined by 2.5 percent. The year 1982 indicates a recession since real GNP declined from the previous year. Thus, the dollar volume of goods and services purchased was lower than the preceding year.

The interpretation of economic data warrants another reminder. The rate of economic growth is always somewhat overstated when the nation emerges from a recession. This is because the base is lower than that of the preceding year. In Table 3-7, real GNP in 1982 is below that of 1981. Thus, it is a lower base compared to real GNP for 1983. To demonstrate this, consider what the rate of growth would have been if the economy had experienced no growth or decline between 1981 and 1982. Real GNP would have stayed at $3,248.8. If we measured 1983 real GNP against this, the rate of growth would have been less than 1 percent. So some of the growth in real GNP was needed to return the economy to its 1981 level of real GNP.

TABLE 3-7
Nominal and Real Gross National Product
($ bil.)

Year	Nominal GNP	Percent Change	Real GNP	Percent Change
1981	$3,052.6		$3,248.8	
1982	$3,166.0	3.7	$3,166.0	−2.5
1983	$3,405.7	7.6	$3,279.1	3.6
1984	$3,772.2	10.8	$3,501.4	6.8
1985	$4,010.3	6.3	$3,607.5	3.0
1986	$4,235.0	5.6	$3,713.3	2.9

Source: Economic Report of the President, 1988.

CONTENT QUESTIONS

1. What is the arithmetic mean income in Table 3-8?
2. What is the median income in Table 3-8?
3. What is the mode income in Table 3-8?
4. What causes the arithmetic mean income to be higher than the median and mode incomes in Table 3-8?

DISCUSSION QUESTIONS

1. What base year is being used in Table 3-9?
2. By what percentage did prices rise between 1977 and 1981?
3. If a person's salary was $10,000 in 1977 and increased to $12,500 in 1981, what was their actual purchasing power in 1981?

TABLE 3-8
Income of Ten Persons

Person Number	Annual Income
1	$100,000
2	50,000
3	20,000
4	10,000
5	8,000
6	8,000
7	8,000
8	6,000
9	5,000
10	5,000

TABLE 3-9
Consumer Price Index for Econville

Year	CPI
1977	100
1978	110
1979	130
1980	140
1981	160

4

HUMAN BEHAVIOR AND THE BASIC INSTITUTIONS OF FREE ENTERPRISE MARKETS

Jill A. Trask[1]
and
Walton Sharp, Ph.D[2]

The basic institution which makes the free enterprise system work is the market. By the market, we mean the interplay of the **demand** for goods and the **supply** of goods.

Consumers, businesses, and units of government generate *demand*. In general, the lower the price of a good, the more demand there is for the good. The higher the price of a good, the less demand there is for the good. Because of this, we say that demand is characterized by an inverse relationship between the price of a good and the quantity demanded.

Producers make goods available. The lower the price of the good, the less of the good they will be willing to *supply*. This means profits are lower. The higher the price of the good, the more of it they will be willing to supply. We say that supply is characterized by a positive relationship between price and quantity.

The interplay of supply and demand tends toward an equilibrium. This is the point at which price will clear the market of goods. Stated another way, there is a price at which goods produced satisfy demand.

The market model assumes that humans are **maximizers**. This means that humans strive to

get the most pleasure from a given expenditure of resources with the least pain. In the workplace, people invent more efficient ways to do the job. As consumers; people shop for the lowest price in relation to quality.

Another dimension of the market model assumes that individuals are **rational**. One brand of compact disc player may carry a lower price tag than another. Does this mean that consumers will prefer it? Not necessarily. They want to know such things as the durability of the product. Will it work when purchased? Does the product have a reputation for quality? The model assumes that people will choose to purchase products based upon rational assessments of all factors, including price.

A third facet of the model is that wants are **insatiable**. This means that people always want more. A time reference distinguishes this unlimited desire. To an eight year old, a bicycle would probably satisfy a want. To an eighteen year old, a new car might be more appropriate. Considering another time perspective, how much satisfaction is derived from a second or a third soft drink? Each soft drink provides less satisfaction during a given period. This exemplifies the **principle of diminishing returns**. Each additional unit of an input provides less satisfaction than the one before, when other things remain the same.

These patterns of behavior are based on the self-interest of individuals. They will tend to

[1]Associate Director, Center for Economic Education, University of North Texas.
[2]Assistant Professor, Labor and Industrial Relations, University of North Texas.

16

maximize their own self-interest. Through millions of individuals acting in their own self-interest, the forces of supply and demand interact. This interaction provides for the exchange of goods and services.

MICROECONOMICS

Microeconomics is one branch of study in economics. It focuses on factors such as cost, productivity, supply and demand. Its emphasis is on one economic actor such as a single consumer, a single business or a single market. It employs many of the basic concepts already presented in this chapter.

For example, a single business firm chooses to maximize profits and minimize costs. The firm attempts to make rational economic decisions. It relies upon the principle of diminishing returns and employs **marginal analysis**. This means that it measures changes in one variable in response to a one-unit change in some other variable. For example, it might concern itself with the change in production resulting from the addition of one worker. Marginal analysis is central to the study of economics, especially microeconomics.

MACROECONOMICS

Macroeconomics is the other branch of study in economics. Its focus is on total aspects of the economy rather than individual units. For example, it may concern itself with total consumer demand rather than the demand choice of one consumer.

One of the primary issues of macroeconomics is economic growth and contraction. When the economy is growing, new jobs are being provided. When the economy is contracting, referred to as a **recession**, jobs are being lost.

Another issue of concern in macroeconomics is **inflation**, defined as a rise in the general level of prices. A low level of inflation, such as 1 or 2 percent, does not cause much concern. Increases in **productivity** and wages will offset small increases in inflation. A high level of inflation causes concern because it cannot be offset. Some consumers will not be able to demand goods because of the increase in prices and because

their wages do not rise at the same rate as the prices.

A recession, when used to reduce inflation, may create a dilemma in the economy. It does this by taking wages out of the economy, thereby reducing demand. However, a small percentage of the labor force pays the price of bringing down inflation for everyone. In this respect, and others, macroeconomics is concerned with the distribution of income in society. Another problem of income distribution is persons who work but still cannot earn enough to purchase the basic necessities of life. Also, some individuals can't find employment to earn an income. This is, of course, the problem of poverty.

OTHER INSTITUTIONAL ELEMENTS

Several other institutional elements shape and strengthen our free enterprise system: *free exchange, private property, consumer control, contracts, the profit motive, competition* and *government*. Two other significant principles, *individual freedom* and *interdependence*, contribute to the successful mixture. Free enterprise encourages people to pursue their own self-interests. The system harnesses these individuals' self-interests to achieve the market goals described earlier. Allowing people to pursue their own self-interests achieves a desired outcome. A discussion of each of these institutional arrangements follows.

Free Exchange

Free exchange provides an orderly method for interchanging ownership or possession. It is important to note that it achieves much more than that. Free exchange provides an automatic, voluntary method of control over the self-interested drives of the economic person. That is, free exchange organizes and promotes cooperation among people, thereby avoiding the restraints of command and traditions.

Exchange is the means by which all elements of society gain mutual benefits. Cooperating with each other, in their own self-interest, people voluntarily exchange goods and services. Using money and prices as a common denominator makes the voluntary exchange of goods and services between millions of people easier.

The individual exchanges of millions of workers, landlords, capitalists and entrepreneurs allows the free enterprise market to solve the economic problem. This social outcome occurs because people act in their own self-interest. The existence of these choices provides each economic role player with a strong sense of security and independence.

Private Property

The effective working of voluntary exchange requires certain rules that permit the granting and withholding of benefits. These rules of law guarantee the rights to **private property** and to liberty. They also provide people with the right and authority to control the fruits of their own labor. Freedom to own property spreads economic power more evenly. Those who own property can expect to benefit from that ownership. Private property rights make free exchange possible. They reinforce the motivation to be efficient, competitive, and responsive to the forces of supply and demand.

Consumer Control

Most important among the variety of exchange relationships is the one between individual consumers and producers. The direction and rate of economic growth result from consumer demand. To some degree, consumer demand also determines who gets the system's output.

Of course, producers produce and market new goods and services for which there is no preexistent demand. This occurs because entrepreneurs are creative, innovative, and inventive. Free enterprise encourages the development of new technology and new goods and services that create new supply. This in turn creates new demand. Although producers are free to produce and market any goods and services, consumers have the last word. Producers cannot force consumers to buy something that they do not want.

Contracts

Free exchange is the cornerstone of the free enterprise market. These voluntary transactions occur between buyers and sellers and between producers and the workers they employ. A free enterprise economy enforces voluntary agreements by legal **contracts**. Enforcement by a legal system makes contracts, and the agreements they represent, more secure. Contracts, enforced by a legal system, stabilize the economic environment and spread economic power more evenly.

The Profit Motive

Entrepreneurial desire to obtain maximum profit benefits the total economic system. The profit motive makes sellers more responsive to consumer will. Only if sellers are responsive to consumer demand can they expect to receive high profits. Producers can lower costs and increase profits only by using the most efficient modes of production. The striving for profit thus achieves two important economic ends: responsiveness to consumer demand and increased efficiency.

Competition

Competition among producers, workers, and consumers also contributes to the success of the free enterprise market. The essence of competition is choice. Choice requires more than one option. Therefore markets are competitive when the economic participants have options. If producers are not responsive to consumer wants, the consumer can go elsewhere to satisfy his or her wants. If producers are not efficient, their prices become too high. Consumers are free to switch to a different supplier or a substitute product. Thus competition between the economic participants causes the market to be more responsive and efficient.

Government

The free enterprise market satisfies the needs of society in an environment of maximum individual freedom and minimum government control. Even though the United States is a free enterprise economy, that does not mean there is no role for government. In a modern, complex, industrial society, government has an important role. Government is necessary to insure property rights and enforce contracts. Government defines and controls the money supply and insures competition. Also, appropriate government involvement is necessary to promote economic stability and growth.

SUMMARY

Many institutional elements contribute to making the free enterprise market system more effective, responsive and free. Included in these interdependent concepts are the economic model of human behavior, free exchange, private property, consumer control, contract, profit, competition and government. The theory underlying the free enterprise market assumes that human beings will act in their own self-interest. The pursuit of these self-interests will benefit the entire economy. Building on these self-interests, the system blends all elements to produce the goods and services consumers want. Furthermore, the system achieves this goal with maximum individual freedom and minimum government involvement.

CONTENT QUESTIONS

1. How are contracts and private property necessary for the smooth performance of the free enterprise system? Cite examples.
2. Why is the free exchange of goods and services critical to the working of the free enterprise system?

DISCUSSION QUESTIONS

1. Most entrepreneurs take pride in doing a task well. Most have a sense of social responsibility. Could these entrepreneurial traits replace the profit motive? Why or why not?
2. Explain the concepts of division of labor, specialization, and exchange. How does the application of these economic concepts make everyone "better off"?

5

DECISION MAKING

William D. Witter, Ph.D.[1]
and
William McKee, Ph.D.[2]

A good grasp of economics serves modern men and women in many ways. One of the more important of these is the advantage that economic methods provide us in making decisions as part of our business and personal lives. Recent research has applied economic methods to issues such as interpersonal relationships. The researchers found that family harmony (and discord) may be examined by the same economic methods as are used in research on standard economic markets. Moreover, marginal analysis and economic concepts like scarcity now are being used by chemists and biologists studying genetic engineering and natural adaptation.

When applied to many everyday issues, basic economic concepts and methods lead to important and interesting results. Economics often can give us information for decision making that is not available from other methods. But, to make use of economic science in this way, we need to be able to distinguish between facts and personal values.

FACTS AND VALUES

A century or more ago, along the Texas frontier, "facts is facts" was sometimes enough to get a man hung for violation of the understood social order. No matter how he came into possession of a stolen horse or stolen cattle, the fact of possession could be used to convict him of rustling. This situation reflects the possible combination of a fact situation (possession of the stolen livestock) with the rationalized value judgment that "whoever has the animals must be the varmint who stole them."

The fact statement usually can be verified or refuted in some objective fashion, such as, "Wild Bill weighed 172 pounds, including noose, when they cut him down from the oak tree." A value judgment, on the other hand, is a statement of what ought to be, rather than what is. For example, the following is a value statement: "Wild Bill would be alive today if he had listened to my advice and not attempted to drive the herd through the Galleria Shopping Center." Obviously, the latter statement, however reasonable, mostly is a matter of personal opinion that cannot be tested in a scientific way.

This sounds a lot like common sense, so what does economic thinking add? Consider the economic problem of health and safety in the workplace. All of us are potential or actual labor force participants who have a vested interest in protecting our bodies (and our unborn children, even) from work-related injuries, traumas and diseases. Two means of insuring this protection are:

1. enacting job-safety regulations, such as that attempted through the *Occupational Safety and Health Act* (OSHA) of 1970, and

[1]Assistant Professor, Institute of Applied Economics; Director, Center for Economic Education, University of North Texas.
[2]Associate Professor, Labor and Industrial Relations, University of North Texas.

20

2. allowing the marketplace to regulate its own health and safety issues.

Which alternative you think is better probably depends on your own values and goals.

As a regulatory arm of government, OSHA requires substantial amounts of the government's general revenues (our tax dollars) to develop and enforce workplace health and safety restrictions. It can help to improve job conditions if provided sufficient funding, but this approach will have the side effect of reducing the freedom of business owners and workers to adopt the practices they feel are most appropriate in their given situations. It also may redirect society's resources away from activities that people regard as more important—such as greater production, increased civil rights enforcement, military spending, etc.

The second alternative promotes individual and corporate freedom and (perhaps) would result in more jobs throughout the economy, but can the marketplace regulate its own health and safety problems? If it could, why did we have the problems that resulted in the passage of OSHA? You could choose this option if you feel that owners and managers are more enlightened now than they were when, say, Upton Sinclair wrote *The Jungle*, an account of the human injustices prevailing in Chicago's meat packing industry at the turn of the century. Perhaps you also would want to consider the fact that today, even with OSHA in effect, more than 12,000 U.S. workers die each year from workplace accidents and exposures, and several hundred thousand more suffer crippling injuries and illnesses. The National Safety Council estimated the 1981 cost of workplace accidents to be $32.5 billion.

NORMATIVE AND POSITIVE ECONOMICS

Another distinction that should be recognized is that between **normative economics** and **positive economics**. Like the concepts discussed earlier, these definitions are not hard to remember if you pay attention to their descriptive titles. *Positive economics* is built around the issue of measurement of variables related to economic concepts and theories. The primary emphasis of this approach is the separation of economic facts from value judgments and the rejection of value judgment from economic science.

Economists who follow normative logic, on the other hand, are willing to accept or reject economic matters on the basis of facts and economic theory *and* on the basis of normative judgments. "A 9 percent unemployment rate is better for the economy than a 9 percent rate of inflation," is an example of a normative consideration. You can see that normative economics is a combination of positive economics with some judgment about what society's objectives should be.

GOALS

The private enterprise system is founded on the fundamental rights of individuals to decide what is best for themselves. As individuals exercise these rights, conflicts of values are minimized and individual expression is accented. Thus, the market system is known to be pluralistic since it tolerates a wide variety of actions, values, and goals.

Fundamental constitutional rights are intertwined with the basic U.S. goals that affect our decisions. The following goals are primarily economic in nature.

- *Freedom.* **Economic freedom** describes the ability of producers and consumers to do as they choose. In many instances, economic freedom is defined in terms of the absence of barriers. Thus, if there are no barriers prohibiting new firms from entering a market, then entry into the market is free. Markets also are defined as free when there is an absence of government intervention. In all these contexts, freedom is limited only by consideration of the rights of others.
- *Efficiency.* **Efficiency** actually can mean more than just the production of maximum output. It has two dimensions, technical and allocative. **Technical efficiency** involves obtaining the largest output from a given amount of resources. This means getting the most for the least. **Allocative efficiency** involves the use of resources in harmony with society's goals. For example, an economy is not allocatively efficient if television game shows are being produced when opera is being demanded.

- *Equity*. **Equity** is simply fairness or justice. In economics, equity is concerned with the income distribution and matters that affect the distribution, like taxation.
- *Community*. **Community** is living in trust and harmony with others. It obviously implies interaction and shared values and goals. Still, community also concerns interdependence and shared responsibilities.
- *Stability*. **Stability** often is used to refer to the extent an **equilibrium** price or set of prices can be achieved. An equilibrium price is the price at which supply and demand are equal to each other in a market.
- *Growth* **Economic growth** refers to the situation in which the nation's output expands at a rate faster than population growth.

A DECISION MAKING MODEL

When disagreements between individuals and groups center on values, reflective decision making can play a vital role. Reflective decision making considers both facts and value and is applied in a step-by-step procedure. Here are the steps in this process.

1. Develop the background and importance of the problem. This step involves identification of the factors and events which caused the problem. An analysis of the economic, political, and/or social consequences of the problem must be included.
2. Develop a statement of the problem. This is a short, concise statement of what is wrong. It usually helps to pose the problem in the form of a question.
3. Develop the possible solutions to the problem. If the problem is economic, this step requires the identification of the relevant economic concepts.
4. Analyze the factual consequences most likely to result from each solution.
5. Choose the goals to be pursued. This is a statement of value preferences. What goals are valued most highly: Efficiency? Freedom? Full employment? Some goals may be in conflict.
6. Evaluate the solutions against the goals you wish to pursue. Use the factual consequences developed in Step 4.

7. Choose the solution most likely to achieve the goals defined in Step 5.

A CASE STUDY: CONCERTS IN THE PARK

The voters in Nowhere, Texas, recently were presented with a number of proposals designed to spur economic development in their community. In the past year, an economic development expert had performed a consulting study for the city. Outlined in his final report was a proposed series of actions the city could take to improve its potential for attracting new employers (and jobs) to the area. The consultant also reviewed the financial well-being of the city and noted that, under the current budget, the city would not be able to supply financial incentives to entice new employers, nor could it afford any significant outlays on city cultural and beautification projects. At the same time, the consultant emphasized that Nowhere could expect little economic growth until it improved its quality of life.

One local recommendation that caught the attention of the city council was the possibility of holding symphony concerts in the public park. Many community leaders were strongly behind this proposal, so a decision was made to study the issue more closely.

The park concert issue involves the well-being and economic security of the citizens of Nowhere. Facts can be gathered to show that companies considering either start-up operations or relocations tend to move to areas which provide musical, dance, and literary expression for their residents. Is the park concert a solution to the cultural deficiency of the area?

Statement of Problem

A. The immediate problem is the lack of new jobs for the unemployed residents of Nowhere. Not only has the city's tax base declined in recent years, but the brightest graduates of the local school district are forced to leave the area if they desire favorable employment opportunities. What can be done to create jobs?
B. Associated with this problem is the longer-term economic health of the area. Falling tax revenues in recent years have forced the city to reduce educational and road improvement

expenditures, as well as to curtail many of the specialty wards of the local public hospital.

Policy Options

1. Rely on the market system alone to create jobs in Nowhere (surely employers will learn about the advantages of living and working in Nowhere, won't they?);
2. Subsidize the park concerts with public funds to assure the fulfillment of the project;
3. Charge reasonable fees to all persons attending the concerts, thereby creating the opportunity for the concerts to be self-sufficient;
4. Conduct a fund-raising drive with an honorary title given those who make substantial financial gifts to the symphony; or
5. Approve the borrowing of private funds, through the bond election procedure.

Predicted Consequences of Policy Options

1. *Rely on the market system.* An advantage of the market system is that regional imbalances normally even out over time. But even these natural forces do not eliminate pockets of poverty and unemployment in more remote areas of the nation unless the residents are willing and able to relocate to areas of better opportunity. A major problem of Nowhere is that it is "nowhere" and offers employers little in geographic or natural resource advantages to move there.
2. *City subsidies.* This could be a reasonable approach, except that the city does not have a surplus fund to draw on at present. To create a surplus fund will require that either taxes must be raised or expenditures reduced. Any combination of these actions could achieve some level of funding, but city officials will come under intense political pressure in making these decisions.
3. *Charge fees for attendance.* On the surface, this appears reasonable. However, a park concert is a special form of service which can be classified as a public good. A public good is a commodity or service which, if supplied to one person, can be made available to others at no extra cost. Hence, people can "consume" the concert and avoid paying the entrance fee by standing outside the gate or

even sitting in the open-air restaurant across the street. The attraction of being a "free rider" will be overwhelming to some who otherwise might have purchased tickets.

4. *Private fund raising.* If enough Nowhere residents are symphony enthusiasts and have some discretionary money, this option could work. However, it is unlikely that people who are not enthusiasts about the symphony will be charitable in their giving. Evidence shows that honorary titles are important only to those who have a personal interest in the activity.
5. *Approve the bond issue.* This option has several positive features. Foremost, it permits the citizens to express their wishes directly. If enough citizens support public symphonies, the bonds could pass. The difficulty with this solution is that residents may conceal their true preference in order to escape any personal responsibility.

Evaluating the Facts, Values, and Options

The options stated in this case may be summarized into three categories:

1. private market solutions;
2. public sector solutions; and
3. a possible combination of government and market.

Both government and private citizens have an interest in economic development, especially in terms of the goals of growth and security. Community is a strong public goal, but it is interesting that businesses express a strong interest in the quality of life within a community when making relocation decisions.

Those who favor freedom and efficiency generally prefer as little government as possible. A public good is a dilemma for people with these values, for providing public goods is a matter of collective choice. In this situation, a combination of public and market interests might be feasible. Government, of course, has the legislated responsibility for enhancing the goals of equity and community.

So, what is the solution? Individual values and goals of Nowhere's citizens should direct the response here. But it is important that there be a more in-depth analysis of the symphony proposal. By itself, it is unlikely that a symphony in the park will entice new jobs to Nowhere. In fact, it is entirely possible that Nowhere's economic destiny will remain dismal, regardless of civic action. If so, the question would then shift to whether the residents want a local symphony for the pure enjoyment of it.

CONTENT QUESTIONS

1. List and describe the steps in the reflective decision making process.

2. When do you use the reflective decision making process?

DISCUSSION QUESTIONS

1. Explain the difference between normative economics and positive economics.
2. Explain the importance of values and goals in the process of decision making. Give at least two examples of how your values and goals affect the decisions you make.

2

ECONOMIC GEOGRAPHY: REGIONS AND CITIES

Since Texas joined the United States under the condition that it could split into five separate states at any time, various methods for dividing the state have been studied.

Texas' great size, together with the cultural, climatic, and geological diversity within its borders, provides ample justification for numerous ways of splitting the state into regions.

The presence or absence of natural resources has created regional diversity in wealth and economic development across the state, with some cities like Midland and Odessa almost totally dependent on petroleum for their recent growth. As in the case of oil production, the use of the land through forestry, farming, and ranching has been crucial to the development of some regions.

The location of Texas on the Mexican border has added cultural diversity to the natural diversity of the state. The Spanish entered Texas from the south via Mexico, and settled first at San Antonio and Nacogdoches. While San Antonio prospered as a Spanish settlement, Nacogdoches, because it was farther from Mexico with a terrain alien to the Spanish, did not attract as many Spanish settlers. Nacogdoches, therefore, was settled more from neighboring Louisiana and the southern United States than from Mexico and

it took on a different character from that of San Antonio. In addition, the plains of north-central Texas received streams of midwestern Americans, while direct immigrants from Europe settled in Central Texas. To this day, these diverse cultures have not completely merged.

Texas lends itself to being divided into economic regions. The natural and cultural characteristics of a region interact and are influenced by external economic events and changes in available technology to determine a particular region's economic base—those products and services which generate income and employment.

Because these economic bases differ from region to region, economic events, such as the oil price decline, the peso devaluation, or a defense spending increase, can be expected to affect the economy of each region differently.

In order to assess more accurately the implications of such events for Texas, the Comptroller of Public Accounts has divided the state into six economic regions—East Texas, the Metroplex, the Plains, the Central Corridor, the Border, and the Gulf Coast—as shown in Figure 1.

East Texas is primarily a non-metropolitan region, mostly dependent on the production and processing of timber, petroleum and coal. The

Metroplex, on the other hand, is almost totally metropolitan with diversified manufacturing and service sectors. The Plains region is the largest and most sparsely populated area of the state, with a petroleum and agricultural based economy. The Border area is characterized by its economic dependence on trade with Mexico. The most populous region of Texas, the Gulf Coast, has an economy centered around petroleum and petrochemicals. Finally, the public and private service sectors provide the economic base for the Central Corridor.

FIGURE II-1
Economic Regions of Texas

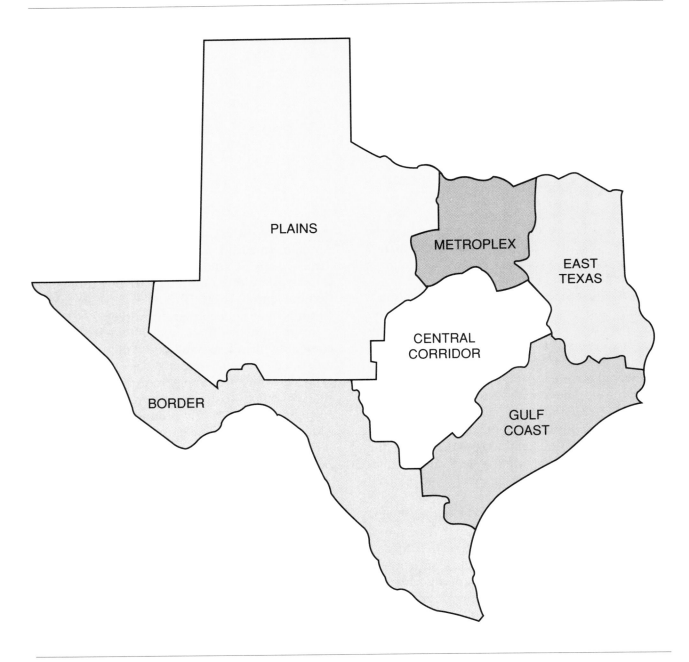

Source: State of Texas Comptroller of Public Accounts.

6
EAST TEXAS
Robert F. Hodgin, D.A.[1]

This forested region of Texas has its economic roots in timber and agriculture. However, the discovery of oil at Spindletop, Texas, in 1901 added manufacturing and oil extraction to the economic base. No large cities dominate the

region but three growing areas continue to show promise. Those three *market areas* are Tyler, Longview-Marshall and Texarkana (see Figure 6-1). A **market area** has a large population where there are strong economic and social ties to a central city. Along with other regions of Texas, East Texas is not immune from the effects of external economic events.

[1]Associate Professor of Economics, University of Houston–Clear Lake.

FIGURE 6-1
East Texas

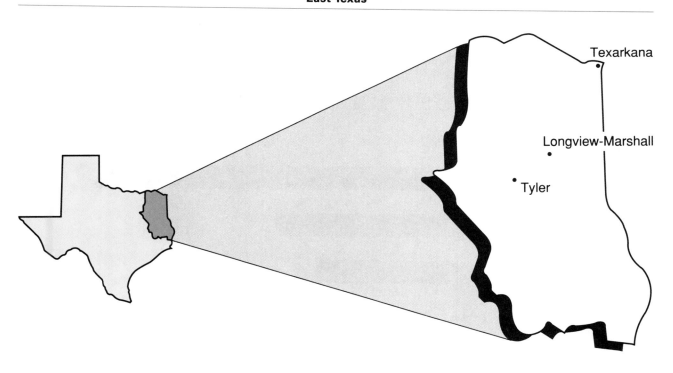

Source: State of Texas Comptroller of Public Accounts, "The Economic Regions of Texas," *Fiscal Notes*, March 1983, p.8.

East Texas firms produce much of the raw resources used in other parts of the state. For example, 80 percent of the timber, 65 percent of the coal, 12 percent of the crude oil and 9 percent of the natural gas produced in Texas come from East Texas. Poultry, cattle and dairy production also contribute significantly to the region's output. As diversified as the economic base appears, the past few years have witnessed significant swings in both total business volume and employment.

Movements in certain economic measures, such as *interest rates*, affect different industries in different ways. The **interest rate** is the cost of borrowing money. When it rises, businesses find it more difficult to undertake investments that will earn enough profit to cover the costs of borrowing. When the petroleum industry was booming in the late 1970s, higher interest rates were virtually ignored by those in the oil patch. However, this rise in the costs of borrowing money created a significant downturn in East Texas construction. Then in 1981–82 the prices of oil and lumber both fell, driving East Texas into a steep recession. When mortgage interest rates began to fall after 1982, construction was once again stimulated and the lumber industry came back. The resurgence of the lumber trade acted as a buffer to the continued slide in the oil sector of the East Texas economy through the mid-1980s.

The outlook for East Texas is still mixed. The petroleum industry has stabilized somewhat but lumber prices have again slowed down as mortgage rates once more ticked upward. A shift from manufacturing and extractive industries to trade, services, and finance is expected to occur as the economic shifts in the region continue. See Figure 6-2

THE TYLER MARKET AREA

Tyler is a bustling middle-sized city whose economy is based on tourism, manufacturing and agriculture. Tyler's population is 135,000. Strong economic growth led by housing construction and some new industry location began in 1983. Tyler is the administrative center for the East Texas oil industry. Tyler is well known for its production of rose bushes and is the largest rose-growing area in the nation. Over half of all rose bushes grown in the United States come from the Tyler area. The rose industry is a major spring and fall tourist draw.

Tyler is a major East Texas medical center. Its education facilities include the University of

FIGURE 6-2
East Texas Employment Profile 1986

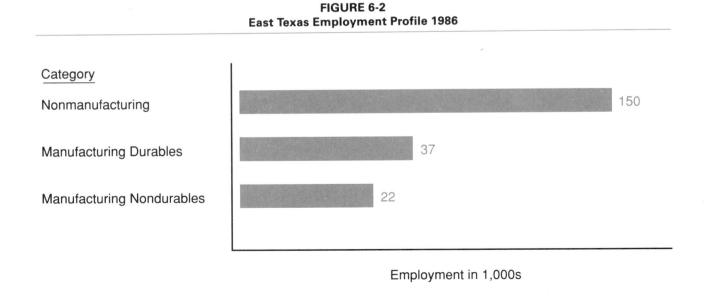

Source: Data from State of Texas Comptroller of Public Accounts.

Texas at Tyler, Tyler Junior College, and Texas College. Tourists, seeking the solitude of the pine forests, also make a significant contribution to Tyler's retail businesses.

THE LONGVIEW-KILGORE-MARSHALL MARKET AREA

The twin cities of Longview and Marshall committed to the oil boom in the 1970s. As a result, they too have experienced the roller coaster effects from world oil price changes. However, other significant industries help to bolster this area. Agriculture, steel, and food-processing activities dominate the sizeable industrial sector of this area in East Texas. Something of a magnet for "footloose" companies, 286 manufacturing firms are located in the Longview-Marshall area. The Texas Piney Woods attract significant numbers of tourists. Educational institutions include Le Tourneau College at Longview and Kilgore College (home of the world famous Rangerettes), in addition to Wiley College and East Texas Baptist at Marshall.

THE TEXARKANA MARKET AREA

Texarkana is a metropolitan area with a population of 126,000. It is located in two states, Texas and Arkansas. The boundary between the states bisects the city. The towns are a transportation and commercial center for Northeast Texas, Northwest Arkansas, Northwest Louisiana and Southeast Oklahoma.

In addition, the Red River Valley is a prosperous farming and ranching area. Crops, livestock, and timber are all major contributors to the economic health of the area. The U.S. Army Depot and Ordinance Plant, plus Texarkana Community College and a branch of East Texas State University are public facilities which add to the economy. Two large lakes are major tourist attractions.

THE FUTURE OF THE EAST TEXAS ECONOMY

Recent estimates from the State of Texas Comptroller's Office indicate that the East Texas region should add 5,000 nonfarm jobs to its labor force in 1988–89. Even though the past two years have been pretty lean, the region escaped some of the drastic downturn experienced by the Gulf Coast during the oil recession. The reason for that was the rising world demand for timber. Aided also by the settling of a trade dispute which restricted imports of Canadian lumber into the United States, East Texas lumber companies took advantage of rising timber demand by gearing up the local mills. The decline in the value of the dollar made Texas lumber cheaper in world markets. This further stimulated demand. For East Texas lumber companies output, prices, and profits were up. Overall, economic capacity is growing and the region is gaining jobs and income. As with most regions of Texas, the future will be shaped as much by world economic events as by the ability of area industry to plan carefully.

CONTENT QUESTIONS

1. What are the two major industries in East Texas?
2. What caused the recovery of the timber industry in the 1980s?
3. What types of new industries have been attracted to the Longview-Marshall area?

DISCUSSION QUESTIONS

1. How has the timber industry acted as an economic buffer for the oil industry in East Texas?
2. What might be done to further enhance the prospects for growth in the eastern region of Texas?

7

THE TEXAS GULF COAST
Robert F. Hodgin, D.A.[1]

The area of Texas known as the Gulf Coast is comprised of four major market areas. These four market areas are Houston, Beaumont-Port Arthur, Galveston-Texas City and Corpus Christi (see Figure 7-1). The largest of these four market areas is Houston. A *market area* is a large population center where the people have strong social and economic ties with the central city. The government's name for officially designated market areas is Metropolitan Statistical Areas. Before looking at each of the market areas separately, an overview of the region's economy will provide a broad perspective.

[1]Associate Professor of Economics, University of Houston–Clear Lake.

FIGURE 7-1
The Gulf Coast

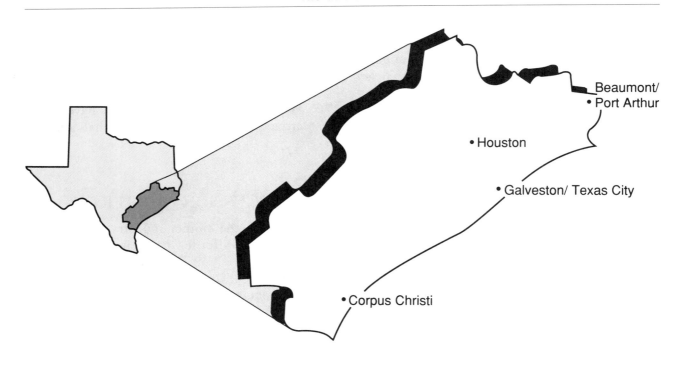

Source: State of Texas Comptroller of Public Accounts, "The Economic Regions of Texas," *Fiscal Notes*, March 1983, p.8.

As with all regions, business leaders capitalize on those industries which have the greatest **comparative advantage**. A region has a comparative advantage if it can produce a product less expensively than another region. The Gulf Coast economy has a natural comparative advantage in petroleum, chemicals, fishing, and selected agricultural products.

Taken as a whole, the Gulf Coast region employment base includes shipbuilding, petroleum refining, steel production, port activity, fishing, and agricultural production. The discovery of oil in 1901, at Spindletop in the Beaumont-Port Arthur market area, launched a new era for Houston and the state of Texas that continues to this day.

The most dramatic economic swings in the state have occurred recently in the Houston area during 1979–1983. During that time, the petroleum industry began expanding rapidly due to rising world demand for oil. Nonagricultural employment in the Gulf Coast region increased by 17 percent from early 1979 to early 1982. The oil industry economic bubble burst in mid-1982. Manufacturing-related employment fell by 18 percent by the end of that year.

Just as the trauma of the oil industry recession began, the Mexican peso was devalued. It then took more pesos to exchange for a dollar, effectively raising the prices of U.S. goods for Mexican citizens. As a result, the previously thriving trade between Houston and Mexico fell significantly. What is more, in 1983 Hurricane Alicia battered the Texas coastline, damaging many businesses and further hindering the fishing and agricultural sectors.

The region continues to slowly work its way out of the effects of the recession even in 1988. Oil prices have stabilized somewhat and business confidence is returning. Employment forecasts indicate a cautious recovery with job growth of 1.3 percent expected in 1989. Houston, by far the largest city in the region, is seeking new economic directions to round out its mainstay petrochemical industry.

THE HOUSTON MARKET AREA

The Houston market area is the industrial and financial center for much of Texas. With 5,000

energy-related firms and 200 chemical companies producing over 400 products, Houston is rightfully called the energy capital of the world. It hosts one of the three largest seaports in the country and is headquarters for the Lyndon B. Johnson Space Center. The Texas Medical Center, an immense complex of hospitals, medical schools and research facilities, is the city's largest private employer, with 55,000 people on the payroll. Several colleges and five major universities are located in the city. Houston still continues to attract many tourists. Currently working to reposition itself, the city seeks by constructing a new convention center to become an even more attractive tourist destination point. The banking sector continues working through some difficult times brought about by the nearly simultaneous collapse of the oil, agriculture, and livestock industries.

Hardest hit of all the cities in the state by the oil industry recession in 1982, Houston is on its way back to full economic vitality. The manufacturing base has stabilized and is beginning to grow again, retail sales are rising and the office vacancy rates which were among the highest in the nation are once again falling. See Figure 7-2.

Houston's leaders are striving to redirect the economy into new and productive endeavors such as space commercialization, biomedical technology, and international relations, without repeating the past mistakes of overbuilding. The city has become quite responsive to the needs of new and entering businesses. Economic development initiatives are strongly focused on targeted industries such as computer technology, aircraft construction and maintenance, pleasure boating, and convention tourism. Still, the future of the Houston economy will likely be determined as much by changing world events as by the efforts of its own development thrusts.

THE BEAUMONT-PORT ARTHUR MARKET AREA

The discovery of oil, as much as anything else, caused this complex of cities to become what they are today. Although the area serves as a major port and agricultural center, its economic base is comprised predominantly of petroleum

FIGURE 7-2
Houston Region Industrial Profile 1986

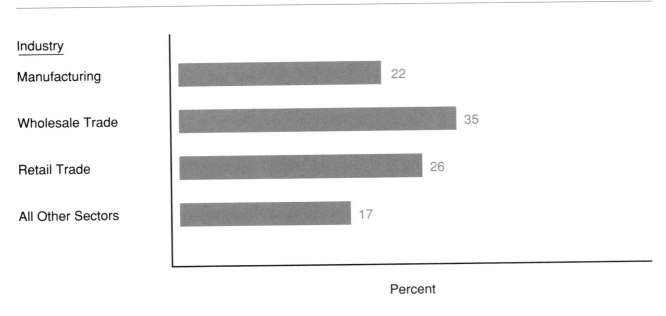

Percent

Source: Data from State of Texas Comptroller of Public Accounts.

refining, oil field servicing, and the manufacturing of oil field equipment. Almost 1 million barrels of crude oil are refined in Port Arthur each day.

Port Arthur is one of five major seafood ports along the Texas Gulf Coast. Over 25 varieties of fish, both fresh and saltwater, are harvested in nearby waters. A sizeable seafood processing industry survives here, too.

Although this region was also hard hit by the oil industry recession, stability has returned and businesses look toward a brighter future. Recent hotel expansion and tourism increases have brought about a rise in retail sales.

THE GALVESTON-TEXAS CITY MARKET AREA

The island of Galveston is a distinctive component of the Gulf Coast, having its own unique ambience. Tourist related businesses and financial enterprises dominate the island economy along with shipping and commercial development. The site of homes over 100 years old, this history-laden strip of real estate hovers between the chance to return to the days of legalized gambling and the costs inflicted upon it from

occasional hurricanes. Hotel, restaurant, and condominium facilities are expanding handsomely to accommodate the rising tide of tourists seeking the sun. Several new events such as the Galveston Mardi Gras and the Dickens on the Strand festival attract ever more participants each year. Economic development leaders are looking for ways to capitalize on the recently passed legislation allowing parimutual wagering. Location of a horse-racing facility could add to Galveston's already rich character as a place to recreate.

Several large businesses dominate Galveston's economy. The American National Insurance Company is the largest financial institution on the island. The University of Texas Medical Branch, also located there, is the island economy's largest employer. Texas A&M University, too, supports its marine science programs in modern academic facilities located at the eastern tip of the island. The port of Galveston is distinguished by being the largest port in the country not supported by public funds.

Texas City, located across the Galveston causeway on the mainland of Texas, is the location of several major oil and chemical firms. Notorious for the massive chemical explosion in 1946,

Texas City's petroleum-based economy is quite sensitive to the swings in world oil prices. Although they too felt the downturn in the petroleum industry, area businesses are rebounding and new industry is slowly moving back. For example, serious negotiations are in progress with a major foreign automobile manufacturer to locate a production plant in Texas City.

The land mass from Texas City up to the city of Houston holds much untapped potential. Known as the Clear Lake area, this tract of land boasts a lake with over 7,000 recreational boat slips, is home to the Johnson Space Center (J.S.C.) which supports over 13,000 aerospace personnel, and houses a populace with higher incomes and more advanced education than almost any other small area in the region. The J.S.C. injects more than $400 million annually into the regional economy as it continues its role as the lead center in the U.S. space program. After these dollars are multiplied (the **multiplier** accounts for the impact of successive rounds of respending of money) throughout the region, the total economic impact is more than $850 million each year.

THE CORPUS CHRISTI MARKET AREA

This city is a major deepwater port for Texas and the future site of the U.S. Navy's homeport facility. The port, one of the ten busiest in the nation, accommodates oil and refined products, grain, cotton, and chemical products.

Tourism ranks as another major industry for the city. Convention facilities are fully booked and condominium construction continues at a robust pace. Nearby North Padre Island attracts many thousands of tourists each year. Major fishing villages also lie within close driving distance of the city, helping to make Corpus Christi a tourist destination.

THE FUTURE OF THE GULF COAST REGION

After three consecutive years of declining employment from 1984 to 1987, the Gulf Coast region is predicted to increase its employment base. In 1988 all cities in the region had significant increases in employment. This economic turnaround is being led by the same broad industry classification that lost most of the jobs during the oil recession—manufacturing. Indeed, the region's petrochemical firms are setting profit records in the face of stabilizing world markets. Houston, Beaumont and Corpus Christi account for 62 percent of the nation's petroleum capacity. Latest reports indicate that some $1.5 billion in new petrochemical construction projects are on target for completion by 1990.

The long-run future for the region rests as much on world oil and chemical market stability as on the direction of new industrial programs. Yet the aerospace and biotechnology industries hold much promise as rising stars in the region's economic plan. With successes in the space shuttle and space station programs of the National Aeronautics and Space Administration (NASA), the future for the commercialization of space could be unlimited. In the words of an economist, the Gulf Coast region of Texas is finding its comparative advantage in the world's marketplace.

CONTENT QUESTIONS

1. What three events hurt the Gulf Coast economy in the early 1980s?
2. What organization is the largest private employer in Houston?
3. How does the Johnson Space Center affect the Gulf Coast economy?

DISCUSSION QUESTIONS

1. What is meant by the term "comparative advantage"?
2. What comparative advantages are there in the place where you are living?
3. What is the multiplier effect and how does it influence a region's economy?

8

THE TEXAS BORDER REGION

Peter P. Pranis, Jr.[1]

The Texas/Mexico border region is unique in Texas and perhaps in the United States. It follows the Rio Grande from El Paso to the Gulf of Mexico. The region begins at the cities of El

[1]Vice-President, Economic Development Research, Council for South Texas Economic Progress.

Paso/Juarez and the high desert country at the border's western end and ends in the east where the Rio Grande empties into the Gulf of Mexico near the deepwater port of Brownsville and South Padre Island. See Figure 8-1. Understanding the economy and economic prospects of today's Texas Border Region requires some knowledge of the region's geography and economic history.

FIGURE 8-1
The Texas Border Region

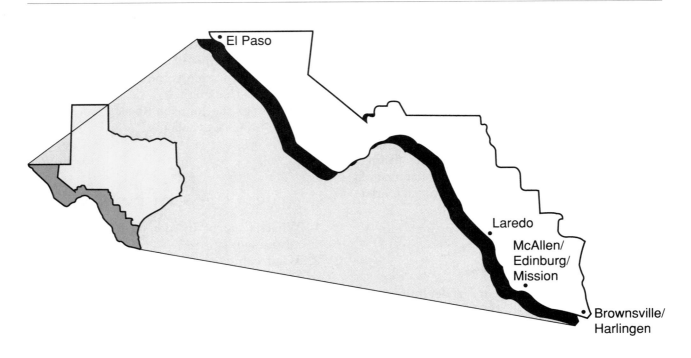

Source: State of Texas Comptroller of Public Accounts, "The Economic Regions of Texas," *Fiscal Notes*, March 1983, p.8.

GEOGRAPHY

A relative lack of rainfall is common to all the Texas/Mexico border lands. With less than 30 inches of rain, farmers usually cannot grow crops without irrigation. Since the Border Region has rainfalls of from 8–10 inches around El Paso in the west to 26 inches in the Lower Rio Grande Valley, without irrigation the border lands would be either deserts or useful only as ranch land.

Farmers can irrigate the flat lands along the river banks such as east of El Paso around Laredo and in the Lower Rio Grande Valley. Except for these irrigated areas the ranch and desert lands form a belt on each side of the river a hundred or more miles wide, separating the border communities from the population centers of both Texas and Mexico. This relative isolation contributes to the region's unique character where the best of both Texas (Anglo) and Mexican (Hispanic) cultures mix in Texas Border communities.

HISTORY

The Border Region has experienced three distinct historical periods. People and machines transformed it from an inhospitable wilderness to a ranching and commercial center which is now emerging as a globally competitive manufacturing frontier. The first period was restricted to ranching. This was followed by a period of irrigated agriculture and commerce. The most recent period includes farming and commerce as well as manufacturing. These periods can be defined by the political and technological changes which spawned them.

The Texas ranching tradition was begun over 200 years ago by the Spanish/Mexican pioneers in the Texas Border Region. Indians had lived in and crossed the Border Region between the Rocky Mountains and Texas to Mexico for thousands of years. However, the first permanent settlements made by whites occurred in 1659 when El Paso was founded as a mission, frontier post, and way station to Spanish/Mexican settlements at Albuquerque and Santa Fe, New Mexico. The El Paso settlement was followed in the early 1750s by similar settlements at Reynosa, Camargo, Mier and Laredo. Matamoros, the last of the major Spanish/Mexican Border communities to be established, was founded in 1796 to protect the border towns at the mouth of the Rio Grande. Because of the lack of rainfall these pioneers had no choice but to turn to ranching as their main source of income.

Texas' independence from Mexico in 1836 and its annexation by the United States created the need for U.S. border forts. These forts supplied the nearby towns with a new market—soldiers. The towns also became a convenient place for trade, legal and illegal, between the two nations. This trade flourished since it was cheaper to transport goods into Northern Mexico from the U.S. border than to import them through Mexican ports or transport them from Mexico City.

Similarly, during the American Civil War, confederate states exported cotton to Europe, and imported war materials from Europe, via Mexico so as to avoid the Northern blockade of Southern ports. And when civil strife broke out in Mexico between 1910 and 1920, war material moved from Texas across the border to both factions. During this period, Mexico's political and economic instability induced many prudent Mexicans to put their money in U.S. banks for safekeeping. This tradition has continued to the present. By 1988 it was estimated that Mexicans had deposited at least $12 billion in U.S. banks, many of which are on the Texas border.

Following Mexican revolution, the U.S. prohibition era set the stage for massive smuggling of alcohol from Mexico, where it was legal. This trade continued until prohibition was repealed in the early 1930s. However, this smuggling established a tradition which persists to the present day.

From the end of World War II until very recently Mexico had much higher tariffs than the United States. Mexico also had quotas on imports to protect her emerging industries, as well as considerable centralized government control of the economy. This led to the smuggling into Mexico of not only consumer goods such as stereos and televisions, but industrial goods as well.

Most of the goods smuggled into Mexico from the United States are flown in. Under U.S. law, written before airplanes were invented, it is only illegal to smuggle goods into another country by boat or land from the United States. No one dreamed that it could be done by air!

The disadvantages of high tariffs and centralized government control of the Mexican economy were brought home to Mexico's citizens by two events in the 1980s: the collapse in the world price of crude oil in 1982 and the amazing economic growth of the Asian countries which followed free market economic policies. As a result, Mexico has recently decided to lower its tariffs, abolish most of its import quotas, and join the **General Agreement in Tariffs and Trade** (GATT). GATT is an international agreement which seeks to reduce trade restriction between nations.

The government is determined to make major reductions in the government's role in the economy. Mexico, seeing the manufacturing and economic success of the Asian free market countries, has freed many industries from government regulation.

TECHNOLOGY

Among the technological advances that have had a major impact on the Border Region was the coming of railroads (El Paso 1883, Laredo, Del Rio, Eagle Pass 1881–82, Brownsville 1904). The railroads eliminated the area's isolation by making it economically feasible to move large amounts of freight to and from the border towns. This meant that U.S. goods could be cheaply sent to Mexico, while live or slaughtered cattle and vegetables could be shipped to U.S. markets in refrigerated freight cars on the return trip or "backhaul."

Another machine-age impact on the Border Region was the introduction of high-volume water pumps in the 1890s. This was especially important to the Lower Rio Grande Valley because it meant that the area's rich soils could be irrigated and land use could be diversified from ranching to more profitable uses of the land such as growing oranges, grapefruit, cotton, and vegetables. These pumps also made it feasible to pump water from the Rio Grande Valley to border cities for human consumption.

The third technological innovation was air conditioning for homes, offices, and factories. Air conditioning has made possible the establishment of factories and offices in hot climates such as that of the border region.

CURRENT CONDITIONS

By the early 1960s, the border communities were modern, solidly established cities and towns with the amount of their economic activity being reflected in the size of their populations. El Paso, having a population of 276,000, had an economy based on the military presence at Fort Bliss (which dates back to the Mexican-American War), serving as a commercial center and border crossing point for Chihuahua, West Texas and New Mexico, and as a major transportation center for U.S. transcontinental rail, truck, and auto traffic. Laredo had a population of 60,000 in 1960 and was heavily engaged in border trade, both retail and wholesale, by truck and rail to south Texas and especially Mexico.

The Valley is the major area for the production of fruit and vegetables in Texas. These products are shipped throughout the nation. In addition, the Valley is a haven for "snow birds." These are people who migrate each winter from the northern states to enjoy the hospitable climate and attractions of the area. The money they bring with them stimulates the economy by creating jobs in both the retail and service sectors.

The economic vitality is reflected in the rapid population growth of the border region. It is the fastest growing area in Texas. In the 22 years from 1960-1982, El Paso grew from 275,000 to 425,000, Laredo grew from 60,000 to 91,000, McAllen grew from 33,000 to 66,000, Harlingen grew from 41,000 to 43,000, and Brownsville grew from 48,000 to 85,000. Since then, the jobs in manufacturing have continued to expand.

This growth is due to the expansion of manufacturing in the border towns. This influx of firms is due to the "twin plant" system, in which a company operates on both sides of the border. Operations on the Texas side involve management, engineering, and high tech production of parts and components. On the Mexican side these parts are assembled into finished products by workers whose wages are low relative to what would be paid in the United States. This system makes the final product highly price competitive.

Even with this growth in manufacturing, unemployment on the Texas Border is the highest of any region in Texas. This is due to a surplus of workers, many of whom came to the United States when the oil industry was booming and jobs were plentiful. Unemployment results in a family income which is below the state average. Low incomes create problems for city and state governments, which must provide health, education, and governmental services.

The economic future of the Texas Border Region is bright for its citizens. However, the future opportunities will be in areas that require knowledge and skills which ultimately rest on a solid education starting in grammar school, expanding in high school, and continuing throughout life.

CONTENT QUESTIONS

1. The city at the western end of the Texas Border is _____ while the deep-sea port of _____ is at the eastern end.

2. Why did trade along the Texas/Mexico border flourish after Texas' annexation by the United States?
3. Where do many Mexicans now deposit their money?
4. After World War II, smuggling in Mexico resulted from what?
5. What three technological events assisted the border economy?

DISCUSSION QUESTIONS

1. What has Mexico done recently to improve its economy? Do you think these are sound decisions?
2. What does the Border Region need to do to improve its economic climate?

9

INDUSTRIALIZATION ALONG THE TEXAS/MEXICO BORDER

Peter P. Pranis, Jr.[1]

In the 1960s, the Lower Rio Grande Valley communities of McAllen, Harlingen, and Brownsville were engaged in trade with Mexico. In addition to the expected truck and rail traffic between our two nations, the deepwater port at Brownsville made it possible to unload cargoes right at the border of southern Texas and northern Mexico. Further, the entire Lower Rio Grande Valley was and still is a year-round farming area specializing in citrus, fresh vegetables, and sugar cane. The mild winter climate also attracted northerners, especially retirees, called "Winter Texans," as a friendly winter alternative to Florida.

THE BRACERO PROGRAM

Since the 1960s, farm laborers from both sides of the border have served as seasonal migrant farm laborers in the United States. The flow of Mexican farm workers had been going on for many decades; it was formalized by the U.S. and Mexican governments as the **Bracero Program** during World War II to help reduce U.S. worker shortages. However, in the early 1960s the U.S. government banned the use of Mexican migrant farm labor on U.S. farms. This was done to increase the employment opportunities of U.S. citizens. The result has been unemployment among Mexican migrant farm workers, who lived mainly in Mexican border towns.

This U.S. policy not only caused great economic hardship in the Mexican border towns, but was the spark that eventually led to the United States/Mexico border region becoming a world manufacturing center. Border firms are now competitive with firms in Japan, Hong Kong, Germany, Korea and Singapore.

THE BORDER INDUSTRIALIZATION PROGRAM

The Mexican government's response to the end of the Bracero Program was to start the **Border Industrialization Program** (B.I.P.) for companies located in the Mexican Frontier Zone along the U.S. border. The purpose of the B.I.P. was to encourage manufacturing plants to be set up along the Mexican border with the United States. The idea behind the B.I.P. is that the United States and Mexico have complementary economic strengths and resources. Combining these resources would create one of the world's most dynamic manufacturing regions.

The economic advantages Mexico brings to the B.I.P. include:

1. A large, willing, and highly productive work force which is equal to or better than that found in many Asian countries.
2. The work force's proven adaptability to new production techniques such as those that have made the Japanese so efficient and quality oriented. This is not always the case with American workers, particularly in areas

[1]Vice-President, Economic Development Research, Council for South Texas Economic Progress.

38

of the United States having a long manufacturing tradition combined with a history of industrial strife.

3. Closeness to U.S. markets and manufacturing centers, which keeps transportation costs low and transport time shorter than if the factories were in Asia or Europe. Goods can be shipped by truck all the way from U.S. and Mexican plants to their U.S. customers. There is no need for an in-between boat trip, as is the case for products made in Asia or Europe.

4. Easy communications. The border is no more than three time zones away from any place in the U.S. This means that people in the U.S. can easily make phone calls to border operations.

5. The Mexican government's allowing participating foreign companies, including those from the United States, to be 100 percent foreign owned. Other foreign companies in Mexico have to be at least 51 percent Mexican owned. There are no tariffs on imported raw materials, parts or components for companies participating in the program as long as all products and equipment are eventually exported. However, to guarantee that this will be the case, the companies have to post bonds, something like jail bonds, to make sure the machines and materials are sent out of Mexico when finished. This feature has given the B.I.P. one of its other names—"In Bond Program."

6. Special assistance. Because companies in the B.I.P. were helping Mexico's economy, the Mexican government made special efforts to reduce the government bureaucratic red tape. The Mexican government also made provisions to reduce these companies' taxes.

The economic advantages the United States brings to manufacturing in the Mexican border region include:

1. Tariff exemption. The border program utilizes the provisions in the U.S. Customs Code to exempt from U.S. tariffs any components and parts made in the United States, but assembled into final products in a foreign country and then brought back into the United States for sale. This is called **production sharing**. Production sharing occurs when an item is partially made in a U.S. plant and completed in another plant located in Mexico. This has been named the Twin Plant System.

2. The knowledge, skills, education, technology, and investment money that U.S. companies can supply to establish the manufacturing plants.

3. The U.S. companies' established distribution channels and business contacts, which enable them to sell the products the twin plants produce.

The first companies established in Mexico were subcontractors who assembled parts into products for U.S. firms. The subcontractors do not own the parts or products they assemble. As a result, the plants are called *maquilas* in Spanish, meaning "mills," like flour mills. The miller did not own the grain he was grinding for the farmer; since the Mexican subcontractors do not own the material they are working on, the Spanish name *maquiladora* (miller) seems appropriate. The B.I.P. program is also called the **maquiladora program**.

The first factories in the program were owned by Mexican subcontractors. Soon the United States realized that the twin plant idea was a real money maker. As a result, U.S. manufacturers set up their own twin plants in Mexico's border communities.

Most of the first twin plants taking part in the program made clothes, assembled electronic goods such as televisions, radios, and stereos, or made all kinds of toys. Some plants were also set up to sort out supermarket cents-off coupons. As time has passed, the type of products made in the twin plants has widened to include automobile parts, machinery, machine parts, medical equipment, minicomputers, and furniture.

There are about 1,300 maquilas along the U.S. border in Mexico. Of these, 400 to 500 are across from Texas. The program grew slowly from 1965 to 1982 when there were 455 plants in the program.

The reasons for this slow growth were:

1. Manufacturers are by nature very cautious in investing large amounts of money for new

plants, especially in foreign countries, even if only across a river.

2. Many manufacturers did not think that unskilled Mexican workers would be as productive as American or Asian workers.

3. Most importantly, Mexican wages before 1982, while low compared to those earned by U.S. workers, were higher than those of Asian workers.

These wage differences meant it was cheaper to make things in Asia and ship them across the Pacific Ocean to U.S. markets than to make them in Mexico and truck them across Rio Grande bridges. This problem of higher Mexican wages was a consequence of the 1979-1982 oil boom which drove up Mexican wages. Additionally, many believed that Mexican workers were competing against American workers, when in fact the Mexican workers were competing against Asian workers, who received lower wages.

This situation started changing in 1982 when the world price of crude oil collapsed and Mexico was forced to devalue the peso in relation to the U.S. dollar. When the value of the peso dropped, so too did the value of the maquila workers' wages in terms of U.S. dollars. For example, if a person made five pesos an hour when one peso could buy one dollar, then the Mexican's wage in U.S. money would be five dollars an hour. If the exchange rate dropped so that it took two pesos to buy one dollar, then the Mexican earning five pesos would only be making two dollars and fifty cents an hour in American wages. When the value of the peso dropped, Mexican wages were lowered relative to U.S. wages. This reduced the cost of maquila goods, which were then better able to compete in U.S. markets against products made in Asia, where exchange rates had not fallen. Recently, this situation has further improved as the value of many Asian currencies has increased against both the dollar and the peso. This increase has made Asian goods even less competitive in U.S. markets when compared to maquila products.

Currently, assembly workers in Mexico earn about $1.10 to $1.20 an hour including all benefits and company-paid taxes such as Social Security. Many people in Mexico have realized that Mexico's maquila program is really competing with Japan, Hong King, Korea, and even Brazil.

As a result, the decision has been made to keep Mexican wage rates competitive with these other newly industrializing countries.

American manufacturers learned that Mexican workers are hard workers having very high productivity and quality standards. American manufacturers also found out that with the maquiladora program they had the best of all worlds. They could keep their research, development, engineering programs, and other operations at their American plants. These could be combined with manufacturing operations in Mexico which use large amounts of low-cost labor. The combined production process is able to produce goods for markets in the United States and other countries which are competitive in quality and price with those made anywhere else in the world.

The success of the B.I.P. maquiladora program has meant that many American companies participating in it have been able to keep major portions of the operations in the United States instead of closing their American factories entirely because of foreign imports. The success of the maquiladora program in keeping American jobs has been confirmed in studies done by the U.S. International Trade Commission and the U.S. Department of Labor.

The success of the maquiladora program has lead to an influx of new manufacturing plants. The number of plants grew from 455 in 1982 to 629 in 1985 to about 1,300 in 1988, with many more companies expected to join the program in coming years. It has been so successful that the Mexican government has extended B.I.P. to cover the entire country. This move is seen as the surest way to develop Mexico's economy.

BENEFITS OF THE BORDER INDUSTRIALIZATION PROGRAM

Given that these factories are located in Mexico, the question has been raised, "How do these plants benefit Texas?"

First, the flow of goods to and from maquila twin plants is helping develop the border region into a major transportation center. This is reducing the cost of transportation not only for maquila products, but also for the other goods Texas border communities bring in or ship out for their own use.

Second, job opportunities in the Texas border communities are increased. The maquilas store parts and completed goods in warehouses on the Texas side of the border. These generate jobs for customs brokers, warehousemen, truck drivers, and office and technical workers.

Third, most American personnel who work as managers, engineers, and other specialized staff in the maquila plants normally live in the Texas communities across the border from the plants. These people and their families add to the local communities' economic growth just as if they worked in Texas.

Another promising development for the Texas border communities is the trend for the American companies which supply parts to the maquila plants to set up factories on the U.S. side of the border to make those parts. These plants offer employment opportunities for border Texans which would not be there if the maquiladora program didn't exist.

CONCLUSION

The maquila plants have demonstrated that the Texas Border Region can support sophisticated manufacturing operations with a skilled, productive labor force while providing all their employees an excellent life style. The program has

encouraged other companies, which have nothing to do with twin plants, to establish manufacturing operations on the Texas side of the border in such fields as aerospace and apparel.

CONTENT QUESTIONS

1. What was the Bracero Program?
2. What is the purpose of the Border Industrialization Program?
3. Mexican workers do not compete with American workers but with workers from where?
4. Explain the twin plant system.
5. What event made Mexican wages competitive?

DISCUSSION QUESTIONS

1. Discuss the advantages that Mexico and the United States bring to manufacturing along the U.S. border.
2. How do you think the maquiladora program has affected U.S./Mexican relations?

10

THE TEXAS PLAINS REGION

Clinton Daniels, Ph.D.,[1]
and
Patrick Kelso, Ph.D.[2]

The Plains is the largest in area of the six economic regions of Texas. This can be seen by looking at the map in the introduction to Part II (Figure II-1). The Plains Region includes 98 of the state's 254 counties. It accounts for 39 percent of the total number of counties in Texas, and about 40 percent of the land area of the state.

In 1987, the population of the region was estimated to be 1,826,400 persons. Given the land area, the Plains is considered to be the most sparsely populated of the six regions, having approximately 17 persons per square mile.

It is important to note that, while the Plains Region as a whole is sparsely populated, over half of its people live in densely populated metropolitan areas. The seven largest population centers (and the counties in which they are located) are: Odessa (Ector), Lubbock (Lubbock), Midland (Midland), Amarillo (Potter, Randall), Abilene (Taylor), San Angelo (Tom Green), and Wichita Falls (Wichita). See Figure 10-1. The biggest of these centers is Lubbock, with a 1987 population estimated at 227,263. The smallest is San Angelo, with an estimated population of 96,400. The federal government calls such population of centers **Metropolitan Statistical Areas** or M.S.A.'s. More information on these M.S.A.'s will follow later in this chapter.

THE ECONOMIC BASE OF THE PLAINS

The State Comptroller of Public Accounts divides the state into economic regions as an aid to analyzing the impact of economic changes on Texas. Regions are defined by differing combinations of natural resources, human resources, and technology. These combinations determine what the Comptroller's Office refers to as a region's economic base, that is, those products and services which provide the sources of employment and income within a region.

The economic base of the Plains is especially related to the presence of two exhaustible natural resources, oil and groundwater. It follows that petroleum and irrigated agricultural products are very significant in the region. Weakened demand for these products creates regional economic problems. Furthermore, since both oil and groundwater are exhaustible resources, the region has good reason to develop a more diversified economic base over the longer term. The economy of the southeastern part of the Plains is currently considered more diversified than other sections of the region.

Petroleum

Discovery of oil in West Texas dates from the 1920s. The economic growth of the region has been based, in part, on the large demand for petroleum products since that time.

[1]Associate Professor of Economics; Director, Center for Economic Education, West Texas State University, Canyon, Texas.
[2]Associate Professor of Economics, West Texas State University, Canyon, Texas.

42

FIGURE 10-1
The Plains Region

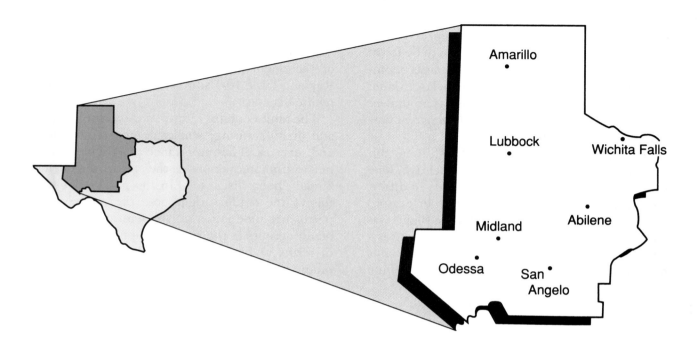

Source: Texas Comptroller of Public Accounts, *Fiscal Notes*, November 1988, p.8.

Oil and gas are the main component of the economic base of the Northern Panhandle, and the west central and southwestern parts of the Plains. The Midland-Odessa area is of major importance in this regard. In 1986, approximately 67 percent of the crude oil and 28 percent of the natural gas produced in the state came from the Plains.

Water

Water resources are essential for the production of agricultural products. Aquifers supplying groundwater are found under more than half of the area of the state. Of special importance is the Ogallala Aquifer which furnishes irrigation on the High Plains (the northwestern part of the region). In 1985, the Plains accounted for about 41 percent of the value of farm production in Texas.

The presence of groundwater has made possible the production of extensive amounts of cotton, grain, sorghum, wheat, and corn. In addition, the area from Lubbock north to Amarillo is recognized as a national leader in feedlot cattle production.

Diversity

The southeastern part of the Plains is described as having smaller farms which are not so dependent on irrigation. Ranching is prominent. Petroleum production is of lesser importance than in other parts of the region. The two population centers here are Abilene and San Angelo, which have diversified local economies. Thus downturns in the prices of oil and agricultural products affect this area less than the remainder of the Plains Region.

EMPLOYMENT AND INCOME

Based on 1984 data, total employment in the Plains Region was 967,626. About 92 percent, or 890,216 persons, were classified as being employed in nonfarm activities and 8 percent, or 77,410 persons, in farm employment.

The unemployment rate for 1984 was 4.7 percent, 1.2 percent below the overall state unemployment rate of 5.9 percent for that year. This should not be taken as a sign that the Plains economy was stronger than the state economy. Unemployment in rural regions tends to be lower than in large metropolitan areas because unemployed workers tend to migrate to large labor markets. Also, the Border Region has an unusually high unemployment due to the constant flow of aliens across the border.

Personal income in 1984 was $22.9 billion. But that figure needs to be put into perspective. One way of comparing the economic vitality of different places is in terms of per capita (per person) income. The per capita income for the Plains was only 3.4 percent lower than that for the state as a whole. Among the six Texas regions, the Plains ranks third in per capita personal income behind the Metroplex ($15,133) and the Gulf Coast ($13,868).

THE PLAINS M.S.A.'S

The following paragraphs provide a brief picture of the major population centers of the Plains Region. Table 10-1 summarizes some basic economic data.

The table contains information on employment and manufacturing, wholesale and retail trade, and services. The importance of agriculture and petroleum production to the entire region has already been discussed. In the paragraphs that follow, the reader might note the influence of petroleum production on the nature of the economic activity in these major population centers, in terms of both raw materials and peripheral products and services.

TABLE 10-1
Selected Economic Statistics for M.S.A.'s in The Plains Region of Texas (1982 figures unless otherwise noted)

Economic Component	Abilene (Taylor)	Amarillo (Potter, Randall)	Lubbock (Lubbock)	Midland (Midland)	Odessa (Ector)	San Angelo (Tom Green)	Wichita Falls (Wichita)
Total Employment (1984)	48,802	75,939	85,077	49,445	50,373	36,092	47,532
Employed in Manufacturing (1984)	5,472	10,060	8,738	3,521	4,495	5,582	8,905
No. Manufacturing Establishments	145	195	292	139	323	101	173
Manufacturing Product Value (millions of dollars)	1,515.8	2,685.4	949.5	427.7	1,561.5	363.1	N.A.
Retail Sales (millions of dollars)	804.3	1,220.5	1,344.8	713.4	993.3	571.4	N.A.
Wholesale Sales (millions of dollars)	1,533.6	2,242.7	2,714.8	2,334.3	1,679.1	621.3	576.4
No. of Service Industry Establishments	804	1,136	1,373	774	871	542	722
Service Industry Receipts (millions of dollars)	223.8	342.6	388.5	329.0	368.5	163.2	231.3

Source: Mike Kingston, ed., *Texas Almanac and State Industrial Guide 1986–87* (Dallas: Dallas Morning News, 1986), pp. 278, 323, 329, 340, 359, 362, 371.
N.A. = not available

Abilene

Abilene is described as being the center of a 22-county area called "Big Country," and is the hub of retail trade, manufacturing, farming and ranching, medical care, the petroleum industry, and other economic activities of this part of Texas. The town was established in 1881 upon the completion of the Texas and Pacific Railway and has experienced steady growth as the "Key City."

Abilene's manufacturers employ 11 percent of the city's labor force and produce a wide variety of products which include clothing, food lines, consumer electronics, brick and tile, concrete, feeds, cottonseed oil products, musical instruments, structural steel, machine shop products, toys, aircraft and helicopter component parts, air conditioners, campers, sporting equipment, faucets and other brass products, and tire retreads.

Abilene is the home of Abilene Christian University, Hardin-Simmons University, McMurry College, an Extension Center of Texas State Technical Institute and a technical center operated under the auspices of Texas A&M University.

Dyess Air Force Base in Abilene is among the most important military installations in the free world. It is home to a wing of B-1B bombers and is the 'schoolhouse' for all B-1B training. Given its several other missions, the base involves the combined efforts of over 7,000 military personnel, civilian employees, and contractors.

Amarillo

Amarillo is considered to be a regional trade center serving parts of five states. While natural gas production and cattle are important segments of the economic base, Amarillo has, in addition, a diversity of industry with 14 percent of its labor force employed in manufacturing. The activities of its largest employers include nuclear assembly (the final assembly point for the country's nuclear warheads), beef slaughtering and packing, rail transport, refining of nonferrous metals, helicopter modification and refurbishment, fiberglass production, dyeing and processing of denim clothing, and food distribution.

Amarillo serves as a medical and educational center for the High Plains region. Its medical center complex occupies the largest land area set aside for that purpose in the nation. Hospitals are among the major employers.

Educational institutions include West Texas State University (Canyon), Amarillo College (Community College), and branches of Texas State Technical Institute and Texas Tech's Medical School.

Lubbock

Lubbock is a regional agricultural, energy, trade, service, and educational center for a large area of the High Plains.

Agribusiness and energy are major economic activities. Lubbock is the home of the world's largest cottonseed processing center. However, the economy is diversified, with 10 percent of the labor force in manufacturing. Major employers include producers of electronic equipment, earth moving equipment, chips and snacks, steel, irrigation pumps, bakery products, fire detection and protection equipment, and soft drinks.

Educational institutions include Texas Tech University, Lubbock Christian University, and South Plains College.

Midland

The Sesquicentennial Edition of the Texas Almanac, in describing Midland, stated: "The petroleum industry dominates the area's economy. Midland is an administrative and operations center for production in the Permian Basin, which for much of the twentieth century has been the nation's most productive petroleum reservoir. Midland was established in the 1870s." Other lines of production include electronic products, bearings, military products, and plastic moldings. Manufacturing of all sorts employs 7 percent of Midland's labor force.

Midland College is located here.

Odessa

Like Midland, petroleum dominates the Odessa economy. Products of major employers include oil and natural gas, hydrocarbons, petrochemicals, synthetic rubber, and oil and gas processing equipment.

Educational institutions include the University of Texas of the Permian Basin, Odessa College, and Texas Tech Academic Health Center.

San Angelo

San Angelo began as a trading post near Fort Concho in 1867 and over time has developed into a center for petroleum and agricultural products. Of particular significance are sheep and wool. San Angelo is recognized as the country's largest primary wool market, with the production, processing and shipping of wool and mohair being of major importance.

Goods manufactured here include surgical sutures and needles, men's jeans, and house slippers. Manufacturing provides 15 percent of the city's employment.

San Angelo is the home of Angelo State University and a Texas A&M Research and Extension Center.

Wichita Falls

The Texas Almanac describes this city as "an important manufacturing, wholesale and retail and distributions center for a large section of north Texas and southern Oklahoma."

Agribusiness and oil production are important here. Manufactured products provide 19 percent of total employment and include fiberglass, clothing, electronic components, aircraft turbine components, and hand tools. Sheppard Air Force Base is also a major contributor to Wichita Falls' economy.

Educational institutions include Midwestern State University and Vernon Regional Junior College.

CONCLUSION

In 1987–88 the Plains Region was the brightest star in the state's economic recovery. Exports of apparel, electronics, plastics, and farm products were booming. Farmers received the best prices in years for grain and livestock. With the stabilization of oil prices even the oil industry showed signs of recovery. Employment was up in every city. Barring another collapse in oil prices, the recovery should continue.

CONTENT QUESTIONS

1. What two resources are most important to the economy of the Plains?
2. How much of the state's oil and agricultural output comes from the Plains Region?
3. How does the Plains Region compare economically with the rest of Texas?

DISCUSSION QUESTIONS

1. Since the economy of the Plains Region is tied to exhaustible resources, what should be done to insure the region's economic future?
2. How are the major cities of the Plains Region similar, and how are they different?

11
THE CENTRAL CORRIDOR OF TEXAS

Calvin A. Kent, Ph.D.[1]

The Central Corridor of Texas stretches along Interstate 35 from San Antonio in the south to Waco in the north. It encompasses many of the state's more prosperous metropolitan areas including San Antonio, Austin, Killeen/Temple/

[1]Herman W. Lay Professor of Private Enterprise; Director, Center for Private Enterprise, Baylor University, Waco, Texas.

Belton, Waco, and Bryan/College Station. See Figure 11-1. For the first six years of the 1980s, the Central Corridor was the fastest-growing of the Texas regions in terms of population, income, and jobs. Almost three million people lived here in 1985. Personal income per capita was $11,859, only slightly less than the state average of $12,798.

FIGURE 11-1
The Central Corridor

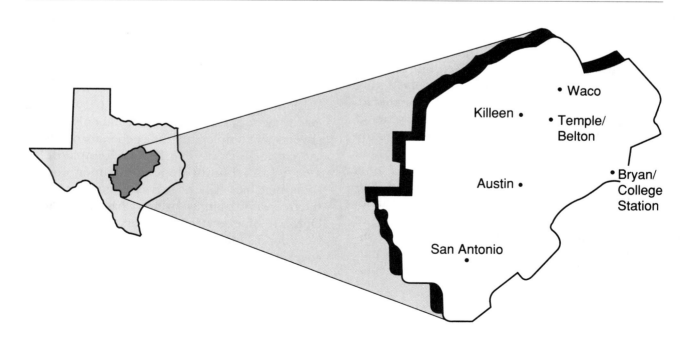

Source: Texas Comptroller of Public Accounts, *Fiscal Notes*, November 1988, p.8.

CURRENT CONDITIONS

The economic growth in this region is primarily due to its economic diversity. Like the Dallas/Fort Worth Metroplex, the Central Corridor is not dependent upon the depressed petroleum industry and relies on fast-growing industries which include services, high technology, manufacturing, national defense, and government. From 1980 to 1985, employment in the area grew by 5 percent while employment for the entire state expanded by only 1 percent.

Economic growth in the Central Corridor has slowed toward the end of the 1980s. This slowing has been caused by two factors. The first is overbuilding. The fast pace of growth in the Central Corridor during the early 1980s caused a building boom for both office space and homes. Supply grew faster than demand, and the resulting surpluses have depressed the market.

The second factor has been the slowdown in high technology. Overproduction of items like computer chips and competition from foreign producers have limited sales. But the prospects for continued growth and expansion of the Central Corridor look good as manufacturing, services, government, and high technology will continue to be strong sources of growth for the nation as a whole.

Manufacturing

The growth of jobs in the manufacturing sector in the Central Corridor has been spectacular during the 1980s. While the rest of Texas lost manufacturing employment during the first six years of the decade, manufacturing employment actually increased by 10 percent in the Central Corridor. A good percentage of these manufacturing firms were in high technology, which generated two-thirds of the new manufacturing jobs. Manufacturing has shifted away from the processing of Texas-grown food and fiber toward the more sophisticated and better-paying high-tech manufacturing industries such as computers and communication equipment.

Services

The Central Corridor provides a wide variety of services to the rest of the state and the nation.

The service sector of the Texas economy includes firms in health care, transportation, communications, public utilities, retail trade, wholesale distribution, finance, real estate, and government. Also included as service firms are the laboratories that design and produce new technologies. Research and development (R&D) firms are attracted to the Central Corridor by its many outstanding colleges and universities. Almost 50 percent of all Central Corridor jobs were in service areas such as these. The service sector to be successful must "export." This means that those living outside the region must purchase the services. When the services are purchased, money flows into the region, creating new jobs and profits for the service-based firms.

Government Services

Not to be neglected is the role of the government in the Central Corridor. Austin is the state capital, and employment in state and related agencies dominates the economy. All state agencies have staffs in Austin. As these employees spend their incomes, they create a demand for retail stores to serve them as well as a demand for insurance, real estate, and medical services. These indirect effects are part of the total impact of government payrolls in a region.

In addition, federal dollars pour into the region's fifteen federal civilian and military installations. The military has nine bases and six military hospitals. San Antonio has the largest federal payroll of all cities in the United States except Washington, D.C. and New York City. Federal government employment is second only to state government employment as a generator of jobs for the city of Austin. The Killeen/Temple/Belton area is also highly dependent upon federal spending since Killeen serves as the gateway for the free world's largest military base, Fort Hood. One out of every four workers in the Central Corridor is employed by the federal or state government. Government spending is more important in the Central Corridor than in any other region of Texas.

Higher Education

The Central Corridor is also the state's largest provider of higher education. There are 27 institutions providing education beyond high school in this region. Almost a quarter of a million students obtain their postsecondary education at one of the Central Corridor's schools. The state's two largest universities, the University of Texas at Austin and Texas A&M University in Bryan/College Station, are in this region. Colleges and universities benefit a region not just because of staff payrolls. When new facilities are built, construction expands. Students spend money on food, housing, and recreation. Professors receive outside grants to support their research. Across the Central Corridor, universities and colleges are the breeding grounds for R&D firms. Many of these firms are founded by graduates. The schools are a source of new employees. Faculty members are available to serve as consultants.

MAJOR METROPOLITAN AREAS

When the government gathers statistics about an area, it does not confine itself to just the major city. Included are all the suburban cities and towns which surround the core city. This grouping is called a Metropolitan Statistical Area (M.S.A.). What follows is a discussion concerning the entire M.S.A.'s, not just single cities.

Austin

Austin, once known as Waterloo, was named after Stephen F. Austin, who founded the first American settlement in the state. It was chosen as the site for the capital of the Republic of Texas in 1839 and later became the capital of the new state. The Austin economy is based on government, education, and tourism.

The Austin M.S.A. had a 1985 population of 726,800. Although state and federal government employment dominate the economy, the attraction of high-tech industries such as computers and semi-conductors in the 1980s has lent both diversification and stability to the Austin area economy. The Austin area is one of the five leading high-tech areas in the nation. One other, Dallas/Fort Worth, is located in Texas. (The other three areas are found near Boston, near San Francisco, and near Raleigh, North Carolina.) The central campus of the University of Texas, regarded by many as one of the twenty best universities in the nation, is located in Austin.

The area's cultural, educational, and historical attractions bring thousands of visitors to Austin each year. The state capitol, the governor's mansion, and the Lyndon B. Johnson Presidential Library on the University of Texas campus are the primary tourist destinations. Nearby are the L.B.J. Ranch, President Johnson's boyhood home, and the picturesque Texas hill country. Austin has been ranked as first in terms of quality of life among Texas cities.

Bryan/College Station

The dominant feature of the Bryan/College Station economy is Texas A&M University. The 1985 population of the area was 120,800. Texas A&M University's schools of agriculture and engineering are the largest and among the most respected in the nation. The presence of the university has led to a boom in high-tech and research-related businesses and manufacturing in the area. Bryan has long been a center for agribusiness serving the highly prosperous farm and livestock region. The future of Bryan/College Station is tied to the continued drive for excellence on the part of Texas A&M University. The future is hampered by less than adequate transportation. It is the only major city in the region not near Interstate 35. Unlike Austin and San Antonio, Bryan/College Station does not have a major airport.

Killeen/Temple/Belton

The cities of Killeen, Temple, and Belton were among the fastest-growing of any in the nation during the 1970s and early 1980s. The 1985 population totaled 233,700. Military payrolls are the cornerstone of the local economy. Killeen is located at the main entrance of Fort Hood, where over 40,000 soldiers are stationed. Health services are also important to the area's economy. The military maintains hospitals in both Killeen and Temple. Temple is an internationally-known medical center. In recent years, Temple has been particularly successful in attracting new manufacturing industry. Recreation is also a growth industry. The nearby city of Salado has capitalized on its history as an old stagecoach stop to become an artist colony known worldwide.

San Antonio

San Antonio is the largest city in the Central Corridor, the third largest in the state, and the eleventh largest in the nation. Of the total population of 1,276,400 in the M.S.A., almost 850,000 live in the city itself. San Antonio also is the region's major tourist attraction. Originally an Indian village, the original Franciscan mission of San Antonio de Valero was one of the earliest permanent Spanish settlements in the state. Later known as the Alamo, and then as San Antonio de Bexar, the city became the capital of the Spanish province of Texas and was also the center for the mission work of the Catholic church.

Mexico, which at that time included the territory of Texas, won its independence from Spain during the revolution of 1821. San Antonio is the home of the Alamo, which became a symbol of Texas fortitude when 187 of its defenders fought to the death against 5,000 attacking Mexicans during the Texas Revolution in 1836. In addition to the Alamo, the Spanish culture makes San Antonio a prime tourist stop. The San Antonio Zoo, the art museums, Governor's Palace, the Tower of the Americas, Hemisphere Plaza, the Institute of Texas Cultures, and the Paseo del Rio (the Riverwalk, beside the river which flows through the center of the city) attract millions of tourists each year.

However, the primary source of income for those in the San Antonio area is the federal government. There are five military installations either within or just outside the city limits. San Antonio also serves as a wholesale/retail, financial, and distribution center for almost all of southern Texas. Recent years have seen a steady growth in manufacturing.

Waco

Deriving its name from the Huaco (Way Co) Indians, whose encampment on the banks of the Brazos River became the site of the city, Waco has long been a crossroads for trade and travel in central Texas. Cattle drives northward along the Chisholm Trail had to ford the Brazos River at Waco. This was the only place where the Brazos could be forded, from its start in the northern part of the state all the way to the gulf. The construc-

tion of a suspension bridge in 1870 further strengthened Waco's position as a center for commerce as well as a rough and tumble cow town. In 1837, the Texas Rangers established a camp which has now become Fort Fisher.

Waco became an agribusiness center when central Texas was one of the world's largest cotton-producing regions. Despite the decline of the cotton industry beginning with the depression of 1920, Waco continues to serve as the principal trade center for the blacklands farm belt.

In recent years, numerous small manufacturing plants, including the world's largest candy factory, have located in Waco primarily because of the city's central location. Once known as the Athens of Texas because of its many educational institutions, Waco is the home of Baylor University, which is the oldest continuing institution of higher education in the state, having been founded in the days of the Texas Republic. Texas State Technical Institute is the largest technical school in the state and is a national leader in high technology. Baylor and T.S.T.I., along with the other two institutions of higher education, serve as the economic base for the area.

CONCLUSION

By the end of 1988 the San Antonio area was booming. The opening of a new major tourist attraction, Sea World, and a major shopping mall were important developments. Killeen/Temple/Belton and Waco gained jobs due to increased manufacturing activity. The Austin economy remained sluggish due to an oversupply of homes and commercial buildings.

The Central Corridor will play a pivotal position in the state's economic development in the future. Over the next decade, nine out of ten new jobs in the United States will be created in services and high technology. The Central Corridor leads the state in providing opportunities in these areas. The excellent research facilities available at the colleges and universities, along with the relatively low cost of labor, indicates further growth for manufacturing employment. The heavy concentration of higher education facilities within the Corridor will continue to be a source of growth and economic vitality.

CONTENT QUESTIONS

1. Economic growth in the Central Corridor is due primarily to what?
2. What types of firms constitute the service sector of the economy?
3. The Central Corridor is the principal location in the state for which two types of spending?

DISCUSSION QUESTIONS

1. How does spending for government services or higher education benefit a region?
2. How do the cities of the Central Corridor compare, and how do they contrast?

THE TEXAS METROPLEX
John B. McCall, Ph.D.,[1]
and
Chee-Ooi Low[2]

The Metroplex is the urbanized area which has Dallas and Fort Worth as its center. The federal government has designated this area the Dallas-Fort Worth Combined Metropolitan Statistical Area. This governmental definition adds together not only Dallas County and Tarrant County (Fort Worth), but also the immediately surrounding counties: Denton and Collin to the north, Parker to the west, Johnson and Ellis to the south, and Rockwall and Kaufman to the east. See Figure 12-1.

[1]Associate Professor of Economics; Director, Center for Economic Education, University of Texas at Arlington.
[2]Graduate Assistant, University of Texas at Arlington.

FIGURE 12-1
The Metroplex

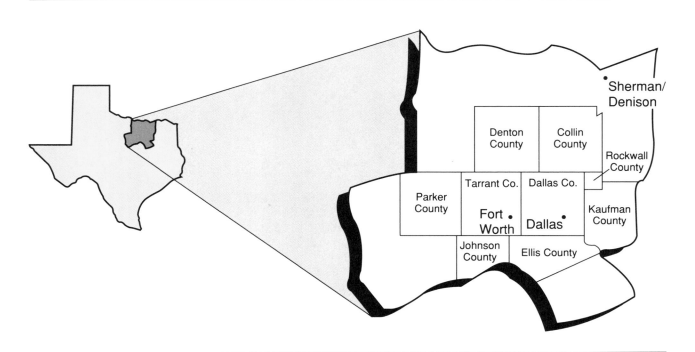

Source: Texas Comptroller of Public Accounts, *Fiscal Notes*, November 1988, p. 8.

Roughly one-quarter of the state population lives in the Metroplex and the per capita personal income is over $15,000 a year, the highest in the state and higher than the national average. Of the six regional economies in the state (the Plains, East Texas, the Gulf Coast, the Central Corridor, and the Border Region are the other five), the Metroplex has the most diversified economic base.

After experiencing spectacular economic growth during the 1950–80 period, the Metroplex has slumped with the rest of the Texas economy during the 1980s. Due to overbuilding, the Metroplex has been the slowest economic region to respond to the state recovery which began in 1987.

The announcement that the federal government will build its new super collider just south of Dallas near Waxahachie is great news. The $6 billion project will create 3,500 to 4,000 new jobs when finished. Most of these will be for professional and technical workers.

WHY DO URBAN AREAS EXIST?

The Metroplex is a good example of the fact that patterns of economic activity do not stop at political boundaries such as county, state, or even national lines. Although political borders may serve as barriers to the flow of goods and services, and although these borders may influence where a business firm chooses to locate, as well as where it buys its inputs and sells its outputs, these barriers are usually weak. The forces that cause economic activity to cluster at certain locations are more likely to involve the following tendencies:

1. Raw materials (including labor in the short run) are not distributed evenly across the map; they tend to cluster in certain locations.
2. Both positive and negative geographical factors are unevenly spaced. In the past, when transport was primitive, a deep river, a mountain barrier, a harsh climate, and many other geographical features influenced where people chose to work and live. Such decisions, once created, tend to survive on their own momentum, even when the forces that influenced them pass away.
3. Both the availability and the cost of transportation (highways, riverboats, railroads, airline routes) will influence where businesses choose to locate and where the workers in these businesses decide to live. Transportation also interacts with geographical factors in determining where cities form. For example, transport routes will tend to intersect at points of favorable geographical conditions. Freight and passengers will, therefore, tend to pause there, and will perhaps be unloaded in the process of changing from railroads to boats, as at a harbor on the coast.
4. As business firms, and the people making their living in these firms, begin to cluster at particular locations on the map, a symbiosis begins to develop—they begin to support each other by their close proximity. Firms now can specialize in what they produce by efficiently subcontracting some of their tasks to others. They no longer have to perform all the steps in manufacturing their product themselves, as they would have to do in an isolated location.
5. At the same time, this clustering of businesses and people will generate a large and ready market for their products, right at hand, and easily and efficiently reached. This, in turn, will cause these businesses to grow larger and perhaps realize economies of scale, with lower costs.
6. To the extent these businesses grow larger and to specialize, they tend to evolve production methods that use relatively more capital (in the form of tools) with each worker. As a result, each worker is able to produce more than would be possible in a location that is isolated by geographical barriers or by poor transportation. So jobs in cities can offer higher wages to workers than jobs in isolated locations. The higher wages attract yet more population from isolated locations, further expanding the local market for goods and services.
7. As a city grows large, it begins to not only serve its own local population but it also to draw shoppers from surrounding locations (from how far away depends upon the quality and cost of transportation into the city). This

further enlarges the local market. Large cities can support professional sports teams, large amusement parks, and large shopping malls, as well as specialized financial and medical institutions which draw upon the surrounding region (and beyond) as a part of their market.

These seven factors, and others, are all mutually supportive and act together to cause some towns to grow into cities.

Each city has evolved from its own particular mix of the above factors. The Metroplex grew from two small towns to its present size as a result of its own mix of factors. Understanding this mix of factors, and the resulting contribution of the Metroplex to both the state economy and the national economy, is a useful learning exercise in economic patterns and relationships.

HOW DID THE METROPLEX GROW?

The Local Context

Understanding the present Metroplex economy first requires a short detour to explore its more recent history as a part of the larger industrialized state and nation. Prior to the coming of the first railroad to Dallas in 1872, the immediate area was in its early stages of organized small-scale farming and ranching. Transportation over land, from the east and northeast, was both slow and expensive. Transport up the Trinity River from the coast was uncertain at best. The unsettled and wild areas to the west in effect formed an economic barrier to the Dallas area, much like a high mountain range. There were no markets out west which could demand goods from or supply goods to the Dallas locale. Even if markets existed there, transport to and fro was so dangerous and expensive that little economic exchange would have taken place anyway. The Dallas area, therefore, was a fairly primitive localized economy on the edge of a nation that was just beginning to industrialize.

The rural families and the villages located in what is now the Metroplex were largely local economies that consumed all they produced, with little export of agricultural products to other areas and little importing of manufactured goods from other areas. Remember that if any area wishes to import goods, it must have something to sell as an export in order to earn the money to buy those imports.

Apart from fairly self-sufficient agriculture, the area was endowed with no natural resources that would allow it to grow into a larger-output/higher-living-standard economy. Three post-Civil War trends at the national level changed this situation and caused what is now the Metroplex to begin to grow.

The National Context

First, U.S. population began to grow both from native birth and, perhaps more importantly, from immigration. Although some of this population moved on westward (including to Texas), most of the growth remained in the Northeast in the established cities. This population growth created a need for food and clothing, and all the other primary things necessary to life, that outstripped the ability of the established agricultural areas (Ohio, Indiana, and so forth) to supply them. The national market for what the Metroplex area in particular, and the Texas area in general, was endowed to supply—agricultural output—began to grow rapidly.

Second, after the Civil War, the nation moved rapidly, if unsteadily, toward industrialization—toward an economic base that was founded upon manufacturing instead of agriculture. The growing population was absorbed by the new factories, which themselves required more raw materials from the West.

Third, the national mood turned inward. The push was to settle the West, to place people out there who would both create products in the process of earning a living and also demand the manufactured products of the industrializing Northeast. Because this new area was arid and encompassed vast distances, the basic tool of settlement was to be the railroad. The post-Civil War building of our railroad network west of the Mississippi River caused the nation to expand westward. Texas, though at a somewhat slower pace than much of the West, was included in this new activity.

Synthesis of the Local and National Contexts

The sleepy local economy that grew into what is now the Metroplex was placed on its growth path by the coming of the first railroad to Dallas in 1872. The Houston and Texas Central was built northward from the Gulf Coast ports to Dallas in that year, opening up the immediate area along its route to an efficient means by which its agricultural products could be exported. This, alone, was not sufficient for the area to grow as it has. The coming of other railroads fairly quickly—the Texas and Pacific from the east, as well as the Missouri-Kansas-Texas from the north—established Dallas as a crossroads point on Texas' developing transport network.

Leaving to the political historians the reasons why Dallas, and not some other town, was chosen by the railroads as a crossroads point, we can assess the economic impact of this intersecting railroad network. The impact went far beyond just providing access to a ready market to the east and to the Gulf Coast ports in the south for the agricultural produce of the local area.

First, because there were several railroads in competition for tonnage both into and out of Dallas, freight rates tended to be cheaper than in other areas of Texas. This allowed local exporters to deliver their products to distant markets at low "laid-down" prices. It likewise allowed local importers to deliver manufactured goods to the Dallas market at attractive prices. The result was a rapid growth of freight tonnage (and passenger traffic) both to and through Dallas. Local businesses of both the import and export variety benefited.

Second, because rail routes crossed at Dallas, this location became a natural place for freight shipments to be loaded and unloaded. Imports were "broken out" here from carload lots to smaller lots for local and regional distribution. Similarly, exports were gathered here from an ever-widening local region. They arrived in small lots and were combined into carload lots for shipment to distant markets. These processes, centered in Dallas, created businesses that spe-

cialized in such break-bulk and make-bulk activity. They provided jobs for local workers, and income which they could spend at other area businesses.

Third, as Dallas grew toward a regional freight-handling center, where shipments both in and out converged for processing, a variety of nontransport businesses began to develop in the area, which were supplementary to the transport activity. For example, the growing volume of agricultural export loading drew forth brokerage and trading firms to act as middlemen in selling these exports. The growing import tonnage likewise created a need for wholesale firms and storage firms to supply these manufactured products to the growing regional market. These businesses, in turn, called forth both specialized and general-service financial institutions to finance and to insure these transactions. As in any business area, the lawyers also found a niche. As the generation of wealth in the Dallas area began to take place, with growing tax payments to government, Dallas began to develop significant political clout at both the state and national levels. Governmental offices and government projects were drawn to the area.

Dallas, in short, was growing into a regional wholesale center for imported goods and was concurrently developing into a regional marketing center for export goods. Supporting these activities were growing financial, legal, and governmental sectors. With practically no local natural resources, Dallas was making a living as a service-driven economy. A similar arrival of intersecting railroads in Fort Worth a decade later promoted, to a somewhat lesser degree, the same activity in that location. The coming of the highway system in the 1920s intensified this growth process for both cities. Local construction businesses developed to support this growth.

The development of Texas' oil industry in the 1920s was initially financed and directed from Dallas, not because there was oil in the immediate locale, but because the city was already a financial and transportation center that could support the management and planning of these activities. New oil-related service businesses were launched in the area and, for the first time, local manufacturing—of oil field equipment—was undertaken. For a time, until Houston took over, Dallas was the business center for Texas' oil activity.

As the airline industry developed nationally in the 1920s and 1930s, both Dallas and Fort Worth became significant air traffic hubs. This development, coupled with the growing political importance of the area, was significant as the nation was gearing up in the late 1930s to fight World War II. Government spending for the manufacture of war-related goods—particularly aircraft and related products—provided a further boost to Dallas-Fort Worth employment, income, and profits. It created additional service-related businesses in the process. More and more people moved from the rural areas to find jobs in these businesses. The area had developed into an active and growing urban concentration of people, economic activity, and opportunity.

The growing population concentration and living standards, in turn, precipitated cultural activity, significant medical facilities, and regionally-important institutions of higher education and training. This provided a local source of skilled labor to sustain economic development.

After the big war, the process continued. As a spin-off from the technological developments in the airline industry, and from World War II generally, electronics manufacturing businesses—originally producing mainly radios and navigation equipment for airplanes—began to develop in their own right. Today, we call it "high-tech" industry. Texas Instruments, Collins Radio, and E-Systems were created, as well as the supporting firms such as that founded by Ross Perot. These firms took their place, alongside the oil field businesses like Dresser and the aircraft firms like L.T.V. and General Dynamics, as manufacturing firms in their own right. Nearly 40 percent of Texas' high-tech employment is located in today's Metroplex.

The completion of Dallas-Fort Worth regional airport in the 1970s, along with the "hub" type of operation of airline routes brought by deregulation, further expanded the Metroplex growth. Not only did many national firms locate their central offices in the Metroplex because of the ready intercity passenger service, but many new businesses that used air freight located here.

Finally, a common thread that runs through the growth of the area from its beginnings to present needs special comment. That common thread is entrepreneurship. Sometimes rowdy, often misdirected, occasionally illegal—but always energetic, the idea people, the risk-takers, the forward-lookers have always provided the catalyst that insured that the Metroplex got its share and more of the national opportunities for advancement.

CONTENT QUESTIONS

1. What event caused the Dallas area to start to grow?
2. List the factors that cause economic activities to cluster in an area.
3. How did World War II contribute to the growth of the Metroplex?

DISCUSSION QUESTIONS

1. How did the forces described in this chapter bring about the settlement of the town where you are now living?
2. What forces will cause the Metroplex to continue to grow in the future?

THE ECONOMIC BASE

Normally, when one thinks about what makes the Texas economy "tick"—if one thinks about it at all—one thinks of business firms paying incomes to people for their labor and for the raw materials that they own, and, at the same time producing useful things for sale to others. If incomes are high and if the things produced for sale are both plentiful and of good quality, then living standards are high; life is good.

For convenience in thinking about how economies function, it is usually helpful to group the various business firms together into clusters, each identified as an **industry**. An *industry* is a group of business firms that is engaged in some common form of economic activity. If a given industry hires lots of labor and uses raw materials, and if it creates a large percentage of the city's (or state's or nation's) economic activity, then it is viewed as a major industry. The impact of a major industry upon its surrounding economy is great. If this industry prospers, so does the surrounding economy, and *vice versa*.

WHY STUDY AN INDUSTRY?

One does not have to take a formal course in economics to understand the fundamental rela-tionship between a large industry and the living standard of its surrounding population. However, the formal learning of the economist's way of looking at things, using examples one already understands, allows one to proceed with the anal-ysis of economic examples that one does not yet understand. In the process, one comes to know more about how one dimension of the world—the economic dimension—works.

Other courses allow one to learn how other segments of our society are put together (politi-cal, engineering, cultural, historical). In time, the student begins to form a personal under-standing about how all these segments fit to-gether to make the world. This process is called education. Intertwined with this process is the learning of some specific skills that will allow the student to make a better living than would other-wise be possible. An understanding of how the world works allows the student to better apply these specific skills toward a favorable outcome.

You want to know how the world works, don't you? Certainly you are interested in how to im-prove the living you make for yourself as you go through life. That brings us back to economics.

Economics, at least in the Western world, is concerned with making money because money represents value created. Money earned is good in that it gives the earner (whether an individual, a region, or a nation) *more choices* in determining how they will make a good life for themselves and others. Economics, then, is fundamentally a study of choices and of the opportunity cost of every choice we make. We have to choose because none of us can have everything we want. Resources (including time) are scarce; they have alternative uses, and therefore scarce resources should be allocated to those economic activities where they will generate the greatest result for what they cost. In a market economy, that result is translated into money earned.

In the chapters that follow you will study the major industries of Texas. Do not think of industry only as a giant plant. As we have said, an industry is a group of firms and individuals who produce a product or service or a group of products or services that are closely related. Industries can be broadly defined, such as "agriculture," "government," or "manufacturing." They can be narrowly defined, such as "oil," "steel," "defense," or "tourism." Remember that if you live in Texas and have a job, you will work for a firm or agency in some Texas industry. Your economic prosperity will depend on that industry's prosperity.

13

THE TEXAS ECONOMIC BASE
Prepared by the Texas Research League
(Gary Wood, Ph.D. President), Austin, Texas

The Texas economy is only suffering a summer cold; last rites won't be necessary. Data recently released by the U.S. Department of Commerce, Bureau of Economic Analysis, show that Texas' gross state product (GSP — the state equivalent of GNP) grew by $49 billion between 1982 and 1986, up 19 percent (see Table 13-1).

At least part of the reason for so much doom and gloom in the past few years is the stark contrast those figures show to the 1972–82 boom to which Texans would have liked to become accustomed. During those 10 years, Texas GSP grew an astounding $189 billion, or 287 percent.

TABLE 13-1
Texas Total Gross State Product by Industry: 1963–1986
(Millions of Dollars)

	1963	1967	1972	1977	1982	1986
Agriculture	$ 1,330	$ 1,097	$ 2,041	$ 3,448	$ 5,378	$ 5,865
Mining	3,515	4,112	5,228	15,007	43,406	31,115
Construction	1,423	2,194	3,688	9,079	14,536	16,226
Manufacturing	5,800	8,649	12,172	24,890	40,980	48,708
Trans./Public Utilities	3,247	4,087	6,541	12,488	24,768	33,273
Wholesale/Retail Trade	4,954	6,784	11,589	21,967	40,824	51,441
Finance/Insur./Real Estate	3,892	5,129	8,996	16,887	30,843	41,403
Services	2,757	4,122	7,249	14,367	30,211	43,190
Government	3,147	4,985	8,243	13,958	23,562	32,289
TOTAL	$30,065	$41,159	$65,747	$132,091	$254,508	$303,510
Percent Distribution:						
Agriculture	4.4%	2.7%	3.1%	2.6%	2.1%	1.9%
Mining	11.7%	10.0%	8.0%	11.4%	17.1%	10.3%
Construction	4.7%	5.3%	5.6%	6.9%	5.7%	5.3%
Manufacturing	19.3%	21.0%	18.5%	18.8%	16.1%	16.0%
Trans./Public Utilities	10.8%	9.9%	9.9%	9.5%	9.7%	11.0%
Wholesale/Retail Trade	16.5%	16.5%	17.6%	16.6%	16.0%	16.9%
Finance/Insur./Real Estate	12.9%	12.5%	13.7%	12.8%	12.1%	13.6%
Services	9.2%	10.0%	11.0%	10.9%	11.9%	14.2%
Government	10.5%	12.1%	12.5%	10.6%	9.3%	10.6%
TOTAL	100.0%	100.0%	100.0%	100.0%	100.0%	100.0%

Source: U.S. Department of Commerce, Bureau of Economic Analysis, *Survey of Current Business*, Vol. 68, No. 5 (May 1988).

TEXAS' NEW LOOK

The GSP data also show that the Texas economy is taking on a new look. Figure 13-1 shows the accumulated percentage growth for the total Texas GSP and for the five industrial sectors that deviated most from that total. (Four other sectors—transportation and public utilities; wholesale and retail trade; finance, insurance and real estate; and government—are not shown on the chart because they follow the total line almost identically.)

The mining segment of Texas' GSP went almost straight up between 1972 and 1982, and only slightly less than straight down in the four years following—the obvious result of a collapsed oil market. The service sector, however, continued its rapid growth pattern and more than offset the loss in the mining area. The other Texas GSP industrial components dawdled along showing the same trend as the overall total.

The mining segment contribution to Texas obviously continues to be tremendously important. That means that the Texas economy always will be significantly different from that of almost any other state.

In other respects, however, the Texas economic makeup is beginning to mirror the national economy. That movement results from modifications both in the state and in the nation. On a national basis the manufacturing sector, for example, dropped from 28.1 percent of total GSP in 1963 to 19.7 percent in 1986, an 8.4 point drop (see Figure 13-2).

That declining pattern also was followed in Texas: manufacturing contributed 19.3 percent of state GSP in 1963, but only 16.0 percent in 1986. Note that the intrastate decline during that period was less severe with the result that Texas was much closer to the national level in 1986.

FIGURE 13-1
Texas' Gross State Product
Accumulated Percent Growth for Selected Industries
(Current Dollars)

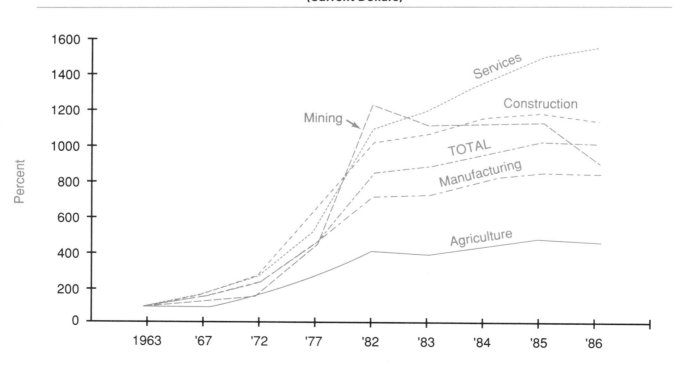

Source: Texas Research League, *Analysis*, August 1988, p.1.
Note: 1963 is the base year.

FIGURE 13-2

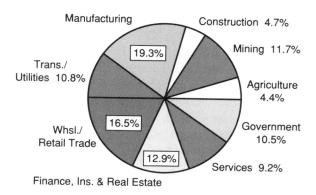

**Major Components
Texas Gross State Product,
1986**

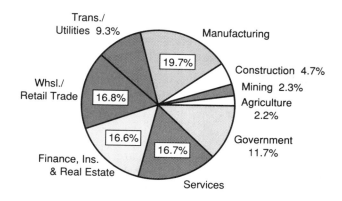

**Major Components
Texas Gross State Product,
1963**

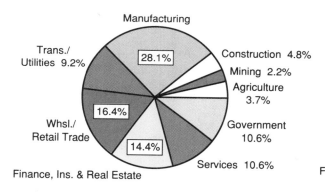

**Major Components
Total U.S. Gross State
Product, 1986**

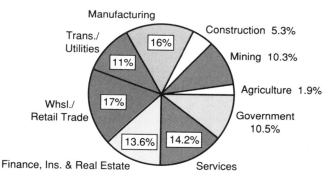

**Major Components
Total U.S. Gross State
Product, 1963**

Source: Texas Research League, *Analysis*, August 1988, p. 2–3.

The service sector follows somewhat the same pattern. Nationally, that industrial segment increased in economic importance from 10.6 percent of total GSP in 1963 to 16.7 percent in 1986. In Texas, the corresponding growth was from 9.2 percent to 14.2 percent. Here, though, Texas moved further away from the national norm—a 5.0 percent increase contrasted to 6.1 percent for the nation as a whole.

One characteristic of the Texas economy, most particularly during the 1970s, was that it was almost impervious to the economic downturns experienced nationally. That is probably no longer the case. As Texas more closely mirrors the

national fiscal pattern, most experts believe that the state will be much more susceptible to economic ups and downs.

DYNAMIC GROWTH IN EVERY SECTOR

In 1963, Texas accounted for 5.0 percent of the national GSP; by 1986, the Texas contribution had increased to 7.2 percent (see Table 13-2). That proportional gain outpaced any of the other 11 major industrial states.

The Texas gains occurred in every industrial sector, as can be seen by comparing the 1986 percentages with the 1963 percentages in Table 13-2. The largest share increase was in mining (6.5 percent), where Texas accounted for almost one-third of the total U.S. GSP attributable to that sector, despite the decline in oil prices. The smallest share increase was in the agricultural sector (.3 percent). In between, the Texas contribution to total GSP grew between 1.5 percent (finance, insurance, and real estate) and 3.3 percent (construction).

CHANGING EMPLOYMENT PATTERNS

Texas' employment patterns are changing as a reflection of movement among the industrial sectors. Between 1982 and 1986 (four years of relatively slow economic growth in GSP terms), Texas added a net 300,000 nonagricultural employees.

Numerically, the largest gain (232,000) was in the service sector (up 20 percent). Proportionately, the big growth was in the finance, insurance, real estate area where net employment increased by 80,000 (up 22 percent). Mining (minus 98,000, or 32 percent), manufacturing (minus 94,000 or 9 percent) and construction

(minus 27,000 or 6 percent) were the industrial sectors showing net employment decreases.

CONTENT QUESTIONS

1. What was the growth of Texas' gross state product between 1972 and 1982?
2. How did the Texas economy differ from the national economy during the 1970s?
3. The biggest gain in employment in Texas between 1982 and 1986 was in which sector? In which sector was the biggest loss?

DISCUSSION QUESTIONS

1. What have been the biggest changes in the composition of Texas' gross state product between 1963 and 1986 and what caused these changes?
2. Do you think the Texas economy will change with the national economy in the future?

TABLE 13-2
Gross State Product: Texas and U.S. by Industry: 1963 and 1986
(Millions of Dollars)

| | TEXAS | | U.S. | | TEXAS/U.S. | |
	1963	1986	1963	1986	1963	1986
Agriculture	$ 1,330	$ 5,865	$ 22,343	$ 92,993	6.0%	6.3%
Mining	3,515	31,115	13,419	95,281	26.2%	32.7%
Construction	1,423	16,226	28,929	197,876	4.9%	8.2%
Manufacturing	5,800	48,708	168,141	824,302	3.4%	5.9%
Trans/Utilities	3,247	33,273	54,805	391,444	5.9%	8.5%
Trade	4,954	51,441	98,224	702,513	5.0%	7.3%
Finance/Ins/RE	3,892	41,403	86,493	694,965	4.5%	6.0%
Services	2,757	43,190	63,275	700,180	4.4%	6.2%
Government	3,147	32,289	63,218	492,151	5.0%	6.6%
TOTAL	$30,065	$303,510	$598,847	$4,191,705	5.0%	7.2%

Source: U.S. Department of Commerce, Bureau of Economic Analysis, *Survey of Current Business*, Vol. 68, No. 5 (May 1988).

14

OIL AND NATURAL GAS

Alan B. Sowards[1]
and
Calvin A. Kent, Ph.D.[2]

Along with the Lone Star and the cowboy, the most recognizable symbol of Texas is the oil derrick. Since the turn of the century the economy of Texas has been based upon oil and natural gas. When the petroleum industry prospered, the state of Texas prospered. The collapse in oil prices which took place in early 1986 severely impacted the Texas economy, costing the state jobs, income, and tax revenues.

The history of the oil industry is one of the most colorful in the state. The Indians used the oil they found seeping from the rocks as medicine. Survivors of the De Soto expedition to the New World in 1543 used thick Texas crude oil to caulk their boats. The first oil well was drilled by Lyne T. Barret in 1866 near Nacogdoches. For the next thirty years most of the oil was found in the northeastern section of the state. In 1898 J. S. Cullennan built Texas' first refinery in Corsicana. On January 10, 1901, Captain Anthony Lucas brought in the world's greatest gusher at Spindletop near Beaumont, which increased the production of oil in Texas to over 3.2 million barrels in 1901. By 1928 Texas was the United States' leading oil-producing state. In 1930 the East Texas oilfield was developed, with the West Texas development exploding in 1948. Texas has been the leading oil-producing state in the nation

for sixty consecutive years. Almost one-third of the nation's output of petroleum comes from Texas.

THE IMPORTANCE OF OIL AND GAS TO THE TEXAS ECONOMY

Oil and gas production is one of the most geographically extensive industries in Texas. Oil is produced in 214 of Texas' 254 counties, while gas is produced in 217. As of 1987 there were 200,055 oil wells producing in 12,281 fields in Texas. There were 68,337 gas wells operating in 17,723 gas fields. Despite the large number of wells, the vast majority of Texas oil and gas is produced from a relatively small number of these. For example, over one-third of all Texas oil came from 13 fields. The vast majority of Texas oil wells are "stripper wells" which produce only 10 barrels or less of oil per day. Early in 1987 there were over 15,000 companies across Texas producing oil and gas.

Even more important is the employment generated by the Texas oil and gas industry. The petroleum industry operating in Texas during 1986 employed over 250,000 people and paid them wages totaling almost $9 billion. This included individuals working in the drilling and well servicing firms, the employees of the oil and gas production companies, those working for pipeline and storage facilities and those

[1]Director of Education and Industry Affairs, Texas Mid-Continent Oil and Gas Association, Austin, Texas.
[2]Herman W. Lay Professor of Private Enterprise; Director, Center for Private Enterprise, Baylor University, Waco, Texas.

employees found at the refining and processing plants.

Each person employed in the oil industry generates $48,198 in wages, dividends, and royalties; $528,059 in gross receipts; and $39,373 in federal, state, and local taxes. Providing goods and services for each of those petroleum industry employees creates jobs for almost four additional workers in the Texas economy. This includes jobs in retail trade; in services such as medical care, accounting, and advertising; in education; and in manufacturing, producing the products those petroleum industry workers consume. Currently, one out of every twelve people employed in Texas works in the petroleum industry. Of the 100 largest firms in Texas, 59 are related to oil and natural gas.

TAXES

In 1987 the Texas petroleum industry paid to the state of Texas $1.3 billion in taxes, which accounted for 11.5 percent of all state tax collections. The principal revenue raiser is the severance tax on Texas crude oil, which is 4.6 percent of the value of the oil at the wellhead. The natural gas tax rate is 7.5 percent of wellhead value. Firms in the petroleum industry also paid to the state of Texas over $130 million in corporate franchise taxes and $1.1 billion in property taxes to support schools and other local governments.

But taxes are not the only way the state gains revenue from the Texas petroleum industry. In 1987 the Permanent School Fund, which is used to support local education, received almost $150 million; and the Permanent University Fund, which goes to higher education, received $77 million. These moneys represent the royalties paid by petroleum companies for the oil and gas they extract from land owned by the state.

THE CRISIS IN THE TEXAS PETROLEUM INDUSTRY

In April 1986 disaster struck the Texas oil industry. The preceding December, oil had been selling for almost $30 a barrel. By spring that figure

had dropped to around $10 a barrel: a decline of two-thirds in less than four months.

There are several reasons for the dramatic fall in price. Like everything else, the price of oil is determined by the laws of supply and demand. The supply of oil in the world is largely controlled by a group known as the **Organization of Petroleum Exporting Countries** (OPEC). These countries are principally located in the Middle East with the biggest producers being Saudi Arabia, Iran, and Iraq. Major oil-producing countries belonging to OPEC outside of the Middle East include Venezuela and Great Britain. In the early 1970s OPEC was established as a **cartel** to control the world price of oil by limiting the amount of oil which could be placed on the market. A cartel is an arrangement whereby producers agree to follow certain guidelines in their production of a commodity. These guidelines allocate to each producer a certain share of the market. No member is to produce more than its assigned share. For almost 10 years the cartel worked. The member nations limited the amount of oil they put on the market, thus keeping oil prices high.

But those high prices led to worldwide conservation. People used less petroleum products and, as a result, the demand decreased. As demand decreased, surpluses began to develop on the market and many of the members began to cheat by producing more than their allotted share. As the worldwide oil surplus grew and demand continued to decline, OPEC fell apart and the world price of oil collapsed. By the end of 1988 OPEC had still not been able to regain control of the market price of oil.

The effects on Texas were immediate and devastating. The price decline caused massive business failures in the oil-drilling business and in companies related to the petroleum industry. There were 850 drilling rigs operating in 1984. By 1986 the figure had declined to 311. Almost 30,000 Texas firms declared bankruptcy in 1986 alone. Employment in the oil industry fell by almost one-half, and income to state government from taxes on the petroleum industry dropped by over one-third.

In terms of petroleum-related industries, the hardest hit was banking. Banks had made loans to Texas businesses in petroleum based on the assumption that high oil prices would continue.

When they did not, many of those loans went bad and could not be paid back. As a result, Texas bank failures soared to levels higher than even those during the Great Depression. Toward the end of 1988 the Texas oil industry had recovered slightly as oil prices had risen to approximately $14 per barrel. But the state's economy had suffered severe damage as witnessed by an unemployment rate which was well above the national average.

REGULATION OF THE OIL AND GAS INDUSTRY

The oil and gas industry in Texas is regulated by the Texas Railroad Commission. The Commission was established in 1891 to regulate the rates charged to farmers and other shippers by the railroads. In 1919 the authority of the Commission was expanded to include the petroleum industry. Major oil companies had integrated operations which included drilling, refining, and transportation by either railroad or pipeline. The law also required that the industry not waste natural resources such as oil and gas.

The Commission now regulates the amount of oil or gas which can be taken from each well. This is done to make sure that wells are not drawn down or depleted too quickly. Until the federal government ordered deregulation of oil and natural gas in 1978, the Commission set the price at which these were to sell in the market.

AVAILABILITY OF OIL AND GAS IN TEXAS

What does the future hold for the oil industry in Texas? For one thing, proven reserves of oil and gas are declining dramatically. Proven reserves are the amount of oil and gas that have been discovered and can be recovered efficiently. Since 1972 the amount of proven reserves in Texas has declined by one-third. New oil and gas wells are not being discovered and developed quickly enough to replace the oil and gas that is being taken out of the ground. In 1987 the proven reserves of Texas oil and gas fields declined by almost 10 percent.

With oil and gas prices depressed there is little incentive to continue or expand drilling. As Figure 14-1 shows, the United States possesses very little of the world's proven reserves which will be available to meet future energy demands. Over one-half of the world's reserves are found in countries in the Middle East. The second largest group of reserves, almost 13%, are found in the Communist countries. The United States possesses only about 4% of the world's reserves.

As Table 14-1 shows, the consumption of petroleum in the United States is again rising in response to falling energy prices. Since proven reserves are declining, this means that the United States will become increasingly dependent on foreign sources of oil. In 1987 oil imports amounted to over 40 percent of all of the oil consumed in the United States. Experts in the oil and gas industry predict that the nation will continue to become increasingly dependent on foreign sources so long as oil prices remain low and the search for new reserves is discouraged. Many predict a coming energy crisis which we will not be able to meet.

TABLE 14-1
U.S. Oil Consumption and Imports

	U.S. Consumption MB/D*	U.S. Oil Imports MB/D*	% of Oil Imported
1972	16.3	4.4	27
1973	17.4	6.3	36
1974	16.5	6.2	38
1975	16.4	6.1	37
1976	17.5	7.2	41
1977	18.4	8.8	48
1978	18.8	8.5	45
1979	18.5	8.4	46
1980	17.1	7.1	42
1981	16.0	5.7	36
1982	15.5	4.7	30
1983	15.7	4.8	28
1984	16.5	5.1	29
1985	15.7	4.8	30
1986	16.2	6.0	37
1987	16.5	6.8	41

*MB/D = Millions of barrels per day

Sources: Department of Energy; American Petroleum Institute *Oil & Gas Journal* (January 25, 1988); Texas Mid-Continent Oil and Gas Association, "Resource Packet," July 1988, p.3.

FIGURE 14-1
World Proven Petroleum Reserves by Region, 1983*

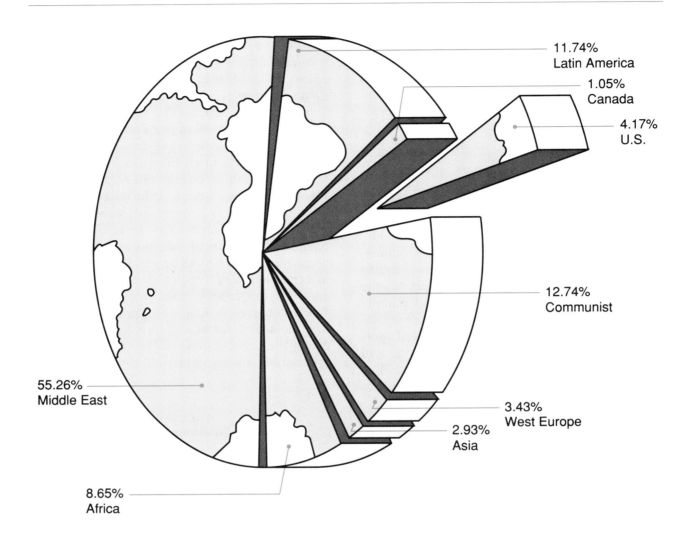

11.74%
Latin America

1.05%
Canada

4.17%
U.S.

12.74%
Communist

55.26%
Middle East

3.43%
West Europe

2.93%
Asia

8.65%
Africa

*Considered economically recoverable at time of data collection; some heavy crudes and bitumens not included.

Source: Texas Mid-Continent Oil and Gas Association, "Resource Packet," July 1988, p.4.

★   ★

CONTENT QUESTIONS

1. Oil production in Texas spread geographically across the state. Where and when were the major developments?
2. How many and what types of jobs are created due to the employment of a worker in the petroleum industry?
3. What is a cartel?
4. Who regulates the oil and gas industry in Texas?

DISCUSSION QUESTIONS

1. Explain how OPEC works and how it contributed to the Texas oil crisis of the early 1980s.
2. Discuss how the collapse in oil prices has affected your community.

15

AGRICULTURE: CROPS

Glenn Jones[1]
and
Bonnie Sjolander[2]

Texas' diverse geography, climate, and soils and its widely varied rainfall make it possible for agricultural producers to grow a variety of different crops, from timber in East Texas to citrus in the Valley. There are approximately 167 million acres of land inside our state border; of this, about 136 million acres (81 percent) are covered by farms and ranches.

DECLINE IN LAND USE

As you can see from Table 15-1, the number of farms and ranches in the state has declined over time while the size of the average farm has increased. The number of acres devoted to agricultural production has gotten smaller and smaller.

INCREASE IN CROP PRODUCTION

The decline in the amount of land used compares with an ever-increasing amount of crops produced. Agriculture has shown one of the largest increases in efficiency of any industry. Table 15-2 shows the rising yield per harvested acre for several major crops.

Gains in productivity are occurring more and more quickly. The Industrial Revolution started the process with increased mechanization in all

areas of our lives. In agriculture this was followed by the Chemical Revolution of 1940–1960, which brought refined vaccines, medicines, fertilizer, pesticides, and herbicides. During the 1970s and 1980s productivity increases will come from widespread use of biotechnology and computers.

Biotechnology is broadly defined as any technique that uses living organisms to make or modify products, to improve plants or animals, or to develop microorganisms for specific uses. The yeasts that make bread, cheese, and wine possible are examples of biotechnology that has been used by man for centuries.

Scientists are using new techniques to manipulate plant genes, bacteria, viruses, and other living things to speed up the process of change and advancement. Changes that once took years to develop are now possible in one generation thanks to genetic selection. Although biotechnology makes very rapid change possible it is important to remember that the laws of nature are still in effect, making the creation of bizarre plants or animals very unlikely.

A bacterium that protects plants from the damaging effects of frost is being perfected. Crops that produce their own pesticides and fertilizer are being created. Potatoes and popcorn that are naturally butter flavored are in the making, as are potatoes that have the nutritional qualities of meat.

Continued advances in productivity are expected to make production agriculture even more

[1]Director, Research, Education and Policy Development Division, Texas Farm Bureau, Waco, Texas.
[2]Research Assistant, Texas Farm Bureau, Waco, Texas.

TABLE 15-1
Number of Farms and Land in Farms
Texas 1950–1984

Year	Farms (thousands)	Land in Farms (thousand acres)	Average Size of Farm (acres)
1950	345	150,000	435
1951	332	151,000	455
1952	318	152,000	478
1953	305	153,000	502
1954	297	154,000	519
1955	298	154,000	533
1956	291	154,000	548
1957	273	154,000	564
1958	265	154,000	581
1959*	252	154,000	611
1960	247	153,000	619
1961	242	151,500	626
1962	237	150,000	633
1963	233	149,000	639
1964	230	148,000	643
1965	226	147,000	650
1966	222	146,000	658
1967	219	145,000	662
1968	216	144,000	667
1969	214	143,000	668
1970	212	142,800	674
1971	210	142,500	679
1972	209	142,000	679
1973	209	141,800	678
1974*	209	141,800	678
1975	189	140,000	741
1976	187	139,700	747
1977	186	139,300	749
1978	185	139,000	751
1979	187	138,600	741
1980	189	128,200	731
1981	189	137,600	728
1982	188	137,200	730
1983	187	137,000	733
1984	187	136,800	732

*For 1959–1974, a farm was defined as any place of 10 or more acres that had annual sales of $50 or more of agricultural products, or any place with less than 10 acres that had annual sales of $250 or more. Beginning in 1975, a farm is defined as a place that sells or normally would sell $1,000 of agricultural produce annually.

Source: Data compiled by Research, Education and Policy Division, Texas Farm Bureau, November 1988.

competitive in the future. Only the most efficient producers will be able to stay in business, perpetuating the decline in farm numbers.

COTTON

Cotton, the number one cash producer for Texas farmers, is also a major export commodity. Texas exports more cotton than any other state. It is grown over most of the state, but is concentrated in the lower portion of the Panhandle and the southernmost tip of the state. A small amount of the Texas cotton crop is woven into cloth at mills inside the state, but most of it is only ginned (the process of separating seed from fiber) here. In most cases the fiber is transported to another state for processing into fabric and finally into clothing, while the seed is used as livestock feed.

Fifty years ago cotton was produced using large amounts of hand labor. Today the process is almost completely mechanized, from planting the seed to weaving cloth.

TIMBER

Timber, Texas agriculture's second largest producer of cash receipts, is a very important industry in the eastern area of the state. Most of our timber crop is pine. Demand for wood products has been increasing nationwide. There are also numerous lumber mills in east Texas which start the process of refining trees into the final product.

GRAIN SORGHUM

Grain sorghum, an important feed crop, is grown throughout a large portion of the state, with production concentrated in the Panhandle, Central, and Rio Grande Valley areas. It is used as feed for animals, and plays an important role in supporting the livestock industry.

HAY

Hay is also grown throughout a large area of the state. It is an essential part of success in the cattle industry. Production of both hay and grain sorghum is geographically dispersed because they

TABLE 15-2
Yield per Acre, Texas 1950–1984

Year	Cotton (pounds)	Sorghum (pounds)	Hay (tons)	Wheat (bushels)	Rice (pounds)	Peanuts (pounds)
1950	211	1,288	1.10	8.0	2,400	675
1951	165	1,064	.99	9.0	2,375	350
1952	171	1,064	.99	12.0	2,500	375
1953	233	1,148	1.13	9.0	2,625	625
1954	245	1,316	.98	10.0	2,675	380
1955	281	1,316	1.10	9.5	3,050	615
1956	280	1,456	.79	12.5	2,900	500
1957	295	1,820	1.20	14.5	3,200	525
1958	383	1,848	1.30	21.5	3,100	730
1959	334	2,016	1.31	17.0	3,150	680
1960	329	2,128	1.22	22.0	3,075	740
1961	350	2,520	1.32	23.0	2,900	730
1962	348	2,184	1.31	16.0	3,550	720
1963	362	2,464	1.13	18.5	4,125	680
1964	348	2,576	1.44	20.0	4,150	950
1965	402	3,136	1.53	22.0	4,600	960
1966	385	3,136	1.61	22.5	4,200	1,400
1967	376	2,856	1.64	16.0	5,000	1,170
1968	410	3,080	1.95	22.0	4,550	1,450
1969	294	2,800	1.76	24.0	3,950	1,310
1970	315	3,136	1.84	24.0	4,500	1,405
1971	265	2,912	1.85	21.0	5,100	1,235
1972	408	3,304	2.03	22.0	4,727	1,565
1973	431	3,360	2.42	29.0	3,740	1,525
1974	269	2,912	2.22	16.0	4,494	1,435
1975	293	2,912	2.33	23.0	4,560	1,525
1976	353	2,828	2.50	22.0	4,810	1,525
1977	408	2,688	2.07	25.0	4,670	1,315
1978	294	2,744	1.82	20.0	4,700	1,450
1979	389	3,024	2.56	30.0	4,220	1,725
1980	234	2,576	2.07	25.0	4,230	1,275
1981	376	3,472	2.46	28.0	4,700	1,625
1982	303	3,080	2.25	24.0	4,690	1,445
1983	324	2,800	2.44	35.0	4,340	1,685
1984	377	2,968	1.78	30.0	4,940	1,665

Source: Data compiled by Research, Education and Policy Division, Texas Farm Bureau, November, 1988.

are so closely tied to the livestock industry which is also scattered across the state.

Dramatic changes in the production of hay, or the various other crops fed to cattle, such as grain sorghum, oats, corn, and cottonseed, affect the cattle industry. Changes such as drought, with the corresponding decrease in supply of available feed causing a sell-off in the cattle industry, are eventually felt by you, the consumer, in the form of higher prices for meat and milk. This cause and effect is not readily apparent because during the actual drought cattle prices tend to decrease due to the larger quantity being sold. This decrease in the cattle herd sometimes is apparent two to three years later when the supply of meat on the market declines because of a smaller number of cows available to produce offspring.

Positive changes, such as improved production methods, that increase feed supplies naturally have the opposite effect on livestock production. Livestock producers tend to expand their herds when feed prices are low, which eventually leads to an increased supply of meat on the market and lower prices for consumers.

FOOD CROPS

Major food crops grown in Texas are wheat and rice. Wheat is produced in the northern half of the state, with concentrations in the Panhandle area. Wheat can also be used as feed for livestock, but rice is not.

Rice is grown only along the coast of the state, in a very small area. This is due to environmental factors such as soil type, temperature, and quantity of rainfall.

Peanuts, soybeans, and sunflowers are oil crops grown in Texas. Peanut production is scattered throughout the state. Successful peanut growth requires sandy-type soils. Soybeans are grown primarily in the Coastal Bend and the Panhandle.

Vegetable, fruit, and nut production are thriving in Texas. Fruit and vegetable growers are diversifying, producing a greater variety of crops than ever before. Citrus and most vegetable production is concentrated in the southernmost portion of the state. Broccoli, cabbage, cantaloupes, sweet corn, cucumbers, cauliflower, carrots, melons, lettuce, onions, peppers, potatoes, spinach, and tomatoes are the primary vegetables grown in our state. Oriental vegetables are gaining popularity, and farmers are moving to meet the consumers' demands.

Peaches are an important crop in south central Texas. Pecans are also an important tree crop in Texas. Producers of tree crops such as pecans, peaches, and citrus must plan far into the future if they decide to expand and increase their production. While growers of annual crops can make their decisions each year, it is several years from the time an expansion decision is made until trees reach maturity and begin producing.

CONCLUSION

The portion of your income spent for food has consistently grown smaller over time. Around the turn of the century more than half of consumers' incomes went for food purchases. Today the average U.S. family spends 14 percent of its income on food. This figure is one of the lowest in comparison with the amount spent in other countries.

Agricultural exports are frequently shipped through Texas ports. This movement of commodities is facilitated by the large interstate highway and railroad systems we have in Texas. Very large quantities of Texas crops are exported to other countries each year. Export sales are very important to the agricultural economy as well as to the Texas economy as a whole. The sale of commodities to other countries brings dollars into the state economy while clearing the market of agricultural products.

Agriculture has played an important role in the development of Texas, and will continue to be a significant part of the state's economy. All industries feel the effect of changes in supply and demand brought on by new products, techniques, or changes in tastes and preferences of consumers, but the agricultural industry can always be sure that people will want food to eat and clothes of natural fiber to wear at the best possible price.

CONTENT QUESTIONS

1. What percentage of Texas land is devoted to farming and ranching?
2. What is biotechnology?
3. What are the two most important Texas crops?
4. What has happened over the past ninety years to the percentage of the average person's income which is spent on food?

DISCUSSION QUESTIONS

1. What are the trends in Texas grain production?
2. Discuss how a drought can affect agriculture.

16

AGRICULTURE: LIVESTOCK

Glenn Jones[1]
and
Bonnie Sjolander[2]

Production of all types of livestock—beef, dairy, lamb, pork, poultry, and mohair goats—plays an integral part in our state's diverse economy. Texas agricultural producers raise more livestock than producers in any other state and they lead all states in cash receipts from marketing of livestock products. These cash receipts amount to more than $5 billion annually for the Texas economy. There is some type of livestock production in all of Texas' 254 counties.

STRUCTURE OF THE LIVESTOCK INDUSTRY

The Texas livestock industry is structured in such a way that a comparatively small number of very large operators (farmers and ranchers) produce most of the output. There are also a very large number of small operators who each produce a small amount of output.

This is illustrated by Table 16-1, which shows the number of cattle operations in the various size groups and the inventory of each. The largest number of operations, those which have 1 to 49 head each, make up more than 70 percent of the total number of operations yet produce only 14.2 percent of the cattle and calves. This compares to large operations having 500 or more head, which make up only 2.5 percent of operations while

producing 46.6 percent of output. The dairy, pork, poultry, sheep, and goat industries have a similar structure.

Texas, with 13.5 million head, leads the nation in number of cattle and calves. Texas beef cattle make up a large share of the nation's cattle industry, representing 14 percent of U.S. cattle numbers, 16 percent of all beef cattle, and 23 percent of fed cattle. Beef cattle are raised in every county, with cow-calf producers concentrated in the eastern third of the state and feeder cattle producers in the Panhandle area. A cow-calf operation is one where a herd of cows are kept year-round for the production of calves. When the calves are weaned (taken from their mothers) they are fed on pasture for several months then shipped to a feedlot, where they are known as feeders. The feeder cattle stay at the feedlot for several months eating grain, before being sent to the slaughterhouse or packing plant. After slaughter the beef is moved to the grocery stores and then finally reaches you, the consumer.

Dairy cattle are raised in the eastern half of the state, with the largest number of producers in Hopkins, Erath, Johnson, and Wise counties. Dairying is important to the Texas economy, especially in the northeast region of the state. Milk production has become very efficient as producers have adopted artificial insemination to improve the productivity of their cattle, and they have a wide variety of feed rations available to get the most milk at the least cost.

Pork producers are concentrated in the Gulf Coast region and the southern portion of the Panhandle. Many of the hog producers are known

[1]Director, Research, Education and Policy Development Division, Texas Farm Bureau, Waco, Texas.
[2]Research Assistant, Texas Farm Bureau, Waco, Texas.

TABLE 16-1
Texas Cattle and Calves:
Operations and Inventory by Size Groups, 1986

Size Group	Cattle and Calves Operations		Inventory	
	Number (thousands)	Percent of total	Number (thousands)	Percent of Total
1–49 head	100.0	70.4%	1,900	14.2%
50–99 head	20.7	14.6%	1,500	11.2%
100–499 head	17.7	12.5%	3,750	28.0%
500+ head	3.6	2.5%	6,250	46.6%
TOTAL	142.0	100.0%	13,400	100.0%

Sources: USDA/TDA; data compiled by Research, Education and Policy Division, Texas Farm Bureau, November 1988.

as farrow-to-finish operations, meaning that a hog is born and raised to market weight on the same farm. Other pork producers own the hogs for a short time before selling them to someone else who completes the next step.

Beef cattle, dairy cows, and hogs also provide numerous important by-products: leather from their hides for belts, gloves, purses, and jackets; bristles from their hair for brushes; various drugs from their glands, such as insulin; creams, soaps, candles, and explosives from their fat; and glue, fertilizer, animal feeds, and bone oil from their bones.

Poultry production in Texas is concentrated in the northeast portion of the state. Most poultry operations specialize and raise chickens for either meat or eggs. Texas is the nation's seventh largest producer of broilers. There is also laying-hen and turkey production.

Chickens are bred at a hatchery to be either egg producers or meat producers. After they are hatched they are moved to houses where the laying hens spend about a year and the broilers about seven weeks before slaughter.

Texas is the nation's leading producer of wool and mohair. Most of this production is concentrated in the area bordered by San Antonio, Abilene, Midland-Odessa, and the Rio Grande.

In addition to meat and the wool which is used to make blankets, sweaters, rugs, and many other items, sheep also provide us with leather, fertilizer, cosmetics, and the catgut used in stringing tennis rackets, to name just a few by-products.

Angora goats provide us with mohair, which is used to make fine sweaters and other clothing. Ninety-seven percent of the mohair produced in the United States and nearly half the mohair produced worldwide comes from Texas Angora goats. San Angelo has the nation's largest sheep and wool market, and is a center for wool and mohair warehouses and for slaughtering plants.

ADVANCES IN PRODUCTION

The technological changes mentioned earlier range from improved management practices to the use of vaccines and feed mixtures. Many fatal livestock diseases have been virtually eliminated through the development of vaccines. Selective breeding has made production of a variety of different types of cattle possible. Today's beef cattle are leaner than those 50 years ago, yet produce far more beef per head than the original Texas longhorn.

Pork production has undergone similar advances with a single hog producing more pork with proportionally less fat than ever before.

Current expectations are for this trend to continue even further due to the introduction of growth hormones in the next few years.

Research into livestock nutrition has allowed ranchers to produce greater quantities of beef, pork, milk, poultry, lamb, wool, and mohair by feeding rations formulated particularly for their purpose, environmental conditions, and age of livestock.

Looking into the future, it is becoming increasingly possible that biotechnology will allow production of animal products with reduced cholesterol, different fat characteristics, and increased production per animal. In the long run it is likely that these and similar changes will make agricultural production an increasingly capital-intensive enterprise.

Other technological changes such as increased use of computer monitoring, increased mechanization, and intensive recordkeeping will contribute to increased efficiency and competition in agricultural production. Scientists estimate that about 50 percent of all technology that we know today has been developed in the last 50 years. Because of biotechnology, technological change is expected to occur 500 times faster than in the past 20 years.

THE PRODUCER'S SHARE OF THE MONEY SPENT ON FOOD

Ranchers have, over the last few decades, put more and more effort into marketing their products in order to increase their income from the very competitive marketplace. Even though the price of food in the grocery store shows a steady upward trend over time, the share of a dollar actually received by the producer has been decreasing. In 1980 producers (farmers and ranchers) received an average of 37 cents out of each dollar spent on food, while in 1987 they received an average of only 25 cents. This widening gap between what you pay and what the producer receives is due to increases in labor, transportation, processing, packaging, and the other costs shown in Figure 16-1.

FIGURE 16-1
What a Dollar Spent on Food Paid for in 1987

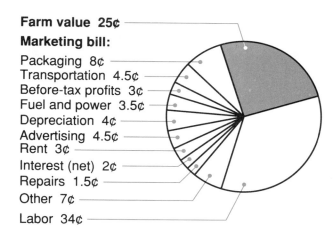

Farm value 25¢
Marketing bill:
Packaging 8¢
Transportation 4.5¢
Before-tax profits 3¢
Fuel and power 3.5¢
Depreciation 4¢
Advertising 4.5¢
Rent 3¢
Interest (net) 2¢
Repairs 1.5¢
Other 7¢
Labor 34¢

1987 preliminary. Other costs include property taxes and insurance, accounting and professional services, promotion, bad debts, and miscellaneous items.

Source: Data compiled by Research, Education and Policy Division, Texas Farm Bureau, November 1988.

Also, the trend is moving from purchase of food to be prepared at home to food that is already prepared and ready for the microwave. In the past a typical shopping basket would contain basic ingredients such as flour, sugar, rice, meat, and similar products, while today that basket is much more likely to contain frozen dinners, mixes, and other prepared items. Figure 16-2 shows the effect processing has on the share of your food dollar that goes to the producer. For items that require minimal changes in form such as milk or meat, a larger share of your dollar is received by the producer than for grain products such as bread. This is also partially due to the fact that bread is made of numerous ingredients which the baker must assemble before the baking process is started.

If you think you would like an opportunity to purchase food at one-third or one-half off store prices, just keep in mind that in the case of beef you would have to drive to a ranch and pick it up yourself. Also, you would have to take the whole animal (800 to 1,200 pounds) and it would still have hide, hooves, and horns attached.

FIGURE 16-2
Farm Value Share of Retail Food Prices

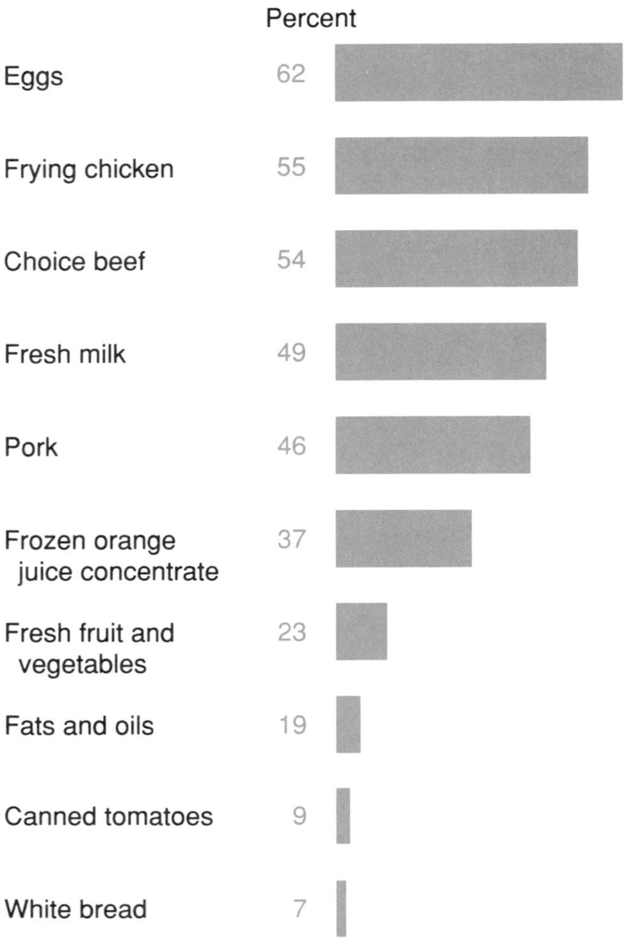

Percent

Eggs	62
Frying chicken	55
Choice beef	54
Fresh milk	49
Pork	46
Frozen orange juice concentrate	37
Fresh fruit and vegetables	23
Fats and oils	19
Canned tomatoes	9
White bread	7

1986 data. Farm value share of the proportion the farmer receives from the dollar the consumer spends. The remainder of the dollar goes to marketing farms.

CONTENT QUESTIONS

1. Texas farmers lead the nation in which aspects of livestock production?
2. What is a cow-calf operation?
3. What are three technological changes that have improved Texas' animal production?

DISCUSSION QUESTIONS

1. What percentage of the food dollar goes to the farmer? Why is that figure so low?
2. What are the trends in livestock raising in Texas? Do you think they will continue?

TOURISM
John B. McCall, Ph.D.[1]
Chee-Ooi Low[2]

Texas' promotion of tourism is probably a good example of how an economy can make the best use of its scarce (and, to a degree, unique) resources. Allocation of these resources (land, labor, capital, entrepreneurship) to the production and selling of a "good time" to people may generate more value—and hence more buying power for those involved in the industry—than allocation of these scarce "inputs" to some other line of business.

Reference to tourism as an industry may give the student pause. Industry, to most, evokes a mental picture of big factories, with smokestacks belching smoke, with workers in rough clothing walking through factory gates, lunch pail in hand, for yet another day of repetitive tasks over an impersonal machine, forming some "thing" from inert raw materials. This is a valid, though quaint, view of what industry is. The broader view of industry recognizes that not only tangible, physical goods are produced, but that intangible services can be produced, also.

ECONOMIC CHARACTERISTICS OF TOURISM

There are some important differences between an industry that creates value by the production of tangible things, such as steel, cars, computer chips, and agricultural products, and an industry that creates and sells an invisible, intangible service, such as a haircut or—the topic at hand—a trip to the beach. These differences affect how well, and how steadily, a given industry can contribute to the economic well-being of its region.

First, and perhaps foremost, manufacturing industries rely on the use of raw materials that are used up in the process of creating value. Once these raw materials are used up, the industry either dies or moves to another location in search of new raw materials, with economic detriment to the region where it was located. Tourism involves the heavy use of those raw materials one could call "natural scenery" (beaches, mountains) and "cultural history" (the romance of the Old West) and similar factors that do not normally deplete and vanish. Tourism, therefore, has a built-in potential to create a good living on a steady basis for any region with attractive scenery and romantic history.

Second, tourism deals directly with people on vacation. This calls for making these people happy and this, in turn, calls for personal attention. In other words, tourism is a **labor-intensive** business—it creates lots of jobs.

Third, tourism is a less cyclical activity than traditional manufacturing. (A **business cycle** consists of a period of prosperity followed by a period of recession followed by a period of recovery.) Generally speaking, whereas a manufactured good can be created in advance of demand and stored until sale, the production of a service must occur at the instant it is demanded. Texas'

[1]Associate Professor of Economics; Director, Center for Economic Education, University of Texas at Arlington.
[2]Graduate Assistant, University of Texas at Arlington.

tourist industry cannot produce trips to the beach in advance of vacation time and then sell these trips as needed. As a result, the problems of overproduction of, say, automobiles, which would cause temporary factory shut-down, unemployment, and lower living standards, may not be present in the tourism industry. To summarize this paragraph, one could generalize that, on the **supply side**, manufacturing possesses more inherent instability than do industries that produce services.

Fourth, service industries, like manufacturing industries, are unstable on the **demand side** of the business. Demanders of goods and services do not seek to buy at a steady pace throughout the day, month, or year. Demand for school clothes peaks just before school starts. Demand for the use of freeway space peaks mainly in the early morning and late afternoon. Demand for trips to the beach peak during warm weather, during vacation. All of these supply activities become relatively idle during off-peak periods of demand, and this may cause unemployment and lower living standards within the industry until demand revives.

This demand-side instability, common to most industries of whatever type, is easier to cure with smart management than supply-side fluctuations. The management of tourism, in particular, may lend itself well to a smoothing-out of demand for its service over the year. Natural factors may help. In Texas, the year-round good climate may attract retired folks to beach areas, for example, during the winter months while their regular homes sit deep in snow. A smoothing-out of the demand for tourist services, then, may respond readily to good management within the industry. The task here is to discover the greatest number of tourist attractions, to then build the facilities to exploit these resources and, finally, to market and promote the availability of these attractions to the nation and the world.

Remember, also, that the tourist industry can also sell its services to local people in small increments—on weekends, on holidays, or even on single nights (a baseball game, for example) if the industry is managed well. This is possible in many cases whether it is winter or summer, whether it is vacation time or not. Furthermore, given a good regional transportation system, even out-of-state visitors may be sold such serv-

ices. Lots of Texas people go elsewhere for a weekend, or even a day, to watch horses race for money. Lots of Oklahoma people come to Dallas during the Texas-O.U. football weekend.

During times when the dollar is weak on world markets, people from other nations can vacation here at very reasonable cost. This is because at such times it does not take much of their money to purchase lots of dollars to spend here. Consequently, for these people our prices are a very attractive alternative to spending their money in their own nations for vacations.

Also, whereas manufacturing industry faces the possibility of both uneven seasonal demand and business-cycle fluctuations, tourism generally has only seasonal fluctuations to confront. So long as family incomes remain reasonably high, families will continue to purchase entertainment and vacations each year. Even if incomes fall (during a business recession, for example), Texas tourism and entertainment sales do not fall to the same extent because people will continue to buy entertainment, only closer to home. Given a national economic slowdown, what Texas tourism would lose in the way of visitors from other states, who might stay home, would be offset by sales to local people who vacation near home, instead of in some other state or nation.

A well-organized and well-managed tourist industry builds on its natural and cultural resources and then seeks to create a steady year-round demand for what it has to sell. Texas has done well in this respect through a partnership between state government and the private sector.

Fifth, the state tourist industry contributes strongly to the state's economic well-being through what economists refer to as **multiplier effects, accelerator effects**, and **spillover benefits**. Each of these three forces differs somewhat from the other two. However, taken together, they refer to the general phenomenon of **linkage** between one person's purchase of something and the resulting economic activity. A good amusement park, for example, not only creates jobs for the people who directly work there, but the activity itself creates jobs and value in other businesses nearby.

The multiplier effect occurs when one person receives a payment and then spends that income with someone else, who in turn spends it. In this way, the original income is respent or multiplied throughout the economy. This respending causes business to expand output and to invest in new plant. This is called the accelerator effect. The multiplier and accelerator effects increase spending, income, and job opportunities which are the spillover benefits from the spending and investing.

Linkage involves both directly-related businesses such as motels, restaurants, and service stations, and more general types of business that locate in the area so their employees will be happier. In this second category, you can readily understand that a national corporation would be more interested in locating near a city with good entertainment opportunities for its workers than near a city where there was almost nothing to do. Stated another way, a business may find that it has to pay a lot more to hire a skilled worker in the boondocks than in a fun city. Businesses will be attracted to these locations because they are more likely to find and retain the quality workers they seek in a fun city.

TEXAS' TOURIST RESOURCES

When one considers just what comprises the Texas resource base for producing tourism it is useful to divide these resources into three major categories: those that occur naturally, those that are the result of Texas' past history, and those that are created by human effort.

The natural tourist resources include a favorable climate; a variety of natural scenery, from forests in the east, plains in the center, beaches in the south, mountains in the southwest, and desert in the west; an abundance of game for hunting and fishing; and the combination of all these special-interest opportunities in one large location.

Texas also possesses a rich and varied cultural history. Countless movies and novels about the history of Texas and Texans have created a demand on the part of vacationers both to see and to be a part of this history. Texas history embraces not only peoples from the Six Flags, but also includes Native American, Czech, and German populations, giving it a broad appeal for tourists.

The man-made element of Texas tourism includes all the facilities developed by private enterprise and by state government to give tourists access to these wonders and to make their visits

easier and more enjoyable. Extensive transportation systems (highway, Amtrak, airlines), provided jointly by the private sector and government, allow efficient access to natural beauties. Supporting motel and restaurant facilities, as well as privately operated tour and guide companies, organize and package tourism for sale. State and national parks and forests provide facilities for the use of natural beauties and historical sites and conserve their continuing availability for the future population.

In addition, the availability of large "theme" amusement parks (Six Flags Over Texas and Sea World, for example) and of professional sporting events creates a draw for tourist dollars. The building of convention centers by local city governments and the building of large regional shopping malls by private enterprise help to attract visitors to the area, both as pure vacationers and for part-business, part-vacation activity.

MANAGEMENT OF TOURISM

The management of tourism in Texas is a partnership between private enterprise and the government. State and local governments, with help here and there from the federal government, provide the basic **infrastructure** to support tourism. Good roads, airline terminals, state parks, convention centers—as well as regional and national wholesale market centers—provide a basis (*infrastructure*) upon which private enterprise can plan its tourist activities for a profit. The dollar vote and the political vote work in partnership. On occasions when this partnership is a success, the tax dollars initially spent on such infrastructure create new economic activity. This activity results in a new tax base. The increase in tax revenue more than repays the state tax payers for the dollars initially spent. This potential for a net payback to the taxpayers is a strong argument in favor of government subsidies of the right kind.

TEXAS TOURIST DATA

The last available data—for the year 1986—suggest that tourist and business travelers in Texas directly spent $17.3 billion on food, recreation, lodging, and souvenirs. Eleven billion of this was for transportation, $4.5 billion was for food and lodging, and more than $1.7 billion was spent on entertainment and incidentals. Spending of this type in Texas has grown over 41 percent since 1981. Since 1987, hotel receipts are up over 80 percent and bus tours are up over 11 percent.

In addition, the various businesses in Texas that supply tourism to these visitors paid almost $5 billion in wages and taxes to the Texas economy and created nearly 300,000 jobs. These workers, spending their earnings at other Texas businesses, helped to create more jobs and incomes, via the multiplier and accelerator effects.

In addition to providing the basic travel/tourism infrastructure, the Texas state government also spends to promote tourism directly. At present, Texas' yearly tourism budget is $12 million, the fifth largest of all 50 states. Millions have been spent by Texas to place advertisements in the media for tourist attractions. The highway department maintains 12 tourist bureaus throughout the state to distribute free maps and literature. This promotion gets results. In 1986, nearly 40 million out-of-staters visited Texas. Although a large proportion of these visitors were here on business, many of these will either buy some tourism while here on business, or will return on vacation later.

ENTREPRENEURSHIP AGAIN

For decades, Texas eked out a living with agriculture. The development of the oil industry in the 1920s led the state quickly toward a high living standard. This living standard was further increased by the large defense-related expenditures from World War II and from the Cold War afterward.

The fall in oil prices in the mid-1980s triggered a great loss of jobs and income in the private sector, and a loss of tax revenues for the state government. Although defense spending had grown to be an important segment of Texas living standards by that time, Texas living standards were still basically tied to the oil industry. If Texas is to recapture the high living standards of the past, it must depend on some other industries in the future.

Along with high-tech industry, the low-tech industry of tourism has developed to help fill the void left by the weakened domestic oil industry. Without active entrepreneurial activity by individuals and groups, both on their own and in partnership with the state government, tourism will not be a successful industry. The success of tourism in Texas has been largely the result of this partnership.

CONTENT QUESTIONS

1. What are two natural resources that tourism makes use of?
2. What three steps are necessary in developing tourism?
3. What role does government play in supporting tourism?

DISCUSSION QUESTIONS

1. Explain the multiplier, accelerator, and spillover effects.
2. What are the three types of tourist attractions? Give an example from your area of each.

18

RESEARCH AND DEVELOPMENT

Thomas M. Stauffer, Ph.D[1]

Research and development (R&D) activity is critical to the ability of the Texas economy to compete in domestic and world markets. This is true more so today than in the past when the economy relied more heavily on extractive industries (oil and gas) and agriculture. Texans will increasingly find their livelihoods and the economic future of the state dependent on advanced technologies. Texas' experience reflects the national pattern.

R&D IN THE U.S. ECONOMY

Technology has been a big factor driving the economic growth of the United States and raising the living standards of the American people. Some studies make the case that 70–80% of American economic growth since World War II has resulted from improvements in technology supported by the research and the education system that created it.

Research and development is credited with making the United States the world's leader in science and technology. In 1988, the National Science Foundation estimated that of the $132 billion being spent in the United States for this purpose, $65 billion came from the federal government, $63 billion from industry, and the remainder from universities and nonprofit organizations. That is more than the combined total being spent by Japan, West Germany, France, and the United Kingdom. For R&D, each country spends about the same percentage of its gross national product (GNP), the measure of the total value of goods and services produced by the nation in a given year. The U.S. rate is about 2.75 percent.

This strength is fortuitous because the U.S. economy must rely increasingly on technology. The ability of the United States to compete with the rest of the world is tied to technology-based industries, such as space travel, electronics, and health care, and technology-based improvements in traditional industries, such as the application of computing to farming and mail delivery. The proportion of the GNP derived from these sectors has doubled over the last two decades.

THE DISCOVERY PROCESS

R&D and technology are interrelated. Research is of two kinds, basic and applied. Basic research occurs when a scientist explores some facet of knowledge without knowing if it will ever be used in a practical way. A basic researcher is only trying to create knowledge for knowledge's sake. Applied research addresses a particular problem to see if scientific knowledge can be used in its solution. Many major innovations start with basic research that took place many years previously, when someone realizes its meaning and how it can be applied to resolve difficulties in daily living. Development is the final stage of the

[1]President and Professor of Public Policy, University of Houston-Clear Lake.

process when a product of applied research is developed into a usable product.

A recent example of this process of discovery is superconductivity. For many decades, scientists tried to increase the efficiency of electrical devices by minimizing the resistance to electrical current in a wire. A large portion of electrical power produced by the world's power stations is lost as a result of this resistance. For decades, neither basic nor applied research on superconductivity produced significant results.

Then in 1986, at an IBM research facility in Europe, a breakthrough occurred and a new material was created by scientists, who won the Nobel Prize for their work. But questions remained about this new substance, and scientists worldwide rushed to duplicate the work of the IBM researchers. The most successful was Dr. Paul Chu of the University of Houston. By putting various materials under pressure, he and his research team were able to lessen the electrical resistance at even higher temperature levels. Previously, superconductivity, or lack of resistance, was possible only at temperatures so low that it was little more than a laboratory curiosity without practical use. Chu's big accomplishment was generating superconductivity at much higher, if still subfreezing, temperatures. The state legislature established the Texas Superconductivity Center, built around Dr. Chu's pursuit of still higher temperatures along basic and applied lines of research.

The ultimate goal is the development of a superconducting wire that could operate at room temperatures. If this goal could be achieved, whole new industries could develop in the computing, defense, electrical, and other fields, and in Texas hope persists that Professor Chu's work could provide a big economic boost for the state.

SCIENCE IN THE UNITED STATES

R&D is a mainstay of the U.S. economy, which soon will be valued at $5 trillion, or a little less than a quarter of the world's economy, a remarkable figure since only about 6 percent of the world's population are U.S. citizens. Americans write over one-third of all the scientific and technical articles published in the world and get more patents and more Nobel Prizes for science than

the rest of the world combined. The top U.S. research universities, numbering about 100, where 60 percent of the nation's basic research is performed, are the best in the world. Even so, the Japanese, West Europeans, and Russians are making great strides, and basic science advances are now global in character.

The U.S. science and technology community is beset by a host of problems. One is cost. New science advances require huge resource investments. Four major proposed projects—constructing the world's largest atom smasher, deciphering the entire human genetic code, studying changes in the world's environment, and building a space station—have a combined price tag of over $25 billion.

This comes at a time when America's scientific work force is under threat. The number of straight-A high school students and college undergraduates taking courses in the hard sciences is declining. At the doctoral level in engineering, physics, and math, about half of the Ph.D. degrees awarded in the United States were earned by foreigners. Even more distressing is the scientific and technological illiteracy of many Americans. A 1988 study for the National Science Foundation, for example, found that more than a quarter of U.S. adults did not know that the Earth revolved around the sun and more than half did not know that it took one year for each revolution. The study placed scientific literacy in the United States at only 5 to 7 percent.

R&D IN TEXAS

Texas is part of this overall pattern, but there exists an extra sense of urgency in the state. When Texas economy went into a slump following the collapse of world oil prices in 1982, there were fervent calls for a more diversified economy. It was not surprising that state and local leaders turned to the potential offered by science and technology.

In recent years, political leaders have begun to recognize the importance of a state commitment to R&D. Propositions pointing in that direction were advanced as early as 1982, during Governor Clements's first term, in the report of the Texas 2000 Commission that dealt extensively with the importance of R&D to the state's future in agriculture, energy, transportation, water development, and other areas of economic potential. Making Texas "a national leader in science and technology development" was a goal stated in 1985 by Governor Mark White, who also established the Texas Science and Technology Council. The efforts of Governors White and Clements to attract major technology companies and support major higher education research efforts attested to their appreciation of the importance of science and technology to the state.

Many other state leaders in public and private life worked to create the right environment for technological innovation, including education and infrastructure improvements, support of vocational and technical training, and economic stimulation for both existing industries and start-up companies.

Still, Texas has more to do before being clearly recognized as one of the national science and technology leaders. While being an industrial power in such fields as energy, agriculture, medicine, aerospace, computers, and electronics, the state lags far behind competitor states in higher-level technologies and scientific disciplines, including several that are vital to the health of established and emerging industries in Texas. The indicators, found in Table 18-1, demonstrate that the state faces important problems in developing its R&D potential, while having significant opportunities too.

TABLE 18-1
Texas Science and Technology Indicators

Disturbing Indicators

• Texas ranks 3rd in population among the states but 10th in total expended research and development (R&D) funds.

• The overall level of research and development activity in Texas is about one-half of the national per capita average. If R&D in Texas were conducted at the national average rate, $4 billion would be added to the state's economy each year.

• The state's four largest higher education systems each receives several times fewer federal R&D funds than the comparable University of California system.

• Only one university department in Texas was rated number one nationally in a recent survey.

• Texas receives a smaller percentage of federal R&D dollars now than it did 10 years ago.

• No major federal laboratory is located in Texas.

• Texas ranks 45th among the states in composite Scholastic Aptitude Test scores and few Texans are named to Sloan Research Fellowships or the Westinghouse Science Talent Search.

Positive Indicators

• Texas has more endowed faculty chairs in public universities than any other state.

• In 1979 there were 1,628 high technology businesses in Texas; by 1988 there were many thousands more: Texas has provided a good climate for advanced-technology economic development.

• Texas has one of the nation's best technical training capabilities, an accomplishment that has been masked by the decentralized system of government and education in the state.

• Texas leaders strongly support the development of R&D capacity in the state.

In examining those areas where the United States holds comparative advantages in its economic position against the rest of the world, the National Commission on Industrial Competitiveness found that only in two out of eight elements did the nation have a lead: technology and human resources. In short, the commission argued, the United States is a nation that is living by its wits but one where extra effort is needed.

Many leaders believe that it is in these two areas, technology and human resources, that Texas can fashion its future economic successes. Only in this way can Texas truly become the master of its own economic destiny. Fortunately, a consensus is emerging among Texas business people, academics, and government officials that, in order to seize the broad-based technological initiative and make science and technology the catalyst for future economic growth, plans for action are mandatory. The Texas Science and Technology Council, the Texas Senate Space Science Industry Commission, the Texas Superconducting Super Collider Authority, and other groups have been hard at work to develop and implement various plans.

Texas can build its new economy from within, using R&D, and not rely on the traditional path to economic development by attracting branch manufacturing facilities. To do the latter would perpetuate too many low-wage jobs requiring minimal education—a "dead-end" scenario. Instead, by depending on Texans themselves to

TABLE 18-2
Ideas for Stimulating Advanced-Technology Economic Development in Texas

1. *Assistance to Business:* funds for innovation; tax abatements, exemptions, and credits; loans of many types; grants for research and training; industrial revenue bonds; enterprise zones, venture capital help or locator assistance; and incentives for R&D activity.

2. *Assistance to Link Companies with University and Other Researchers:* information dissemination, data banks of expertise and other resources, university linkages with business, university research assistance, and technology transfer programs.

3. *Assistance to People:* technical training help, special programs for gifted and talented students, high-technology education, rosters of available experts, improved education at K–12 level, and stronger mathematics and science programs in the schools.

4. *Assistance from State Government:* high state requirements for math and science education, state requirements for computer literacy, new job creation programs, R&D industrial parks, legislation favorable to advanced technology development, and general economic development promotion.

5. *Assistance to Researchers:* help in obtaining patents, science/technology advisory services, consulting help, research extension services, and access to research equipment and facilities.

6. *Assistance in the Form of State Initiatives:* general economic development promotion; research foundations; government-business/industry-labor-education forums for cooperative activity; industrial technology institutes; capital corporations for industrial financing; help with energy alternatives; help with productivity enhancement; economic development foundations; task forces and other bodies on advanced technology; higher education assistance for advanced technology; centers for genetic research, biotechnology, microelectronics, and lasers; innovation loan banks; university-industry centers for small businesses; centers for high-technology excellence; advisory councils on high technology; and general programs to advance new and expanding industries.

spread new technologies throughout the state's economic sectors, a more prosperous economy is possible. Advanced technologies combined with the traditional entrepreneurial abilities of Texans can form the base for a new Texas economy.

There is no lack of ideas on public policy initiatives that can be taken to strengthen the role of R&D in the state's economy. Table 18-2 lists many of the proposals. But expanding R&D activity in Texas ultimately turns on three issues: the strength of the state's thirty-seven senior-level universities and a similar number of private ones; the degree to which Texas-based corporations invest in R&D activities in the state; and the success of state leaders in bringing major R&D centers to the state.

Most research grants to state universities and health science centers result from national competitions for funds, competitions that can be fierce. Hence, universities need to have underlying strength, and it has only been in the last decade that many state universities have become nationally competitive.

Table 18-3 lists the ten largest research programs among senior state universities and the five largest research programs among health science centers. Many Texas state universities have ambitious plans to expand their research activities sharply. In addition, some private institutions such as the Baylor College of Medicine and Rice University have impressively large research activities.

The extent of corporate R&D work is often difficult to chart since much of it, especially in the energy industry, is considered an industrial secret. Still, there is evidence that the overall rate in Texas is less than in other industrial states. Hence, much excitement was generated when major private research programs for the computing industry were attracted to Austin in the mid-1980s. This complements the established Southwest Research Center in San Antonio, the Johnson Space Center in Houston, and research in the defense and electronics industries in the Dallas-Fort Worth region.

The state's leaders frequently joined together in the 1980s to attract major R&D assets to Texas, around which other economic activity could develop. Some proposals have been successful, and others not. Probably the most dramatic was the commitment of $500 million by the

TABLE 18-3
Largest State University and Health Science Center Research Programs in Texas, 1986–87

State Universities		Millions of dollars
1.	Texas A & M University	172.8
2.	University of Texas at Austin	130.6
3.	University of Houston	25.1
4.	Texas Tech University	17.9
5.	University of Texas at Dallas	11.2
6.	University of Texas at Arlington	7.9
7.	University of North Texas	7.9
8.	Prairie View A & M	5.4
9.	University of Houston-Clear Lake	3.3
10.	University of Texas at San Antonio	3.0

Health Science Centers (HSC)		
1.	University of Texas Cancer Center	65.3
2.	University of Texas HSC at Dallas	52.3
3.	University of Texas HSC at Houston	28.0
4.	University of Texas HSC at San Antonio	25.8
5.	University of Texas Medical Branch at Galveston	24.1

Source: Data compiled by author.

voters to the supercollider atom smasher when that giant national research laboratory is successfully located in Texas.

In summary, the economic competitive position of Texas will be heavily influenced by the strength of research and development programs in the state. Currently, the state has its share of pluses and minuses in this regard. But strenuous work is under way to correct the deficiencies. Many believe that the economic future of the state will depend, in no small part, on the outcome of these efforts.

CONTENT QUESTIONS

1. What percentage of American economic growth is due to improvements in technology and education?

2. What is the major problem facing R&D in the United States today?

3. What are the three issues that will determine R&D activity in Texas in the future?

DISCUSSION QUESTIONS

1. Speculate about how superconductivity may change the way we live.

2. After reviewing Table 18-1, discuss what is positive and what is negative about the future of R&D in Texas. What can be done to improve on the negatives?

19

THE HEALTH CARE INDUSTRY

Melinda Muse[1]

Texas is renowned as one of the world's providers of the most sophisticated and technologically advanced health care. The state's medical facilities attract patients from other states and from foreign countries drawn by the facilities' mission to honor the dignity of life and to delivery the finest quality health care.

ECONOMIC IMPACT OF THE INDUSTRY

Health care is Texas' fastest growing industry. Employing more than 440,000 people statewide, it is advancing at an annual rate of almost 4 percent. In 1986, the health service industry paid out approximately $7 billion in wages. The same year, state government expenditures for conservation of physical and mental health and sanitation totaled $1.2 billion. Texas collected more than $7 billion in facilities, examination, and professional fees.

As major purchasers of goods and services and payers of insurance premiums and property taxes, hospitals and other health-care facilities also support other industries from high-tech firms to florists. Food suppliers, laundry vendors, and construction firms, just to name a few, all benefit from health-care facilities.

More than 2,300,000 patients were admitted to Texas health-care facilities in 1986. The secondary economic impact of this is reflected in the vast amounts of money spent locally for lodging, meals, and transportation by family members accompanying patients.

Education and research are important to the Texas economy. According to a 1988 study by University of Texas medical economists, academic medical centers in Texas generate more than $4 billion a year in economic activity and are responsible for bringing $800 million to Texas from outside the state. This provides more than 7,600 jobs and more than $1.3 billion in household income.

HOSPITAL COSTS

Texas health-care facilities and employees are committed to restoring, maintaining, and preserving the highest level of care for all citizens of the state. However, dramatic changes and trends are sweeping the industry, threatening the citizens' access to the medical treatments that remain the hallmark of Texas health care. Spiraling costs of medical equipment and supplies, declining occupancy rates in hospitals, depressed local economic conditions, and increased demand for discounted rates by private insurance companies are jeopardizing the survival of many health-care facilities.

DECREASED GOVERNMENT FUNDING

The profit margins for Texas hospitals have been severely affected by continuing cuts of **Medicare** funding by Congress. (Medicare is the federal government's health insurance program for individuals receiving social security.) Promised

[1]Vice-President of Marketing and Communications, Texas Hospital Association, Austin, Texas.

updates in payments for inflation and cost increases over the past several years have raised payments by only 10 percent, while the hospital market basket cost has risen more than 21 percent. Nationally, hospital costs have risen an average of 9–10 percent in the past three or four years. During that time, the federal government changed the way it paid hospitals for care to elderly patients. The crisis arises from the prospective payment system, phased in during the mid-1980s. Under that system, hospitals are no longer paid a fee based on the cost of each service provided. Instead, they receive a flat fee for care based on a patient's diagnosis. If the hospitals' costs for providing care are less than that payment, they profit. If the care costs more, they lose money on that patient.

Government reimbursement for Medicare and Medicaid patients is inadequate and inequitable. (Medicaid is a federally funded, state administered program that pays the medical bills of poor people.) The Texas Department of Human Services has cut **Medicaid** funding by 10 percent even though Texas is 48th among 50 states in the level of funding medical costs for the indigent. Over a million people in the state received uncompensated care in 1987 for a total amount of $1.4 billion. The industry is waging a battle at both the state and federal levels to receive more equitable payment for care of elderly and indigent patients. The reduction in the payments to hospitals for Medicare patients has had an effect on all hospitals, especially small and rural Texas facilities. Texas leads the nation in the number of hospital closures; since 1984, seventy hospitals have closed their doors with the expectation that more will follow suit. Many were the sole providers of health care in their community.

SHORTAGE OF PERSONNEL

There is a critical shortage of health-care personnel, including registered nurses, occupational and physical therapists, lab technicians, and respiratory therapists, in Texas and across the nation. Some of the reasons for the shortage are: declining patient occupancy rates, lower compensation and career advancement tracks as compared to other industries, and a greater choice of career opportunities both within and outside the health-care setting. A statewide task force of

nurses, professionals in the allied fields, educators, and hospital administrators is at work to resolve the complex issue and alleviate the shortage.

Professional liability issues have forced many physicians to either change their specialty or, in some cases, cease to practice medicine. The aging population of the United States is expected to make a steady annual contribution of about one percentage point to the rise in costs.

New technology accounts for more than one-half of the yearly increases in health-care costs. The high cost of advanced medical technologies will be the focus of effective cost-containment strategies by health care facilities but will also involve very difficult choices. Artificial hearts, new drugs, genetic engineering, and other advances will accelerate the rate of technological change while raising costs. If health-care costs continue to soar, medicine may eventually face a difficult choice: the rationing of services using a variety of criteria such as age, the cost of care, and the potential effectiveness of treatment.

The Texas health-care industry is committed to caring for the sick, injured, and dying. It has far-reaching economic effects on the lives of many Texans. Health-care leaders across the state are waging a critical battle to ensure the continued delivery of the finest medical care in the world.

CONTENT QUESTIONS

1. What is Texas' fastest-growing industry?
2. What is the prospective payment system?
3. Why is there a shortage of health-care personnel in Texas?
4. What criteria could be used for rationing health care?

DISCUSSION QUESTIONS

1. What are the trends sweeping the health care industry and how do they affect you?
2. How can Texas and the nation prevent the rationing of medical services mentioned in this chapter?

20

FINANCIAL INSTITUTIONS
Sue Lynn Sasser, Ph.D.[1]

Financial institutions are intermediaries between people with money saved and people needing credit. The financial industry has a long history in the United States. It is a dynamic industry which continually responds to legislation, technology, and consumers.

One of the most significant pieces of legislation affecting financial institutions during the post-World War II period is the Depository Institutions Deregulation and Monetary Control Act of 1980. Since its passage, the financial industry has experienced customer innovations, rapid change, and perhaps its most intense competition.

DEPOSITORY FINANCIAL INSTITUTIONS

Financial intermediaries include a wide variety of organizations and businesses. The most common type is the depository financial institution, which includes commercial banks, savings and loan associations, and credit unions. Depository institutions accept customer deposits, make loans, and provide other services such as electronic fund transfers, safety deposit boxes, trust management, and short-term investments. The orderly operation of our modern economic system depends upon the functions performed by these and other financial institutions.

Commonly called banks, **commercial banks** were developed in England and later introduced in the American colonies to accept deposits from and make loans to businesses. Today, there are about 14,000 banks in the United States. Approximately 10 percent of them are in Texas.

Commercial banks provide a wide variety of services. They accept deposits from individuals, businesses, and governments, while also making loans to them. Prior to 1980, they held a monopoly over the creation of checking accounts. Commercial banks remain a major source of short- to intermediate-term loans for companies and individuals.

Savings and loan associations are thrift institutions which specialize in providing funds to homeowners. The number of savings and loans has grown significantly since 1945, paralleling the national expansion in home building and home ownership. While their original purpose was to accept savings deposits and use those funds for mortgage loans to homeowners, savings and loans have become more involved in commercial real estate loans, such as apartment complexes and office buildings, since 1980. In addition, savings and loans now offer almost the same services as commercial banks, including checking accounts and many types of savings accounts.

During the 1980s, their rapid expansion into long-term loans has decreased their profits. Many savings and loans are being merged with stronger partners in the industry. While savings and loan associations have broadened their services since 1980, they remain the dominant mortgage lenders and their competitive position has increased their potential to compete in the marketplace. At the same time, however, their lack of capital has impaired their ability to improve their competitive position in the financial industry.

[1]Education Specialist, Federal Reserve Bank of Dallas.

87

FINANCIAL INDUSTRY REGULATORS

The number of regulators in the financial industry is as varied as the different types of financial institutions. Following is a partial list of federal regulators and a brief explanation of their responsibilities. Each has a district or regional office in Texas.

Federal Reserve System

The **Federal Reserve System** (the Fed) requires all banks and thrifts to maintain a percentage of their deposits as reserves. Although all national banks must be members of the Fed, it is primarily responsible for examining bank holding companies and state member banks.

Office of the Comptroller of the Currency

The **Office of the Comptroller of the Currency** (OCC) heads a bureau of the U.S. Treasury Department which carries out all federal laws regarding national banks. OCC examines national banks annually and requires reports of financial condition. Also, OCC approves or disapproves all applications to charter national banks, establish new branches, or merge with other banks.

Federal Deposit Insurance Corporation

The **Federal Deposit Insurance Corporation** (FDIC) insures the deposits of all member banks up to $100,000 per account. FDIC requires regular reports of financial conditions from its member banks. FDIC relies on examinations conducted by OCC examiners.

Federal Home Loan Bank Board

The **Federal Home Loan Bank Board** is responsible for enforcing laws and regulations pertaining to thrifts. It shares enforcement responsibility over savings banks which are members of the Federal Home Loan Bank System.

Federal Savings and Loan Insurance Corporation

The **Federal Savings and Loan Insurance Corporation** (FSLIC) insures deposits up to $100,000 from all federal savings and loan associations as well as most state savings and loans. FSLIC supervises and examines its member thrifts and may also arrange acquisitions or mergers of closed or failing institutions.

In addition to the federal agencies, the Texas Banking Commission is charged with the responsibility of chartering and regulating state banks.

THE BANKING INDUSTRY IN TEXAS

In financing the Texas boom of the late 1970s and early 1980s, Texas financial institutions became high-return, high-risk banks and concentrated their lending on energy, agriculture, and real estate ventures. With the decline of these industries and the subsequent negative effect on the Texas economy, financial institutions began to suffer in the mid to late 1980s.

Several forces combined to produce a sharp decline in profits. The financial stress due to the downturn in the state's economy has increased the number of borrowers who have delinquent loan payments. As a result, bank profits have declined. Profitability among the state's banks has been decreasing for the past five years.

RECENT LEGISLATIVE CHANGES IN TEXAS

The structure of banking laws in Texas prior to 1986 limited the banks' abilities to diversify their loan portfolios. Texas banking laws did not allow branching or interstate banking, thus inhibiting opportunities to expand efficiently. State voters, however, approved legislation in 1986 permitting both branching and interstate banking.

These legislative changes allow banks more freedom to diversify their loan portfolios and streamline their daily operations, which tends to result in a more efficient banking system. As efficiency increases, costs tend to drop and profits rise. The legislation has also resulted in a gradual decline in the number of banks in Texas because many existing banks have either merged or been converted to branches. This practice also tends to increase efficiency in the system.

The reduction of profits for Texas banks had increased the need for capital input from out-of-state banks. With the passage of the interstate banking provision, the needed capital can be obtained from sources within Texas as well as outside the state. Interstate banking legislation removes geographic barriers to raising capital and allows more players to become involved in mergers and acquisitions.

There are three recent examples in Texas where out-of-state banks purchased Texas bank holding companies: First Interstate Bank of California purchased Allied Bancshares; Chemical Bank of New York purchased Texas Commerce Bank; and North Carolina National Bank purchased First Republic, which now operates as NCNB Texas.

Examples of interstate banking include three purchases of Texas bank holding companies by out-of-state holding banks, such as First Interstate Bank from California (which purchased the Allied Bancshares holding company); the purchase of the Texas Commerce Bank by Chemical Bank of New York; and the merger of Republic Bank and InterFirst Bank to form First Republic, which is now managed by NCNB of North Carolina.

Added capital should make Texas banks more resilient to future economic shocks and place them in a more competitive position with larger banks across the nation. Texas banks are expected to grow and become more competitive as more and more people, bankers and nonbankers alike, expand into the state.

BANK CLOSINGS

Problems at individual banks can occur regardless of bank size, branching rules or other situations. Regulators examine banks regularly to determine their solvency. If the regulators determine that a bank is insolvent, it can be closed. Usually, an insolvent bank is sold to new owners who are able to infuse the capital necessary to reopen the institution. These banks are renamed and reopened with new management in a day or two. Occasionally, however, banks are closed permanently because no one bids for them.

The number of bank closings in Texas during the late 1980s continues at a record pace. The figures for 1988 set an all-time high with the closings of over forty First Republic Bank offices. As shown in Figure 20-1, Texas accounts for a substantial percentage of the nation's closings in recent years.

THE THRIFT INDUSTRY IN TEXAS

The Texas banking industry has not suffered alone. Thrifts in the state have also experienced major problems. In a 1988 study conducted by the Financial Industries Department of the Federal Reserve Bank of Dallas, it was reported that Texas thrifts lost $6.9 billion in 1987, with insolvent thrifts reporting losses of $9.2 billion. Additionally, of the 345 thrifts nationwide which are insolvent, 124 were in Texas.

Faced with these problems, the Federal Home Loan Bank Board (FHLBB) of Dallas has implemented the **Southwest Plan** to address the industry's financial difficulties. The plan is designed to reduce the operating costs of Texas thrifts while preserving the basic structure of the industry. Under the Southwest Plan, approximately one hundred insolvent thrifts will be consolidated and the number of savings and loans branches will be reduced from 1,800 to 1,400. Unprofitable branch offices will also be closed. The plan divides Texas into fourteen regions to ensure adequate competition and service throughout the state.

The primary purpose of the Southwest Plan is to reduce expenses and control the losses of troubled thrifts. The FHLBB expects to decrease expenses by eliminating overlapping, unprofitable, and duplicate facilities. Losses will be controlled by retaining the most competent managers when thrifts are merged. The agency also hopes to attract an influx of private capital to

FIGURE 20-1
Bank Failures (Includes Open-Bank Assistance)

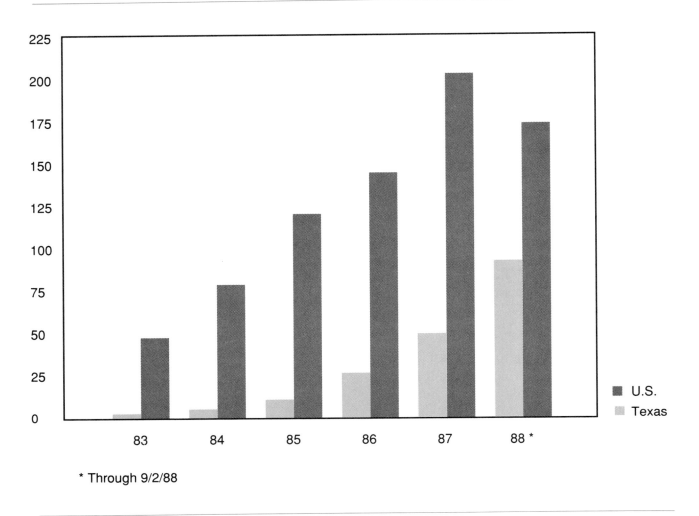

* Through 9/2/88

Source: Data from Research Division, Federal Reserve Bank of Dallas.

sustain those savings and loans which remain in operation.

SUMMARY

Since the condition of the financial industry is a lagging economic indicator, the crisis for banks and thrifts in Texas is reflective of the recent downturn in the state's economy. The past growth of Texas banks and thrifts has provided the necessary financial resources to support the state's previous periods of expansion. It is impor-

tant to the people of Texas, and in the state's race for regional strength, that the financial industry remains competitive and ready to provide the necessary services to facilitate economic expansion.

CONTENT QUESTIONS

1. What are the major regulatory bodies for the financial industry?

2. In what areas did Texas banks concentrate their lending with resulting problems during the 1980s?
3. What is the Southwest Plan?

DISCUSSION QUESTIONS

1. How has recent legislation changed banking in your town?

2. What services do commercial banks perform and how do they differ from savings and loan associations?

21

TRANSPORTATION
John B. McCall, Ph.D[1]

Every business firm both buys its raw materials and sells its products at a variety of locations across the map. Transportation links these buyers and sellers together and makes the economy work in the same way the human body's system of veins, arteries, and capillaries allows the human body to live. An economy with a limited and inefficient transportation system cannot grow or prosper—living standards are low and life is dull and boring.

Look at the world around you. Hardly anyone who earns their own living produces the things they need to stay alive and be happy. Maybe there is a hermit who has to do this, but the rest of us earn our living by **specializing** in the production of a limited line of goods or services. Then we each exchange some of this production for the specialized production of others. That hermit's living standard is very low and has no variety. To the extent we have a good transportation system, we are able to exchange what we produce for a broad list of things produced by others. As a result, our living standard is high and has variety.

Transportation—of both goods and people—can either facilitate the creation of value and economic progress or it can serve as a very real limiting factor that diminishes economic growth. This is true for the world's economic progress and the United States economy. It is also true for the Texas economy and the economy of every city and county within Texas.

THE BEGINNINGS

Prior to the Civil War, most Texas transport used either trails or virtually nonexistent roads. This was slow and raised the cost of delivering goods to market to a level such that only a few Texas families could live beyond self-sufficient subsistence. Where there were rivers, a modest amount of small-scale steamboat and flatboat transport could open up interior areas to the beginnings of economic development. What railroad routes there were in Texas at the beginning of the Civil War were both short in length and low in efficiency. For the most part, these routes radiated out from the Houston-Galveston area.

After the Civil War, conditions were slow to change. Cattle were driven long distances north to market. Cotton was produced in areas close to navigable rivers and around the small seaports that dotted the Texas coast. Other agricultural production was consumed locally. There was no other market because of the lack of transport to move the product to a distant point where it could be sold. Life was hard and poor.

RAILROADS

The coming of the railroads changed this. Between 1870 and the turn of the century, a number of long-distance railroads were built to crisscross major portions of the state. The Houston and

[1]Associate Professor of Economics; Director, Center for Economic Education, University of Texas at Arlington.

Texas Central was built north from Houston to Dallas and on up to Sherman. The Texas and Pacific was built westward from St. Louis to Texarkana, through Dallas and Fort Worth to El Paso. The Texas and New Orleans was built across the southern part of the state—coming from New Orleans—through Beaumont, Houston, and San Antonio to El Paso and on to Los Angeles. The Missouri-Kansas-Texas was built from both St. Louis and Kansas City down through Indian territory to Dallas, Houston/Galveston, and Austin/San Antonio. The Gulf, Colorado & Santa Fe was built north from Galveston, through Temple and Fort Worth, to connect with a railroad from Chicago at a point in Oklahoma. The Fort Worth & Denver City was built from Cowtown up through Amarillo to Denver.

In addition, these major railroads and a number of small companies built short-distance branch lines to many small towns to feed freight into their main lines. In the process, Texas land that was previously worthless could now be used for farming because railroads could get the product to market fast enough so that it would not rot, and cheap enough so that the product could be delivered in a national market at competitive prices. Land values across Texas increased.

Cattle no longer had to be driven overland to market, losing weight and market value in the process. The efficiency of the Texas cattle industry was increased greatly by the coming of the railroads. The Fort Worth stockyards would never have developed without railroads.

Agricultural activity began to spread out over the Texas map. As more output was sold outside the state, Texans could afford to buy more from the rest of the nation and the world. Living standards began to rise. Cheap railroad passenger service attracted new immigrants from out-of-state. With an expanded labor force Texas could produce more value because there were more people around to do the work.

Today, railroad mileage in Texas continues to decline due to competition from highway and air transport. Currently, 29 railroads (7 main lines and 22 branch lines) operate on 14,000 miles of track. While mileage is falling, freight tonnage is increasing, which indicates that Texas railroads are alive and well.

HIGHWAYS

Texas' road system began before the turn of the century to feed agricultural products to the nearest railroad. As automobiles and trucks developed, more and more travel and freight went by road. Federal monies began to supplement state and county funds in the building of roads in 1916 and, by 1920, the beginnings of the national highway network had started. Highway transport broadened opportunities for economic development across Texas and furthered Texas' commercial links with the rest of the nation in a manner which the coming of the railroads only began.

During the Great Depression of the 1930s, much effort was expended on both major highways and on farm-to-market roads in Texas. This effort was financed by federal and state money designed to put people to work. After World War II, the building of the Interstate Highway System, as well as continual upgrading of Texas' other roads, further improved the state's ability to create value.

Texas currently has one of the most extensive highway systems in the nation and one of the highest taxes on gasoline (15 cents a gallon) to pay for them. Currently, there are 275,000 miles of roads in Texas—more than in any other state. Almost 6 million Texans now have driver's licenses.

WATER TRANSPORT

Almost from the beginning of non-Indian settlement in Texas and Galveston, the seaports along the Texas coast served as the region's major contact with the outside world. From the United States, both people and trade came down the Mississippi to New Orleans and over to Texas by ship. It was more efficient than overland travel into Texas from the northeast, and these ports fed the early development of the southern parts of the state.

Similarly, the primitive road systems in the northeastern parts of the state, around Dallas, were fed by water transport from the Mississippi up the Sabine by steamboat to the port of Jefferson, Texas. With the coming of railroads, water transport generally gave way because trains were both faster and more direct transport to the markets in the northeast.

The development of railroads, and the expansion this prompted in agricultural and manufacturing activity in Texas' interior, made the development of the ports of Galveston, Port Arthur and Corpus Christi feasible as major, heavy-tonnage, international seaports. It took the railroads to feed these ports. As a part of this development, a canal able to take ocean-going vessels was built from Galveston Bay up to Houston. Houston soon eclipsed Galveston as the major port in Texas.

During World War II, the Intercoastal Canal was finished. This federally-financed water route allowed barge traffic—moved by towboats—to transport basic tonnage between the northeastern United States and all Texas ports. At the same time, it kept this tonnage away from predatory Nazi submarines operating in the Gulf of Mexico. It was slow, but it was safe.

PIPELINES

Concurrent with the development of Texas' oil industry in the early 1920s, pipelines were built to gather the oil from the wells and to ship this oil directly to market without reloading it onto trains. Development of the pumping technology necessary to move oil long-distance allowed these major pipelines to be efficient. During World War II, when oil was needed in the northeast and when rail and ocean-going transport was inadequate, great pipelines four and six feet in diameter were built from Texas to the northeastern United States to supply their factories. Texas economic activity soared and the state became richer.

AIR TRANSPORT

Nationally, air transport began in 1918 with Army pilots flying the mails for the Post Office Department. By 1920, these airmail routes were operated by a number of small entrepreneurs as a government-subsidized market activity. Dallas and Fort Worth were a part of this primitive airmail service almost from the beginning. As these early small airlines merged and became larger, they began to carry passengers along with the mail. Passenger air travel did not take off in the United States until after the Second World

War. The development of jet aircraft in the late 1950s and 1960s increased speed and reduced cost. Today, Texans make more use of air travel than do any other people. One out of every ten airplane passengers is a Texan.

The growth of air freight as a business furthered these benefits. Not only did a growing number of Texans find jobs in the airline industry, but Texans found larger numbers of jobs in new industries devoted to the design and manufacture of aircraft. Further, many businesses located in Texas because of the benefits good air transportation lends to efficient business operation. Just as the development of railroad, pipeline, and water transport helped growth of our basic manufacturing industries of agriculture, oil, and other raw materials, so the development of the airline industry prompted growth of Texas' high-tech, service, banking, and fashion industries.

Today, every major Texas city has a commercial airport. Lack of adequate air service is a major problem for many cities seeking to develop. Since airline deregulation in 1978, this problem has been reduced by the growth of smaller commuter airlines which serve these cities. The Dallas/Fort Worth airport is one of the world's busiest and is the home base for many airlines. Houston's Intercontinental is an expanding international facility. Almost 80 percent of all Texans who use air transport pass through these two airports.

CONCLUSION

Transportation is a major influence in the standard of living of all Texans. A state as large as Texas cannot survive without an excellent system of moving goods and people. A good transportation system reduces costs and makes the cost of doing business and the cost of living less for all Texans.

CONTENT QUESTIONS

1. What two benefits does a good system of transportation provide for an economy?
2. What event first changed the way Texans transported goods and services?

3. How did the railroads affect Texas agriculture?
4. Which state has the most miles of roads? Which city has the largest port? Which city has the largest airport?
5. Pipelines were developed during _____ to ship _____ to the northeastern United States.

DISCUSSION QUESTIONS

1. How do rail, road, and water transport complement and compete with each other?
2. How does a good transportation system benefit a state?

22

GAS AND ELECTRIC UTILITIES

E. R. Brooks[1]

In the eighteenth century, the English economist Adam Smith wrote that business competitors "are led by an invisible hand to promote the public interest even though this is not their intention." In a nutshell, Smith's idea was that the combined self-interest of competitors would lead to the common good. The result would be lower prices, greater supply, and more opportunity. Across the Atlantic Ocean, the free enterprise system that Smith had described with such conviction took a firm hold in the young United States of America. It remains the mainstay of our economy today.

NATURAL MONOPOLY

Perhaps ironically, an essential element of our free enterprise system is something Smith did not foresee and might not have condoned: natural monopolies. It was not until the middle of the next century that another English economist, John Stuart Mill, developed the idea that some services are best provided through a **natural monopoly**, either because of the essential nature of those services or because the cost of providing them is so great that competition would make the services *more* expensive, not less. In such cases, one firm can provide the product at a lower cost than could many competing firms. One large firm could use larger, more efficient plants.

In the American economy, gas and electric utilities are classic examples of such natural monopolies, because they are highly capital-intensive businesses. Building power plants and gas pipelines is an expensive process. In fact, between 1986 and 1996, the capital expenditures of the electric utility industry alone are expected to exceed $275 *billion*! Given this high cost of producing and distributing power, can you imagine how much more your family's monthly electric bill would be, if several different companies *each* built their own power plants and transmission and distribution systems to serve your town and then competed to provide service to your family?

Natural monopolies like gas and electric utilities provide basic services needed by the rest of our economy. So, they are not only *economical*, they are also *essential* to the free enterprise system, even though they do not function in a free market environment themselves. For instance, without reliable, low-cost utility service, how could we produce high quality, competitively priced computers, automobiles, or farm products?

ELECTRIC AND GAS UTILITIES IN TEXAS

The first electric power plant in Texas was built in 1882 in Houston. But until 1910, most electric power plants served only a city or a small area. In that year, Texas Power and Light built the first high-voltage transmission line from Waco to Fort Worth. This began the age of modern electric utilities in Texas.

[1]Executive Vice-President, Electrical Operations, Central and South West Corporation, Dallas, Texas.

Here in the United States, the link between utilities and free enterprise is particularly strong, since—unlike in most other countries—the majority of our electric and gas utilities are private businesses, rather than government agencies. In Texas, the twelve major privately owned—or, as they are called in the industry, *investor-owned*—provide about 70 percent of the state's generating capacity. The remaining 30 percent is supplied by public power (municipally or federally owned) and by rural electric cooperatives. There are now 138 electric power plants in Texas. Ninety-three are steam plants using coal as a fuel with an additional fifty-one using natural gas. Twenty are hydroelectric plants and the rest are nuclear powered.

Almost 300 gas utilities operate in Texas. The gas utility business is divided into three phases. The first is gas-gathering at the well site, and the second is transmission by pipeline to the city where the gas is to be used. The final phase is the distribution to local customers. Some gas companies are integrated, providing all three steps under one company. Other gas utilities provide only transmission or local distribution, buying their gas from others.

HOW UTILITIES DIFFER FROM OTHER BUSINESSES

Since most suppliers of natural gas and electricity in this country are investor-owned utilities, exactly how do they differ from any other private business? The answer, in a word, is regulation. For the sake of efficiency and economy, a utility is given the exclusive right to serve an area. In exchange for that privilege, the utility submits to government regulation. This regulation takes the place of the free market in keeping the *cost* of service low and the *quality* of service high.

The utility also obligates itself to serve all willing and able buyers of its service in that area. Even if serving the area proves to be unprofitable, the utility is not permitted to pull up stakes and abandon its customers. Furthermore, the utility must be prepared to provide its service on demand. When you turn on the light switch, the light comes on instantly. And, since electricity cannot be stored, that means the power for your light had to be produced and transmitted instantly—even if everyone else in town turned on their lights at the same time.

BUT THE SIMILARITIES OUTWEIGH THE DIFFERENCES

In other respects, an investor-owned utility operates much like any other business. It competes on the open market to attract capital through the sale of stocks and bonds. As we saw above, gas and electric utilities are capital-intensive businesses; in fact, about a third of all long-term corporate financing in the United States goes to electric utilities.

THE REGULATORY BODIES

Utilities are responsible to regulatory bodies at both the state and federal levels. In Texas, electric utilities are regulated by the Public Utility Commission, a three-member board, whose members are appointed by the governor to serve six-year terms. Gas utilities are regulated by the Texas Railroad Commission, whose three commissioners are elected to six-year terms. The Railroad Commission was created in 1891, and was given regulatory authority over gas utilities in 1920. The Public Utility Commission (PUC) is much younger. It was created in 1975 with the passage of the Public Utility Regulatory Act. Prior to 1975, rate-making was handled by the cities and the electric utilities, with the option of appealing to the courts.

At the federal level, gas and electric utility rates come under the jurisdiction of the Federal Energy Regulatory Commission. However, many other federal agencies also regulate utilities. The key ones are the Department of Energy and the Securities and Exchange Commission.

To illustrate how complex the regulatory environment can become for a utility, let me use my own company as an example. Since the Central and South West Corporation has electric utilities in Oklahoma, Arkansas, and Louisiana, as well as Texas, and has a gas pipeline in Oklahoma, we are responsible to four separate *state* utility commissions. At the *federal* level, we are also regulated by the U.S. Department of Energy. And, since we sell power across state lines, we come under the jurisdiction of the Federal Energy Regulatory Commission. Finally, as a public utility holding company (a company that owns other utilities), we are regulated by the Securities and Exchange Commission.

RATE MAKING

Regulatory bodies oversee a wide range of activities in a public utility, but the one that attracts the most attention from regulators, customers, and utilities is setting rates for utility service. The rate-making process begins when someone—whether the utility or the regulatory body—wants to change the existing rates.

For gas utilities, cities—not the Texas Railroad Commission—have primary responsibility for setting rates in incorporated areas. If the city government and the utility cannot agree on the rates, either party can appeal to the Railroad Commission. However, in unincorporated areas, the Railroad Commission has the primary rate-making authority.

In setting electric utility rates, a city also has primary responsibility, *if* that city has retained what's known as "original jurisdiction" over electric rates. Since most of the larger towns and cities in Texas *have* retained their original jurisdiction, their rate-making process works much the same way as rate-setting for gas utilities. If the utility doesn't agree with the rate ordinance passed by the city, it can appeal to the PUC. However, in towns and cities that have waived their original jurisdiction and in the unincorporated areas, the PUC has the primary responsibility for electricity rates. Rate cases can drag on for months. In fact, by the time new rates go into effect, they are often already out of date.

RATE OF RETURN: A FISHING LICENSE

Utility rates in Texas—as in most other states—are required to be "just and reasonable." That means the rates must produce enough revenue to let the utility stay in business. Since investor-owned utilities are private businesses that compete with other private businesses for investor's money, investors must be allowed to earn a fair rate of return or profit on their investment.

Some people mistakenly assume that when a city, the PUC, or the Railroad Commission *allows* a certain rate of return, it has somehow *guaranteed* that rate of return. That's simply not true; the utility still has to *earn* the rate of return that the regulatory body has *allowed*. Many factors might keep the utility from earning that return. Large industrial customers served by the utility may cut back, shut down, or even relocate their operations. The damage from an ice or snow storm may drive operating expenses up. Or an unseasonably warm winter may reduce the amount of electricity customers use. So, the rate of return is no *guarantee*; it's more like a *fishing license*. Having that license does not ensure that you will catch fish; it just lets you keep them if you do.

CONCLUSION

Gas and electric utilities provide economical, reliable service to the citizens of Texas, despite unpredictable weather and population shifts. They do this through a combination of free enterprise and regulation that offers the benefits of both to the consuming public.

CONTENT QUESTIONS

1. What is a natural monopoly?
2. In Texas, most power is produced by _____ _____ electric companies.
3. What takes the place of the free market in keeping utility rates low and quality of service high?
4. In Texas, who regulates the electric utilities?

DISCUSSION QUESTIONS

1. How do cities and state regulatory agencies in Texas share the responsibility for rate setting in Texas?
2. Why does the author call rate of return regulation a "fishing license"?

23

RECREATION AND ENTERTAINMENT

Calvin A. Kent, Ph.D.[1]

Texans love to have a good time. Providing them with that good time has created one of the major industries in the state. The ideal climate of Texas and the entertainment and recreational opportunities it offers have attracted a significant number of tourists to enjoy the good life that Texas represents. There is recreation and entertainment for virtually every person with every type of taste. Few states offer as much recreational diversity or quality as does Texas.

HUNTING, FISHING, AND BOATING

Hunting and fishing are two of Texas' prime recreational activities. There are 1.7 million Texans who hold either hunting or fishing or combined licenses. Over 125,000 out-of-state people hunted or fished in the state in the mid-1980s. Texas offers a wide variety of hunting and fishing. It is the nation's leading state for this form of recreation. The principal animals hunted are white-tailed deer, mule deer, wild turkey, ducks, and javelinas. At the last count, Texas hunters bagged almost one-half million animals.

Texas anglers fish for sport as well as food. Their favorites are largemouth bass, crappie, sunfish, white bass, catfish, walleye, smallmouth bass, and striped bass. All of these are found in the lakes and rivers of the state, which is why this activity is referred to as freshwater fishing.

Saltwater fishing abounds on the inshore waters of the Texas coast and in the Gulf of Mexico. Saltwater fishing is a major industry in Texas, as well as a major sport. Saltwater fishing provides a livelihood for those who own boats and rent them for fishing expeditions. Others make their living supplying fishers with the bait and tackle they need.

Texas' 5,700 lakes provide numerous opportunities for boating and water sports.

CAMPING AND HIKING

Texas offers unusual opportunities for those who like to camp and hike. There are almost 200,000 acres set aside in ten national wildlife refuges. An additional twenty-three wildlife management areas are administered by the state. These run all the way from the beautiful desert of the Palo Alto Canyon and the majestic vistas of Big Bend National Park to the piney woods of East Texas to the sand dunes of the islands off the Gulf Coast. Over 20 million visitors came to the national and state parks in Texas last year to hike or to camp or to just enjoy the tremendous views these provide.

THE FINE ARTS

The fine arts in Texas are a combination of activities provided by both the profit and the nonprofit sectors. Besides recording artists such as Willie Nelson, commercial profit-making firms include

[1]Herman W. Lay Professor of Private Enterprise; Director, Center for Private Enterprise, Baylor University, Waco, Texas.

nightclubs, record companies, and private galleries which sell fine art such as paintings and sculptures. The commercial sector also includes private dance and music halls which are open to the public.

In addition, Texas has extensive cultural resources which are provided by nonprofit organizations. These nonprofit organizations are dependent on the donations of the public and business, as well as on state and local government funding. There are five Texas agencies which support such activities. One of these, the Texas Commission on the Arts, was established in 1965 to attract outstanding artists to Texas and to improve the environment for the fine arts of the state. It seeks to accomplish its goals by providing financial and technical assistance to nonprofit companies conducting theaters, media events, arts festivals, musical performances, visual arts displays, and dance recitals.

Virtually every major Texas city supports one or more nonprofit arts organizations. These include orchestras, museums, dance companies, operas, theaters, and cultural centers. The art museums in Dallas, Fort Worth, and Houston have international reputations. Schools and colleges have fine arts programs which not only train students but provide programs for the public as well. It has been estimated that at least one out of every two Texans attends a cultural event sponsored by one of these community-based organizations every year.

MOVIE MAKING

Filmmaking has become a big business in Texas. The state is one of the most frequently-used locations for the filming of major motion pictures. Many of these are feature films designed for theaters or television. In 1984 three of the Best Picture nominees for the Academy Awards were made in Texas: Silkwood, Tender Mercies, and Terms of Endearment. More television commercials are produced in Texas than in any other state. In addition, Texas filmmakers produce a wide variety of educational films used in schools and for industrial training programs.

Texas now rivals both California and New York as a filmmaking capital. The reasons for this are the variety of great outdoor locations, an excel-

lent year-round climate, and picturesque places and historic old towns such as Waxahachie. The cost of making films in Texas is usually about 30 percent lower than the cost of producing films on either coast. Texas has developed a large number of experienced and talented people who work in the film industry. There are currently 700 companies in Texas making films and more than 1,000 actors have their homes in the state. All this has generated over $82 million for the Texas economy.

SPECTATOR SPORTS

It would be impossible not to mention spectator sports when one talks about recreation and entertainment in Texas. Football at both the high school and collegiate levels is a well-documented passion in the state. Most Texans attend at least one high school, collegiate, or professional football game each year. State high school football championships in Texas are major news stories. No one takes football more seriously than do Texans.

High school football is supplemented by the presence of two professional football teams. The Dallas Cowboys during the 1970s were the most successful franchise in National Football League history. In recent years they have fallen on hard times, but those same years have seen the rise of the Houston Oilers to become contenders for the national championship.

While football dominates the fall, baseball and softball dominate the spring. The good weather in Texas allows baseball to begin in early February and to continue into November. It is virtually a year-round sport. Almost every high school has a baseball team and most communities have recreational slow pitch softball leagues. In fact, more people participate in slow pitch softball in Texas than in any other state in the nation. There are two major league baseball teams, the Rangers in Dallas representing the American League, and the Astros in Houston representing the National League.

Basketball is also important although it tends to be overshadowed by the other two sports. The Dallas Mavericks, the Houston Rockets, and the San Antonio Spurs are the three professional basketball franchises in the state. All have been contenders for national titles in recent years. Pro basketball has helped increase the popularity of high school and collegiate basketball within the state.

The Southwest Conference (S.W.C.) is the major collegiate athletic conference within Texas. It was organized in 1914 and arose out of the special needs of the larger colleges to promote sports within the state. The founding schools were Arkansas, Baylor, Southwestern, Oklahoma A&M, Texas A&M, Texas, Rice, and Oklahoma. Southwestern dropped out in 1917, Oklahoma in 1918, and Oklahoma State in 1925. SMU joined in 1918, TCU in 1923 and Texas Tech in 1953. The University of Houston was the last addition in May 1971. 1989 is the seventy-fifth year and the diamond anniversary of the Southwest Conference. The S.W.C. is one of the premier athletic conferences in the nation and sponsors the Cotton Bowl each New Year's Day.

HORSE RACING

In 1987, Texas legalized horse track betting. This was a very controversial issue. Proponents felt that it would create a major new recreational industry in the state, being of particular value to horse breeders and related businesses. They also felt that the state treasury would benefit by receiving a portion of the amount bet at the tracks.

Opponents raised the issue of the morality of gambling. They felt the economic advantages were overestimated and that betting would attract a criminal element to the state. They also pointed to statistics that indicate horseracing is a declining industry nationwide. Whether or not this new form of recreation will pay off for Texas will be decided in the future.

CONCLUSION

There is something for everyone in Texas. Whether your tastes are for ballet and opera or for hunting and football, Texas provides the opportunity you seek. Texans are fortunate to have this variety available to them, for it not only enriches their lives, it also stimulates the state's economy by providing jobs and income.

CONTENT QUESTIONS

1. What are the major types of recreation and entertainment available to Texans?
2. How many people come to Texas to camp and hike each year?
3. What are the fine arts activities provided by the nonprofit sector?
4. What are the three major filmmaking states?
5. What are the three major spectator sports in Texas?
6. Which schools are now part of the Southwest Conference?

DISCUSSION QUESTIONS

1. What recreational and entertainment opportunities are available in your area? Do you use them? What new ones would you like to see developed?
2. What explains the growth of the film industry in Texas?
3. How do you feel about horse-race betting in Texas?

24

THE TELECOMMUNICATIONS INDUSTRY

Pres Sheppard[1]

In the nineteenth century, the railroad was essential for economic expansion. In order to take advantage of economies of scale, American industry needed a way to tie together markets in different parts of the growing United States. Since the products of the day were, for the most part, raw materials and mass-produced goods, the "silver ribbon" of the railroad provided the ideal way to link suppliers with manufacturers and to tie the manufacturers' small, scattered markets into one large regional or national market.

Today, telecommunications performs a similar function in the American economy. A smaller percentage of our products are mass-produced goods, since more and more of those are being produced overseas where labor costs are lower.

In fact, according to most estimates, companies in the information industry produce over half of our Gross National Product and employ about 60 percent of our workforce. As a result, we have less need to *transport* heavy products to market and more need to *transmit* information and services to those who need them.

Telecommunications makes this possible and, in the process, it creates many of the conveniences we take for granted today, such as automatic tellers and automated credit card verification. Telecommunications improves the quality of life for a growing number of workers through "telecommuting," which lets people work at home and transmit data to and from the office.

And telecommunications reduces the development time and the manufacturing costs of a great many products through computer-aided design and computer-aided manufacturing (CAD/CAM).

So it is not surprising that, just as the railroad was in the last century, telecommunications today is a rapidly growing industry. In fact, in the Dallas-Fort Worth area alone, the telephone communications industry now employs roughly 60,000 people, 6,500 of whom work for the American Telephone and Telegraph Company (AT&T). By 1995, the number of people employed by telephone communications firms in Dallas-Fort Worth is expected to jump to 72,000.

In 1984, approximately 15 percent of the Texas workforce was employed in telecommunications-intensive industries, such as finance, insurance, real estate, and data processing.

FROM MONOPOLY TO COMPETITION

Probably no other event has had a more far-reaching impact on telecommunications than the government-ordered **divestiture** of AT&T in 1984, which separated AT&T and the local Bell telephone companies. Prior to 1984, AT&T was the mother company which owned almost all the regional telephone companies in the United States. In long-distance service AT&T was the largest and, in many cases, the only company. The intent of this ruling was to promote competition in the telecommunications industry.

[1]Vice-President, AT&T, Austin, Texas.

After divestiture, the regional telephone companies became independent firms. As regulated monopolies, they became the sole providers of local telephone service. Under the terms of the divestiture agreement, these regional companies were prohibited from engaging in manufacturing or long-distance services outside their region. Texas is served by Southwestern Bell whose territory includes other southwestern states.

AT&T was thrust headlong into the competitive marketplace. In exchange for divesting the regional companies, AT&T was allowed to keep its manufacturing arm, Western Electric Co., and AT&T Bell Laboratories, the nation's premiere research and development facility.

Divestiture allowed AT&T to enter new competitive markets, such as the computer business, and to provide domestic and international long distance services under regulation by the Federal Communications Commission. The sudden move from regulated monopoly with minimal competition to full-fledged competitor was dramatic. AT&T had faced only a handful of long-distance competitors prior to 1984. Today, there are over 400 firms offering long distance services throughout the country. About 90 of these firms are established in Texas.

NEW INDUSTRY PRICING STRUCTURE

The divestiture of AT&T imposed new pricing schemes for long-distance service. Prior to the breakup, customers paid the local telephone company the entire cost of handling a call, whether the call was local or long distance. But divestiture meant that local and long-distance service would now be offered through separate entities. A system had to be developed to separate the various elements of a long-distance call and compensate the provider accordingly.

That system has become known as **access charges**. In principle, long-distance carriers provide the long-haul communication of messages between cities, or exchanges. But in order to originate or complete a call, local facilities, or switches, must be accessed on the originating and terminating ends of the call. Since local companies complete the call on both ends, they are compensated through access charges.

THE IMPACT OF REGULATION

One effect of regulation on the industry has been to employ social pricing philosophies in place of economic pricing. In representing the needs of its constituency, a regulatory body may implement price subsidies which favor certain social segments (such as residential vs. business customers or rural vs. urban consumers) in a manner that it deems fair.

Social pricing often has little to do with economics. Policymakers in Texas, for example, believe that rural customers should pay the same for telephone service as urban customers pay, even though the cost of serving rural customers is much higher, and the revenue much lower. To meet this goal, telecommunications providers average their prices statewide, so that all customers pay the same regardless of geographic location.

Texas regulators are also committed to keeping the cost of the basic telephone service among the lowest in the nation. In order to accomplish this, they are willing to tolerate the highest access rates in the nation, in effect subsidizing local service through high intrastate long-distance rates.

The result of social pricing is pricing distortion, or customer prices that are either much higher or much lower than the cost of providing that service. Texas access charges rank among the most expensive in the nation for calls within the state—about 70 cents of every consumer's long-distance dollar goes to cover this cost. The high cost of access results in Texans having among the highest intrastate long-distance rates in the nation.

THE IMPACT OF TECHNOLOGY

As with most high-technology industries, advances in microelectronics, software, and lightwave technology are enhancing the capabilities of telecommunications carriers to provide service at a lower cost.

It was only 25 years ago, for example, that most calls in this country were provided over standard copper circuits, capable of handling less than twenty conversations at one time. Today, advances in digital transmission and fiber-optic technology allow up to 24,000 simultaneous conversations, and very high-speed data transmission at

1.7 billion bits per second—the equivalent of sending ten 30-volume sets of the Encyclopedia Britannica in one second.

In 1987, AT&T invested $2.7 billion to improve its Worldwide Intelligent Network. Another $6 billion was invested in 1988 and 1989. In Texas, the company has an accumulated investment of more than $2 billion in digital switching, lightwave routes, and other transmission facilities.

Other carriers have invested heavily in their networks as well, resulting in the development of more than 500 million circuit miles of long-distance capacity in Texas, 35 percent of which is fiber-optic cable. Additionally, more than 2,100 satellite earth stations in Texas move video, voice, and textual information.

The tremendous availability of capacity has resulted in an abundance of choice for long-distance customers, and substantial reductions in the cost of handling long-distance communication. AT&T's interstate rates, on average, have declined 38 percent since 1984.

FUTURE MARKET DEVELOPMENT

Consumers should benefit from increasing competition in the telecommunications industry. Competition, coupled with increasing network capacity, will result in lower interstate long-distance rates—and corresponding lower profit margins for carriers.

On an intrastate basis, however, high access charges will continue to keep the cost of long-distance communication within Texas artificially high. A case in point: a five-minute, daytime, direct-dialed call from Dallas to Houston is priced at $2.23 plus tax—about 29 cents more than a similar call to Honolulu, Hawaii.

There are precedents to show that use of regulation to impose such subsidies can be a strong disincentive in attracting new business to a state. Similar pricing disparities between interstate and intrastate long-distance in California resulted in at least one business incorporating in neighboring Nevada, even though the bulk of the company's business was done via telephone in California.

California lost crucial tax revenue and about 450 jobs.

CONCLUSION

Like the railroad during the last century, telecommunications provides a critical service that American industry needs for growth. Telecommunications is a technology with national and global significance. It creates a competitive advantage for individual businesses. And as more and more foreign countries are discovering, a farsighted national telecommunications policy can create an important competitive advantage for an entire national economy.

As yet, the United States has no national telecommunications policy. Instead, we have the telecommunications regulations of 50 states. Most of the states have no true, comprehensive telecommunications policy themselves. And in many cases, the regulations of one state contradict those of another. Without a strong coherent national policy, the United States stands to lose its leadership in telecommunications at a time when it most needs the economic diversification the industry can offer.

CONTENT QUESTIONS

1. The telecommunications industry performs the same function today as did the _____ industry one hundred years ago.
2. What percentage of the Texas workforce is employed in telecommunications-related industries? What are some of these industries?
3. What is the name of the regional telephone company which was established to serve Texas after the AT&T breakup?
4. What was the purpose of the breakup of AT&T?
5. What is an access charge?
6. What are the results of the technological advances in telecommunications?

DISCUSSION QUESTIONS

1. In what ways has telecommunication affected your life?

2. Explain what happened when AT&T was forced into divestiture.

3. What is social pricing and how has it affected the telecommunications industry?

4

PEOPLE IN THE TEXAS ECONOMY

People are what really matters in economics. An economic system provides people with the security of a job, with opportunity for achievement, and with the goods and services that they desire. People are also the movers and shakers in an economy. They are the ones that make the decisions about what goods and services are going to be produced. Behind every decision made in the marketplace there is a person who made it.

This section of the book looks at some of the roles of people in the Texas economy. The first chapter concerns that rare breed of Texans called "entrepreneurs." These Texans are the change makers in our economy who have developed the new ideas and products which are responsible for the progress and prosperity of our state. Without these individuals who had visions and were willing to take the risks to implement their visions, Texas would have gone nowhere.

The second chapter concerns the Texas labor force. It asks: Where are the jobs? Where will they be in the future? What skills will be necessary for future generations to participate fully in the Texas labor force? It raises issues about unions and union membership in our state.

The last chapter in Part IV concerns people problems in Texas. Not everyone has shared equally in the prosperity of our state. There are significant numbers of people who have been dealt out of the economic system, because they lack either the skills, the motivation, or the ability to fully participate. This chapter looks at the particular problems of education, unemployment, and immigration as they have affected our state's economy. It raises the question of how these people are to be fully included in the state's growth and prosperity.

25
TEXAS TYCOONS: THE ROLE OF THE ENTREPRENEUR IN THE TEXAS ECONOMY

Calvin A. Kent, Ph.D.[1]

When one thinks of Texas, three things come to mind: cattle, oil, and entrepreneurs. This chapter is about those creative geniuses who founded and molded the state. Even today, Texas' entrepreneurs continue to be the prime movers in the state's economy. Blessed with vision, creativity, and dogged perseverance, Texas' economic history has been written by the men and women who dared to have dreams and to follow them.

TEXAS' FIRST ENTREPRENEUR

Texas as we know it was founded by an entrepreneur, Stephen F. Austin. Austin's father, Moses Austin, had suffered a severe setback in the financial panic of 1818 and applied to the Mexican government for the right to bring a group of 300 families into Texas. For his efforts he was to receive an **impresario** grant of land which he hoped would restore his fortune. Moses Austin died in 1821 and his son, Stephen F. Austin, took over. The 27-year-old was well educated, had served in the Missouri legislature and was a judge in the Arkansas territory. His original colony was a tremendous success because of his diligence in following the Spanish law and his honesty in dealing with the Spanish government. He became the most successful empresario (the Spanish term for entrepreneur) in the Texas of his

time, and continued to bring more families to settle in Texas. By 1831 the population of his settlements was almost 6,000. Stephen F. Austin had a vision and acted upon it.

WHAT DO ENTREPRENEURS DO?

The term *entrepreneur* is a French word which literally means "one who begins." While we usually think of entrepreneurs as individuals who start their own businesses, the term embraces much more than that. It refers to anyone who sees what other people have overlooked and acts on the insight. To be an entrepreneur two things are required: vision and courage. Entrepreneurs are niche-finders seeing what others do not see. It may be the new technology yet to be developed or the new product no one yet knows they want because it has not been introduced yet. But seeing is not enough. Entrepreneurs act upon their vision by taking the risk of bringing their products or technology to the marketplace. They not only see opportunity, they seize it.

Introduce New Goods, Services, or Technologies

What is it that entrepreneurs do as they act upon their visions? First, they introduce new goods, services or technologies into the marketplace. Such a person was Bette Graham. Her life illustrates how creativity and personal initiative can

[1]Herman W. Lay Professor of Private Enterprise; Director, Center for Private Enterprise, Baylor University, Waco, Texas.

create a whole new product. She started as a secretary whose hobby was art. As a secretary she faced a problem. When mistakes were made it was difficult to correct them neatly. Not only did the finished product look bad, but office productivity was slowed by multiple erasures and strike-overs. Working in her kitchen, Graham concocted several compounds which could be painted over typing errors, then typed over when dry. Despite having a full-time job and being a single parent she overcame repeated failures and in 1951 developed what is known today as Liquid Paper. The major office machinery companies rejected her invention and failed to see its potential. Rejection did not stop her. She began her own business and marketed the product herself. Her winning personality and tireless effort soon produced results and Liquid Paper became a multimillion dollar firm. In 1975 she opened her corporate headquarters in Dallas and in 1979 she sold her company for $47.5 million.

Ninfa Laurenzo also saw the niche for a new product in the Texas market. In 1948 she and her husband started the Rio Grande Food Products Company, wholesaling pizza dough and tortillas in Houston. When her husband died she tried for four more years to run the business, but it failed. Using a mortgage on her house and all of her savings she opened the original Ninfa's Restaurant in the corner of her abandoned factory. With only her children and family as help she opened with just $16 in the cash register. The restaurant was an overnight success, due particularly to her new product, tacos al carbon (marinated, charbroiled beef wrapped in a soft flour tortilla). In 1976 she opened a second restaurant and the chain spread across Texas, becoming one of the most successful purveyors of Mexican food in a state where appetites for this product seem insatiable.

Discover New Resources or New Uses for Old Ones

A second function that entrepreneurs performed in the Texas economy was to discover new resources or new uses for old ones. January 10, 1901, may be the most important day in Texas history because on that day a gusher called Spindletop, located near Beaumont, blew a column of

oil 200 feet into the air. Spindletop was brought in by an entrepreneur named Anthony Lucas. Lucas was more than a risk-taker. He was also a mechanical genius. He developed the telescoping system of casing for well pipe which made it possible to keep the sand from the Texas salt domes from filling the hole as it was drilled. Lucas not only brought in Spindletop, but he also brought Texas into the industrial age. In 1930, C. M. (Dad) Joiner discovered the oil riches of the East Texas field which covered 200 square miles. In its first year of operation the East Texas field yielded over 100 million barrels. Perhaps no other segment of the Texas economy has produced as many entrepreneurs as has oil. Entrepreneurs like L. F. McCullom, Bill Noel, Joseph Zeppa, and Eddy Scurlock have made the Texas oil industry what it is today.

Today, environmental concerns across Texas are breeding a whole new group of entrepreneurs who recycle garbage, discover ways to dispose of hazardous material, generate electricity by burning the waste products of city dumps, and devise other methods to convert waste products into useful resources. A resource isn't a resource until it is seen to be one. What is required is for some entrepreneur to discover ways to make worthless waste useful and valuable.

Develop New Technologies

The third thing that entrepreneurs have done in Texas is to develop new technologies. Texas became one of the world's leaders in computer technology because of the vision of entrepreneurs. In the 1950s the growth of computers was stymied by a problem. Computers were huge because they used vacuum tubes which were unreliable and emitted enormous amounts of heat. Electronic companies across the nation were in a race to develop a transistor. The transistor, like the vacuum tube it replaced, is a device used to control electric current. The first commercial transistor, developed by Bell Laboratories in 1948, was made of germanium, which broke down under intense heat. Researchers felt that a transistor made out of silicon could operate reliably at either intense heat or intense cold, but no one could design one that worked.

In 1954 Gordon Teal, who was director of Research and Development for Texas Instruments, demonstrated the breakthrough developed by his firm. Teal had two transistors, one of germanium and the other of silicon. He connected these to a record player. When the germanium was dropped into boiling oil the playing stopped. But when the silicon transistor was used, the playing continued. This breakthrough made Texas Instruments the giant of the computer industry. Under the inspired leadership of J. Erik Jonsson, Texas Instruments expanded and grew, generating thousands of high-tech jobs for people in the northern part of the Dallas metroplex.

Open New Markets

The fourth thing that entrepreneurs have done in Texas is to open new markets. One of the most interesting examples is Clint Murchison, Jr. Born in Athens, Murchison made a fortune through his dealings in oil and finance. After the Second World War, Murchison and Sid Richardson (another well-known Texas entrepreneur) formed a business partnership leasing and developing oil fields across the state. But despite Murchison's success in the oil business he may best be remembered for understanding better than anyone else the Texan's love for football. In the late 1950s he decided to bring a pro football team to Dallas, as an existing franchise was leaving for Kansas City. He tried to purchase both the San Francisco Forty-Niners and the Washington Redskins. Both of those deals fell through, but he was not easily turned back. For the sum of $600,000 he bought the rights to form an expansion team, the Dallas Cowboys. Over the years, the Cowboys have become the most successful franchise in pro football history. As "America's team," almost half of all National Football League novelties sold in the United States bear the Dallas Cowboys star. When Murchison sold the team in 1984, the price was $60 million dollars.

Reorganize Existing Businesses

The final thing that entrepreneurs do is to reorganize existing businesses. Two examples will illustrate. The first is Mary Kay Ash. Her life was a constant struggle against adversity through her childhood years. Her first marriage ended in divorce and left her with three small children to support. Wanting to be able to maximize her time with her children, she went into the world of direct sales as a dealer for Stanley Home Products and soon became their top salesman in the nation.

But Ash saw what others had not seen. She realized that women's cosmetics could be merchandised in the same way as home products. Using cosmetics she developed in her own kitchen, she began to apply the direct sales principles she had learned at Stanley to the sale of cosmetics. The result revolutionized the industry. Today, over 200,000 women in pink "think mink," making Mary Kay Cosmetics the giant of the industry.

The same can be said for T. Boone Pickens. The controversial Panhandle oil man recognized that the big money was to be made not in drilling and exploring for new oil, but in reorganizing companies which were performing poorly. In Wall Street terms he is known as a **raider**. He looks for companies whose management is weak and where the managers own only a small percentage of the company stock. Holding only a few shares, these managers are more concerned with their own security than they are with the success of the company. Pickens's philosophy is to take over these poorly managed companies, reorganize them by replacing the stagnant management, and restore the companies' dynamism and competitive edge.

TEXAS ENTREPRENEURS TODAY

Don't think that all entrepreneurs are multi-millionaires. Most entrepreneurs are not. Over half a million new businesses are founded each year in the United States with almost 50,000 of these being formed in Texas. Most of these entrepreneurs are not seeking big bucks, but are desirous of controlling their own financial future. Each of the 50,000 new firms started in Texas each year generates a minimum of five additional jobs for people who otherwise would not find work in the Texas economy. While these entrepreneurs generate profits for themselves, they generate prosperity for all Texans.

In 1986 the price of oil in Texas collapsed, going from over $30 a barrel to less than half that amount. Texas' economy was dependent upon high oil prices and thousands lost their jobs. *Texas Business* called these people the new Texas "desperadoes." Many of them, faced with unemployment for the first time in their lives, turned to entrepreneuring. They started restaurants, construction companies, waste disposal firms, became independent computer programmers and business consultants, thus turning adversity into opportunity.

CHARACTERISTICS OF ENTREPRENEURS

The brief sketches of Texas entrepreneurs contained in this chapter give important insights into the characteristics of entrepreneurs. First, most entrepreneurs do not see setbacks as failures. Almost all entrepreneurs fail, many more than once. They see these failures as learning experiences upon which they can build their future success.

Second, entrepreneurs are persistent. They keep on trying. They understand that success does not come easily. Almost all entrepreneurs have faced situations where they could have given up, but instead continued chasing their dreams.

Third, entrepreneurs are willing to take risks. They are not fools willing to try anything. They do not gamble. But they are not seeking security or safety. They are fully committed to their vision and will risk their money and their position to achieve it.

Fourth, like other entrepreneurs, Texas tycoons are self-confident and self-reliant. They trust in their own judgment. It is this self-confidence that allows them to take risks and to face failure without abandoning their dreams.

Finally, entrepreneurs are creative. In designing new products, services, or technologies they see what others do not. Even more important, they figure out how to solve the problems which the new idea presents. While others say, "Someone ought to," entrepreneurs "do it."

CONCLUSION

Texas owes its life to the entrepreneurs of the past and the present. As long as there is opportunity, there will be entrepreneurs with the vision to see that opportunity and the courage to act upon it. So long as Texas tycoons are given the freedom to operate, Texas will continue to prosper.

CONTENT QUESTIONS

1. What two things are required for entrepreneurship?
2. List the five things entrepreneurs do, and give an example of each.
3. What are the five characteristics of entrepreneurs?

DISCUSSION QUESTIONS

1. How do entrepreneurs differ from other people?
2. What are the benefits of entrepreneurship to Texas?
3. What areas are in need of entrepreneurial activity in Texas today?

26

THE TEXAS LABOR FORCE
Ruth Ellinger[1]

Who does the work in Texas? What kind of work do they do? What will jobs be like when you are looking for work? This chapter will give you some facts about the Texas workforce now, and a look at the direction in which the job market is moving.

WHERE THE JOBS ARE

Everyone who is working now or looking for a job is counted in the workforce. Of seventeen million Texans, about eight million are in the workforce.

A large part of these jobs are in clerical and administrative support. These clerical jobs, of course, are found in every kind of industry and service. Bank tellers, insurance adjusters, bill collectors, court clerks, and teacher aides are some of the jobs in this category, as well as secretaries and general office and warehouse clerks. Even more of these jobs will be available by 1995.

Another large category is the professional and technical sector, which includes doctors, dentists, nurses, lawyers, teachers, computer programmers, architects, accountants, air traffic controllers, engineers, and scientists. Here again the prediction is for growth. By 1995, almost half the jobs will be in these two fields.

The "hard hats" who work in skilled construction, repair, and maintenance make up only about 13% of the workforce now. These are well-paid jobs that may be the goal for some of you. A small increase in these jobs is expected as we come out of the slump in construction.

Some Texas factory jobs have disappeared as manufacturers moved their plants out of the country. Fewer than a million out of the eight million in the Texas workforce are fabricating steel, tires, gasoline, glass, plastic, paper, clothing, and other basic commodities. There will be a drop in the percentage of factory jobs (called "operatives and assemblers") by 1995, but the total number of manufacturing jobs will increase.

Many of you will probably work for a while in retail sales jobs. For those of you who enjoy sales work, there are opportunities in real estate, stocks and bonds, as travel agents, promoters, even "sales engineers."

A large piece of our workforce chart, and the piece growing most rapidly, is the service sector. Your conception of service jobs may be maids and janitors, but actually this big sector also includes all the protective services like fire fighters and police, health aides, personal service like barbers and flight attendants, and food and beverage occupations. This sector is growing because our population is growing, although not as fast as formerly. There will be more children to feed, clothe, and educate. At the other end of the life span, there will be an increasing number of elderly living longer and requiring health care. Both parents will be working in more families; and the convenience industries, like restaurants and microwave dinners, will grow rapidly. In all these examples, the numbers are growing. In Table 26-1, the Texas Employment Commission lists the twenty fastest-growing jobs. These jobs don't necessarily employ the largest numbers of

[1]Education Director, Texas AFL-CIO, Austin, Texas.

112

people, but have the greatest *increase* in the number of workers. See Figure 26-1 for an overview of Texas employment trends to 1995.

JOBS AND SKILLS

Most jobs will require more skill in the future than they do now. For example, a typist will need to become a word processor, a clerk will need computer skills to track inventory, and an auto mechanic will need highly technical training to repair a computerized engine.

Will this mean that these jobs will be better paid than at present? Probably, if the job market is **tight,** meaning a large demand for a small number of workers. And even though we will have a higher birth rate than the nation as a whole, and many mothers will decide to go to work, it appears that well trained young people will be in demand.

A rather high unemployment rate of 6 percent is predicted for the future, but this is because

TABLE 26-1
Growth of Job Opportunities in Texas 1985–1995

Occupational Title	Growth Rate
Paralegal Personnel	63%
Home Health Aides	53%
Registered Nurses	52%
Medical Record Technicians	50%
Social Welfare Service Aides	49%
Medical Assistants	47%
Electrical & Electronic Engineers	46%
Flight Attendants	46%
Computer Programmers & Aides	45%
Respiratory Therapists	45%
Surgical Technicians	45%
Ushers, Lobby Attendants, & Ticket Takers	44%
School Bus Drivers	43%
Electroencepheralograph Technicians	43%
Physical Therapists	43%
Taxi Drivers & Chauffeurs	42%
Teacher Aides & Education Assistants	42%
Nonvocational Education Instructors	41%
Occupational Therapists	41%

Source: Previously unpublished data given to author by Texas Employment Commission.

Texas has so many new immigrants and such a big high-school dropout rate.

LABOR UNIONS

How are wages set, anyway? Do unions make a difference? Let's look at the part unions play in the Texas economy.

Unions have existed in Texas for more than 100 years. Traditionally, some unions felt that their most important function was to limit the labor supply and thereby keep wages stable. Skilled craft unions like carpenters and electricians controlled the number of young entry-level members by apprenticeship training.

The craft unions still have highly respected three- or four-year apprenticeship programs which produce thoroughly trained people with a broad knowledge of their field. This accounts for only a small part of the union membership in Texas today, however.

Most union members in Texas work in factories, transportation, communication, or government. The biggest union in Texas is the one which represents people working for the telephone companies and their suppliers.

The aerospace, automobile, and tire plants are also organized. This means that the people working there have decided to use the collective bargaining process to negotiate a contract with the company, which sets out in detail their wages and working conditions.

Most of the oil refineries and about half of the big chemical, glass, plastic, paper, cement, and food-processing companies in Texas operate with a union contract.

Railroads, airlines, and bus systems have union members in all categories—engineers, pilots, flight attendants, counter clerks, mechanics, and others.

Most civilian U.S. government employees belong to unions. They work on military bases, for the Internal Revenue Service, Social Security, Veterans Administration, and other government agencies. Letter carriers and postal clerks are also represented by unions.

Retail clerks, nurses, police, fire fighters, city bus drivers, and teachers belong to unions—but not all of them. Union membership is voluntary in Texas since Texas is a **right-to-work** state.

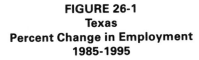

FIGURE 26-1
Texas
Percent Change in Employment
1985-1995

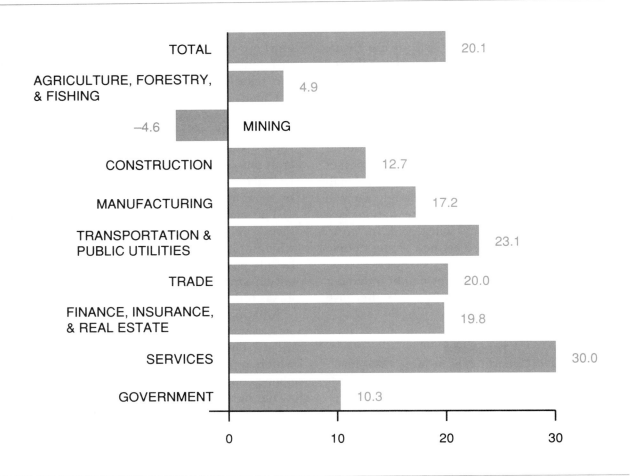

Source: Research Division, Texas AFL-CIO.

This means that even if the majority of workers vote to have a union represent them, those who do not want to join the union cannot be forced to join. But the union represents all workers, both members and nonmembers, and the contract the union negotiates is binding on all the workers. Altogether, there are fewer than a million union members in Texas, but there are far more than a million jobs where the union is bargaining for everyone, even though some do not belong to the union.

The success of the unions in obtaining higher wages, fringe benefits, and better working conditions has led to a higher standard in general. The average manufacturing wage in Texas is about the same as the national average now. There is evi-

dence that union workers are more productive on the whole than non-union members. Therefore, employers of union workers are able to pay good wages and still compete.

Whether or not you will belong to a union depends in large part on what sort of work you choose. If you are self-employed, run a small business, or become a manager in a large firm, a union would not be appropriate for you. If you work at producing basic commodities like steel, or in transportation or communication, or for the government, you will probably be represented by a union.

Your first job will probably not be your lifelong career, but if you are aware of the possibilities, you can direct your job hunting toward work that will train you for advancement in your chosen field.

CONTENT QUESTIONS

1. How many Texans are in the workforce? How many belong to unions?
2. In which sector of the Texas economy are jobs growing most quickly? What are some examples of those types of jobs?
3. Which industries are most highly unionized in Texas?

DISCUSSION QUESTIONS

1. What is the relationship between jobs and skills?
2. What does it mean that Texas is a "right-to-work" state?
3. What job opportunities exist for students in the Texas economy? Will that change in the future?

27

PEOPLE PROBLEMS IN THE TEXAS ECONOMY

B. Joan Dodds, Ph.D.[1]

Texas has a productive economic history. Its natural resources include land suitable for farming and ranching, and large forested areas which are sources of wood and paper products. Its waterways support both fishing and recreational industries, and provide new energy resources for the future. Oil and natural gas deposits contribute billions of dollars to the Texas economy. Manufacturing industries have developed as new raw materials became available and as the demand for products grew. A large segment of the nation's space program further adds to the state's economic wealth.

In order to achieve economic prosperity, Texas has made valuable use of the two other factors of production, **human resources** and **capital**, as it has used its natural resources. A skilled labor force has met the human resource needs of the various industries of the state. Careful decisions have been made regarding the use of capital in developing more effective and efficient methods of production. Throughout its history, the Texas economy has clearly illustrated the necessary and complex interaction of the three factors of production: natural resources, human resources, and capital.

CURRENT ECONOMIC CONDITIONS

Change has contributed to problems in the current Texas economy. Farming and ranching patterns have changed, high technology has caused the costs of farm and ranch production to increase, and fewer individuals are involved in these activities. At the same time as Texans continue to seek oil and gas sources, questions regarding the future availability of such sources result in new conservation measures. The nation's increasing energy needs are met partly by imported supplies. Fishing activity is frequently limited due to the diminished supply or quality of some types of fish. Large migrations of new people to the state have increased the demand for products, and large numbers of products are imported to meet the state's needs. Capital has diminished, natural resources now are more carefully used and conserved, and human resources have grown or become displaced.

Because of the complex interaction of the factors of production, explanation of the causes of current economic conditions is not easy. One cannot simply say that if there were more natural resources or capital the economic problems of the state would be solved. A mere increase or decrease in the labor force will not solve the state's economic problems. Each of the factors must be carefully studied as the state's economic problems are addressed.

[1]Department of Curriculum and Instruction, University of Texas at Austin.

116

HUMAN RESOURCE PROBLEMS IN TEXAS

In this chapter we will look at the characteristics of the labor force, or the **human resources** factor of production. We will try to determine how the nature of this force has contributed to or is itself affected by several of Texas' current economic problems.

Generally it may be said that problems related to the human resources factor of production relate to the *quantity* and to the *quality* of those resources. Quantity refers to the number of people in the labor force. This number may be too large, resulting in high unemployment, or it may be too small, resulting in worker shortages. Ideally, it will be of an appropriate number to reach **full employment**, generally defined as an unemployment level of 4 to 6 percent.

The workers in a labor force must have appropriate skills to meet the economic needs of the state. The labor force may be underqualified, lacking enough skills to meet the economy's human resource needs. The workers may be overqualified, having skills which match a higher level of work and which do not match the needs of the economy. Ideally, workers have skills which fit the economic activity of the state.

These two factors are interactive. The best situation is to have the appropriate number (quantity) of workers with the appropriate skills (quality) to maximize the state's economic productivity. Even if Texas has the appropriate number of workers in the labor force, the situation will not be satisfactory if the labor force does not have skills which match the needs of the state's economy. For example, as Texas moves more and more into a high-technology economy, its skills need to change. If the labor force does not develop the skills necessary for this new economy, it becomes an inadequate human resource.

Let us look at some specific people problems and determine which of these two factors, quantity and quality, are of concern in the problem.

MIGRATION

Several problems relate to the movements of large groups of people *within* the state or *into* the state in the 1970s and 1980s. In the twentieth century, Texas' rural population has diminished from approximately 80 percent to approximately 20 percent of the total population. The current farm crisis, in which farms are becoming larger and more mechanized operations, indicates that this reduction will continue, perhaps even faster, through this decade. This movement within the state has changed a largely rural state population to a largely urban population.

Another problem, related to the movement of groups of people within Texas, is the large **migration** of new inhabitants, mostly Hispanic, into the state. These people have migrated to escape economic, political, or social problems in their own countries. For example, in the 1970s a large population of Vietnamese refugees, primarily seeking political asylum, immigrated to Texas, generally to the Gulf Coast. Currently, large numbers of Mexican citizens continue to arrive, seeking the economic well-being which a healthy Texas economy offers. New Cuban and Salvadoran immigrants seek both political asylum and economic well-being.

Finally, large groups of people from economically depressed regions of the United States have entered Texas' labor force in the past decade. These workers left their home regions or states to seek work which used their skills which were no longer needed in the old labor force. This movement to the Sun Belt was a major economic occurrence in the late 1970s and early 1980s. What do these migrations mean for the Texas economy? At any time that groups of people migrate from one area to another, the demand for products in the new area increases, and the demand in the old area decreases unless other groups move in and replace those who are leaving. Those who migrate should be able to enter the workforce and thereby contribute to production which meets the increased demand. For example, those who have moved from rural to urban areas affect the demand of both areas for products. More products must be produced to meet their needs in the new urban environment, and, simultaneously, the old rural area has a smaller demand and must make supply adjustments. If these new urban inhabitants lack skills which allow them to move into the urban workforce and thereby help to meet the increased demand for products, unemployment in that urban area grows and costs of products increase because of the high demand. Similarly, those who have migrated to Texas' urban areas from other regions of the United States and from other countries increase the demand for products and must possess skills which contribute to the new production demand.

Herein lies the problem. These new groups do not have skills which meet the production needs of regions within the state and of the state as a whole. The quantity of the labor force of the state has increased, and the quality of the labor force has decreased. Unemployment has risen, and the state's productivity has fallen.

DISPLACEMENT

Another general area of concern is the **displacement** of people in the labor force because of market changes. A decreased demand for a product, whether because of product obsolescence or because new markets are available elsewhere, greatly affects the Texas economy. Three options are available to the displaced worker: to seek employment in the production of other products which require the same skills, to develop new skills for other work, or to move to another geographic area where the demand for the worker's skills is high.

Let's look at three examples of such displacement. Many of those people who moved to Texas from the north and eastern regions of the United States in the late 1970s and early 1980s were construction workers. They were brick masons, carpenters, framers, plumbers, and roofers. The demand for their skills had decreased in the north and east because of a slow economy. Texas was experiencing an economic boom, and construction was increasing. When the economy of Texas slowed, construction decreased, and these new workers were again without work. They were displaced.

Another example of displacement is those individuals who were involved in the prosperous energy industry prior to the crisis of the 1970s. Natural resource curtailments and concerns about conservation affected the human resources of the state. Many of the workers—engineers, secretaries, landmen, geologists, and drillers— were forced to leave the energy segment of the labor force, seek work elsewhere, develop new skills, or move to other places when the energy industry declined. Some have moved to the Mid-

dle East and are employed in energy production for foreign governments.

Recently, the banking industry in Texas has undergone severe crises. Many people in banking are now seeking employment in other segments of the Texas economy, are developing new skills, or are considering moves to other regions of the United States where their skills are needed.

Often a displaced worker will take a job which requires lesser skills in order to wait and see if the demand for the old job will increase. These people are then overqualified for the work which they are doing. In these cases, the state has lost potential production; it is not effectively using the skills which these workers possess.

EDUCATION LEVEL

A serious people problem in the current Texas economy relates to the levels of education which its population has attained. The Texas population includes an unsatisfactorily high number of people who have inadequate knowledge and skills to be productive members of society.

Students who drop out of high school comprise a large faction of these unqualified workers. Because they enter the labor force early and without quality skills, the Texas economy suffers.

A large segment of the Texas labor force has been identified as being illiterate. These adults cannot read and write. Some of them are school dropouts; some received a high school education but still cannot read or write. Others are members of the migration populations which were discussed earlier. The absence of literate skills handicaps the individual when entering the labor force. Most jobs require reading and writing, such as writing technical papers, filling out retail sales slips, reading directions, or writing a communication to a co-worker.

Another factor contributes to the inadequacy of education levels in the labor force of this state. As new technologies develop, new skills and skills levels are required. There is a growing concern that the labor force of Texas is not adequately prepared to meet the challenge of the new energy and information industries which are developing in the state. In this instance, we see decisions related to capital investments affecting the human resources factor.

SOLVING THE PEOPLE PROBLEMS

Other people problems exist, and you may choose to examine some of these in the future. Women have entered the labor force in ever increasing numbers, and this movement has raised questions about such topics as family stability and child care. More and more teenagers are entering the labor force before finishing high school, and teenage unemployment is a major problem in the Texas economy.

As the state works to conserve as well as to improve its use of natural resources, it must also work to more effectively manage and develop its human resources. Government agencies, such as the Texas Employment Commission, monitor the movements of people within the economy and the levels of skills which these people possess.

Such information should be used in making economic development decisions. Where should capital be invested to maximize the use of skills which the labor force has? What natural resources can be used in new ways? Where can new markets be developed for products which the Texas labor force can skillfully produce?

Finally, those in the field of education should focus on the needs of the Texas economy. What skills should be taught? Should these skills be attained prior to finishing high school or in technical school settings? Is this education and training the responsibility of the public or of the private sector?

These are just a few of the questions which must be asked as Texans attempt to more effectively and efficiently manage and develop the human resources of the state.

CONTENT QUESTIONS

1. What are the two dimensions of the human resource problem in Texas? What do they mean?
2. List the types of migration which have occurred in the Texas economy.
3. What are examples of displacement of workers in Texas?

DISCUSSION QUESTIONS

1. What has been the impact of immigration into Texas?
2. What steps does Texas need to take to deal with its people problems?

5

GOVERNMENT IN THE TEXAS ECONOMY

Over the last 100 years the most significant event in American economic history has been the growth of government. Texas has not escaped this trend. Gone are the days when state government provided courts and police protection, with minimum commitment to public education and highways. Governments now provide a variety of goods and services which determine the quality of life of the citizens of the nation and of the state. The issue is no longer, "Should we have government participation in the economy?" but rather, "How much should government participate and has the government gone too far?"

The first two chapters look at where the state of Texas gets its money and how it spends it. Every two years when the Texas legislature meets, public attention is focused on the demands the people are placing upon government and the ability of government to meet those demands out of existing revenues. In recent years the composition of Texas taxes has changed. The sales tax has become more important, while taxes on the oil and gas industry have become less important. The economic crisis has made it difficult for the state to provide high quality in a wide

range of services. Court decisions in the area of mental health and prisons have placed additional burdens upon the state which must be met out of tax dollars. Like people in other states, Texans want to have the best in public services, but are reluctant to pay for them.

Perhaps the most controversial issue in Texas is how to pay for elementary and secondary education. The mystery surrounding state aid for education is partially unraveled in the chapter dealing with school aid and the property tax. As continued pressure is placed upon the schools to reduce the dropout rate and upgrade quality, the need for additional money will accelerate rather than diminish.

The Federal Reserve System controls the nation's supply of money and, thereby, the nation's economic health. One of the regional Federal Reserve banks is located in Dallas and is responsible for money matters throughout Texas and other parts of the Southwest. What it does and how it works is the subject of Chapter 30.

The final chapter in this section looks at fiscal federalism. State and federal governments cooperate in providing a variety of programs to the people of Texas. Usually, all or part of the funding comes from the federal level for programs that are administered by the states. Texans send taxes to Washington and in return the federal government spends money in Texas. Much of that federal money is spent for national defense and other federal purposes. But some of it is also spent to support local schools, highways, higher education, and welfare. Do Texans break even? This chapter answers that question.

28

SOURCES OF TEXAS STATE REVENUE

Bob Bullock[1]

Most high school students are well aware of the sales tax—it's that extra amount of money retail stores add to the price of a pair of jeans, tennis shoes, or the latest record album. In addition to the 6 percent state sales tax, local taxing authorities (which include cities, counties, and metropolitan transportation authorities) can add retail sales taxes of up to 2 percent.

Those pennies tacked on to everyday purchases add up to big dollars for state government, making the sales tax Texas' most important source of income. This one tax brings in almost one-third of all state **revenue**.

Texas collects revenue from many other sources as well, including other taxes, federal funding, interest and dividends, licenses and fees, and other miscellaneous receipts (see Figure 28-1).

The relative importance of these revenue sources shifts with the economic winds and the changes in the tax laws. For example, declining oil prices have reduced the importance of oil and gas tax income while recent increases in the sales tax rate have increased the importance of sales tax collections as state revenue.

TAX COLLECTIONS

Tax collections are the mainstay of Texas revenue, bringing in about 60 percent of revenue over

[1]Texas Comptroller of Public Accounts, Austin, Texas.

the past several years. Tax revenue depends on a variety of factors, including the rate of various taxes, what goods and services are taxed, and the health of the Texas economy.

Tax collections provided $12.4 billion in revenue for **fiscal** 1988 (Sept. 1, 1987, to Aug. 31, 1988). The amount of money collected through taxes accounted for 60.6 percent of all state revenue—virtually unchanged from 60.3 percent in fiscal 1982. Tax collections generally have grown from year to year, although they declined in response to the state's weakened economy in 1983 and 1986.

Fiscal 1988 total tax collections grew a healthy 20.4 percent because the 1987 legislature increased tax rates and expanded the number of services covered by taxes. The improved state economy also boosted revenue from several tax sources.

In addition to taxing the sales of a variety of goods and services, Texas taxes motor fuels (gasoline, diesel, and liquified petroleum gas), motor vehicle sales and rentals, corporations (through a franchise tax), oil and natural gas production, insurance companies, cigarettes and tobacco products, alcoholic beverages, and other miscellaneous items.

SALES TAX

State sales tax revenue totaled $6.2 billion in fiscal 1988—a substantial 35.2 percent increase over 1987 collections. This increase was due to a

FIGURE 28-1
State Revenue by Source
Fiscal 1988
Amount and Percentage of Total

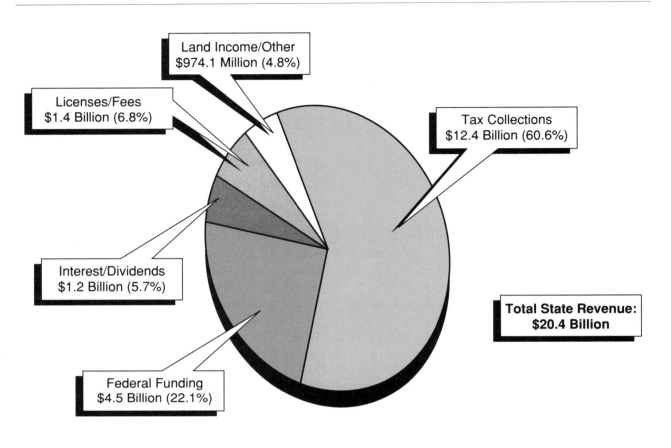

Land Income/Other
$974.1 Million (4.8%)

Licenses/Fees
$1.4 Billion (6.8%)

Tax Collections
$12.4 Billion (60.6%)

Interest/Dividends
$1.2 Billion (5.7%)

Total State Revenue:
$20.4 Billion

Federal Funding
$4.5 Billion (22.1%)

Source: Texas Comptroller of Public Accounts, Economic Analysis Center, November 1988.

higher tax rate and broader tax base as well as an improving Texas economy. The state sales tax rate increased to 6 percent from 5.25 percent in October 1987 and the tax was applied to a variety of previously untaxed services.

Sales tax is collected by retail and other businesses and then remitted to the Comptroller of Public Accounts. The sales tax (as well as other state revenues) are deposited into funds—or accounts—in the State Treasury.

Some items are specifically exempt from the sales tax. Such necessities of life as food, prescription drugs, and residential rent are exempt. Texas' dependence on sales tax revenue has increased dramatically in recent years. Sales taxes

now bring in 50.5 percent of total tax collections compared to 40.0 percent in fiscal 1982.

MOTOR FUELS TAX

Every gallon of gasoline or diesel fuel pumped into a gas tank at the neighborhood service station contributes to state revenue through the motor fuels tax—the second-largest source of tax revenue for the state.

Motor fuels taxes have been an increasingly important source of revenue to the state over the past few years. Motor fuels taxes added $1.5 billion to state revenues in fiscal 1988, making up 11.9 percent of total tax collections. By contrast, motor fuels taxes in fiscal 1982 accounted for 5.7 percent of all tax collections and were the fifth-largest source of tax revenue for the state.

Higher tax rates and more people driving more cars have contributed to the increased importance of motor fuels taxes to state revenue. In fiscal 1988 motor fuels were taxed at 15 cents per gallon. Three-quarters of the money generated by this tax is used for highway construction and maintenance. The other quarter goes to public schools.

MOTOR VEHICLE SALES AND RENTAL TAXES

Texas collects a 6 percent tax on the sale or rental of motor vehicles and on certain interstate motor carriers doing business or living in Texas.

Motor vehicle sales and rental taxes accounted for $947.1 million in revenue during fiscal 1988. This was the third-largest tax source for fiscal year 1988.

This tax also has shown a gradual increase in importance as a revenue source for the state, growing from 6.7 percent of tax collections in fiscal 1982 to 7.7 percent in fiscal 1988. A higher tax rate boosted revenue from this tax 18 percent over fiscal 1987 collections.

The tax rate on motor vehicle sales increased from 5 percent to 6 percent on September 1, 1987. The higher rate applied to motor vehicle rentals and interstate motor carriers on October 1, 1987.

CORPORATE FRANCHISE TAX

Texas levies a franchise tax on corporations for the privilege of doing business in the state. This tax raised $932.6 million in state revenues during fiscal 1988.

Franchise tax collections are tied directly to the health of the state economy. If business falls off and bankruptcies rise, franchise tax collections suffer.

In 1987 the legislature temporarily increased the franchise tax rate and minimum tax. The franchise tax rate increased on January 1, 1988, from $5.25 to $6.70 for each $1,000 of a corporation's "taxable capital" in Texas. Taxable capital is the value of the firm's assets after adjustment. It includes plant, equipment, inventory, and money. The minimum tax rose from $68 to $150 per year. This rate is scheduled to expire in January 1990.

Franchise taxes accounted for 7.5 percent of total tax revenues in fiscal 1988, compared to 5.6 percent in fiscal 1982.

OIL AND NATURAL GAS PRODUCTION TAXES

Texas has relied on the energy industry as a major source of revenue for many years. But when oil prices crashed—dropping from $27 per barrel in late 1985 to about $11 per barrel in July 1986—it became clear that this dependence on oil and gas production taxes was leaving the state overly dependent on one sector of the economy.

Fiscal 1988 revenue continued to underscore this lesson as oil and gas production taxes totaled $1.1 billion, the lowest amount since 1979. This lower revenue reflects the continued effects of lower oil prices in the world market. Production taxes are tied directly to the value of the product—the oil production tax is 4.6 percent of the market value and the natural gas tax is 7.5 percent of the market value.

Revenue from the oil production tax climbed until 1982. Natural gas production taxes continued to rise as a source of revenue until 1986, when lower prices and declining production combined to reduce receipts from this source by 30.6 percent.

In fiscal 1988, the oil production tax accounted for 4 percent of state tax revenue, compared to its peak of 16.7 percent in fiscal 1981. The natural gas production tax contributed 4.5 percent of total taxes collected in fiscal 1988, compared to 11.8 percent at its peak in fiscal 1984.

The energy industry will continue to play a vital role in the state's economy and tax revenue. But the legislature has diversified the state budget's reliance on sources of tax revenue so that a setback in one economic sector won't have the same devastating effect on the state's revenue in the future.

OTHER TAXES

Other major sources of state tax revenue include cigarette and tobacco sales, alcoholic beverage receipts, hotel and motel occupancy charges, and insurance companies. These and other miscellaneous taxes accounted for $1.7 billion in fiscal 1988, or 13.9 percent of total tax revenues.

FEDERAL FUNDS

The federal government represents the second-largest general source of income for the state of Texas.

A total of $4.5 billion in federal dollars flowed through the Texas Treasury in fiscal 1988. Federal funding has ranged from 17 percent of total net state revenue in fiscal 1982 to 22.9 percent of total revenue in fiscal 1987. In fiscal 1988, federal money accounted for 22.1 percent of net state revenue.

A wide variety of state programs benefit from federal funding. Welfare programs traditionally have received the largest chunk of federal revenue. Over the last couple of years, highway projects have claimed the next-largest number of federal dollars. Education received the third-largest portion of federal funding in fiscal 1988, although this program category has been the second-largest recipient of federal funds in past years.

INTEREST AND DIVIDENDS

The state earns interest and dividends on state funds deposited in interest-bearing accounts, corporate securities, U.S. government securities, and corporate stock.

Much of the state's interest and dividend income is earned by the state funds that help support public education and higher education in Texas—the Permanent School Fund and the Permanent University Fund.

Interest and dividend income totaled $1.2 billion in fiscal year 1988, up from $1.1 billion in fiscal 1987. Interest income has varied little as a percentage of total revenue, ranging from a high of 6.2 percent in fiscal 1982 to the current 5.7 percent of total revenue.

LICENSES AND FEES

Revenue from licenses and fees added $1.4 billion to state coffers in fiscal 1988, equal to 6.8 percent of total new revenue. Most license and fee receipts come from motor vehicle registration fees and higher education registration fees. Also included in this revenue source are the license fees paid by medical and legal professionals, inspection fees, and business regulation fees.

Revenue from licenses and fees accounted for 6.8 percent of total net revenue in fiscal 1988, up from 4 percent in fiscal 1982.

LAND INCOME AND OTHER REVENUE SOURCES

Texas earns income on the land it owns in various ways. For instance, some state-owned land is rented, some earns income from oil and gas royalties, and some revenue is earned when the state sells property.

State land income totaled $288.6 million in fiscal 1988, up 2.6 percent from $281.3 million earned in fiscal 1987. This revenue source suffered in fiscal 1987 from the oil price decline of 1986 and has not yet recovered.

Other revenue sources contributed $685.5 million in fiscal year 1988. The main source of other revenue is gains in the value of investments made by the Permanent School Fund and the Permanent University Fund, the state funds that help support education in Texas.

Land income and other revenue sources accounted for 4.8 percent of the total state revenues compared to 7.3 percent in fiscal 1982.

REVENUE GROWTH FROM 1982 TO 1988

Total net revenues increased by $7 billion between 1982 and 1988. This represents a 51.9 percent increase (see Table 28-1). Total tax collections rose by $3.7 billion for a 42.9 percent increase.

Most of the increase in tax revenue can be attributed to sales taxes, which increased by $2.8 billion or 80.4 percent. Between 1982 and 1988

TABLE 28-1
Net Revenue by Source
Fiscal 1988 (FY88) vs. 1982 (FY82)

	FY82 Actual	FY88 Acutal	Amount Difference	Percent Difference
Tax Collections By Major Tax				
Sales Tax	$ 3,461,092	$ 6,242,907	$2,781,815	80.4%
Oil Production Tax	1,316,790	499,916	− 816,874	−62.0
Natural Gas Production Tax	1,057,057	555,647	− 501,410	−47.4
Motor Fuels Taxes (Gasoline, Diesel, LPG)	496,416	1,473,821	977,405	196.9
Motor Vehicle Sales and Rental Taxes	575,337	947,093	371,756	64.6
Franchise Tax	481,219	932,587	451,368	93.8
Cigarette and Tobacco Taxes	346,038	416,999	70,961	20.5
Alcoholic Beverages Taxes	267,680	315,535	47,855	17.9
Insurance Companies Taxes	200,116	546,764	356,648	173.2
Utilities Taxes	188,130	185,336	− 2,794	−1.5
Inheritance Tax	107,849	108,410	561	0.5
Telephone Tax	79,876	22,500	− 57,376	−71.8
Hotel and Motel Tax	42,634	90,101	47,467	111.3
Other Taxes	29,793	27,005	− 2,788	−9.4
Total Tax Collections	$ 8,650,026	$12,364,619	$3,714,593	42.9%
Revenue By Source				
Tax Collections	$ 8,650,026	$12,364,619	$3,714,593	42.9%
Federal Funding	2,433,895	4,515,129	2,081,234	85.5
Interest Income	832,331	1,169,006	336,675	40.4
Licenses and Fees	540,021	1,384,109	844,088	156.3
Land Income: Rents, Royalties, Sales	741,821	288,599	− 453,222	−61.1
Other Revenue Sources	240,384	685,491	445,107	185.2
Total Net Revenue	$13,438,478	$20,406,952	$6,968,474	51.9%

Source: Texas Comptroller of Public Accounts, Economic Analysis Center, November 1988.

the sales tax rate increased 50 percent, from a 4 percent rate to a 6 percent rate. The remainder of sales tax growth was due to economic growth in Texas.

Motor fuels taxes increased by $0.9 billion, or 196.9 percent, between 1982 and 1988. These taxes accounted for 17.7 percent of total state revenues and 27.4 percent of all taxes in 1988.

In 1988, oil and natural gas tax collections together totaled $1.1 billion, down $1.3 billion (55.5 percent) from 1982, These taxes accounted for only 5.2 percent of total state revenues and 8.5 percent of all taxes in 1988.

Federal funding increased by $2.1 billion between 1982 and 1988, an 85.5 percent increase.

Federal funds accounted for 22.1 percent of total revenues in 1988, up from 18.1 percent in 1982.

DEDICATED REVENUES

Much of the revenue deposited in the State Treasury is set aside or **dedicated** for specific purposes. About two-thirds of all state revenues are dedicated by federal law, the Texas Constitution, or state law. Major revenue dedications include:

1. Federal funding of public assistance, highways, and other programs;
2. Public and higher education programs;

3. Construction and maintenance of state highways.

CONTENT QUESTIONS

1. What percentage of state revenue comes from taxes? What is the biggest state tax in terms of revenue raised? What is the current state sales tax rate? How much additional sales tax may local governments add?
2. What is the second-largest tax in the state of Texas? What is the current tax rate? Revenue from the gas tax is divided between which activities of government?
3. Between fiscal 1982 and fiscal 1988 what happened to income from the oil production tax? What happened to the revenue from the natural gas tax?
4. What is the second-largest source of revenue for the state of Texas? How much of the total state revenue does this source supply?
5. List the sources of state revenue other than taxes and federal aid.

DISCUSSION QUESTIONS

1. What factors determine state government income in Texas?
2. What are the advantages and disadvantages of dedicating state revenue?

29

WHERE TEXAS SPENDS STATE DOLLARS

Bob Bullock[1]

It's pretty clear where the state gets most of its revenue; as outlined in the last chapter, taxes are levied on a variety of day-to-day purchases familiar to every Texan. Just where those tax dollars end up may be a little tougher for the average person to see.

Keeping a close watch on spending has always been important, but it has become more critical over the past few years as the shock waves from the oil crisis reduced state revenue from several sources. State spending is determined by many factors including the priorities of taxpayers, legislators, the governor, and special interest groups.

Recently in Texas, federal and state courts also have had a role in determining where state dollars are spent. For example, the state's mental health and mental retardation and prison systems have been operating under federal court orders in recent years. The public school system also recently came under judicial scrutiny.

PAY AS YOU GO

Balancing the needs and priorities of all of these groups is further complicated by the underlying structure of the Texas budget process, which is based on a constitutional prohibition against deficit spending. This **pay as you go** provision of the constitution requires the Texas Comptroller of Public Accounts to certify that the state expects to have enough revenue to cover spending before a state budget can be approved.

[1]Texas Comptroller of Public Accounts, Austin, Texas.

This doesn't mean the state can't end a year with a negative cash balance in the General Revenue Fund—which it did in fiscal 1986 and 1987. It does mean that any revenue shortfall that may have occurred since the legislature last met must be made up before legislators can approve the next budget. Since the legislature is only required to meet every other year, it must pass a two-year budget and the comptroller must project revenues over the two-year period to certify the budget.

WHERE IS THE MONEY SPENT?

While the specifics vary from one budget to another, several areas of state spending traditionally have claimed the most state dollars. Education has been far and away the top priority for spending in Texas. Services such as welfare and mental health also made up a large portion of the state budget. Improvements to the state's roads and parks account for a hefty chunk of the remaining money. See Figure 29-1.

Education

Texas generally commits about half of its spending for a given fiscal year on education. In fiscal 1988, Texas spent $8.3 billion on public schools and universities, that is, 46.6 percent of net expenditures. Overall education funding has grown steadily over the past few years.

The state's Foundation School Program, which is the main source of state funding for public

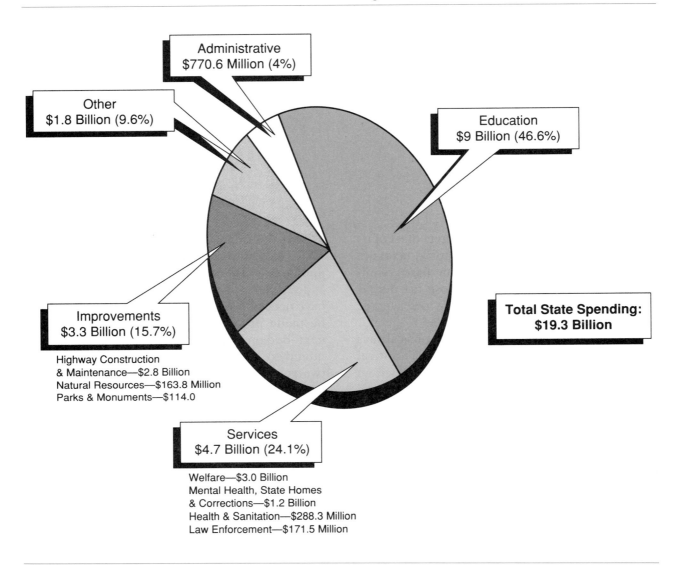

FIGURE 29-1
Expenditures by Function
Fiscal 1988
Amount and Percentage of Total

Administrative
$770.6 Million (4%)

Other
$1.8 Billion (9.6%)

Education
$9 Billion (46.6%)

Total State Spending:
$19.3 Billion

Improvements
$3.3 Billion (15.7%)

Highway Construction
& Maintenance—$2.8 Billion
Natural Resources—$163.8 Million
Parks & Monuments—$114.0

Services
$4.7 Billion (24.1%)

Welfare—$3.0 Billion
Mental Health, State Homes
& Corrections—$1.2 Billion
Health & Sanitation—$288.3 Million
Law Enforcement—$171.5 Million

Source: Texas Comptroller of Public Accounts, Economic Analysis Center, November 1988.

schools, claimed $4.9 million in fiscal 1988. In general, Foundation School Program grants also have increased at a steady pace. One unique element of the Foundation School Program is the Permanent School Fund, a constitutionally protected fund established by Texas' founding fathers and held in trust for Texas school children. Only interest, dividends, and land income earned from investing the $6 billion fund can be spent. Money earned by the fund's investments are distributed to the local school districts along with other state dollars based on a variety of factors, particularly enrollment.

In addition to the regular education program, Texas funds special, vocational, and bilingual education programs. The state also provides money for programs for gifted and talented students, and special funds for remedial training or tutoring. Education dollars also support the schools for the blind and deaf.

Human Services

The second-largest chunk of state money is spent on services for the state's needy, mentally ill, troubled youths, health programs, and law enforcement. State spending on these services accounted for 24.1 percent of all state outlays in fiscal 1988, compared to 23.7 percent in fiscal 1982.

Services spending totaled $4.7 billion in fiscal 1988. Most of this money—$30 billion—goes to welfare programs to help the state's needy. Mental health, state homes, and corrections spending added up to $1.2 billion for the fiscal year. Services provided by the state include health care, care for the elderly and disabled, and child day care. Income assistance is available in the form of food stamps and **Aid to Families with Dependent Children** (AFDC) grants.

Texas provides services for people with mental disorders at eight state mental hospitals. Thirteen state schools house and educate the mentally retarded, and centers statewide provide residential and community services. Services spending also covers preventive health care services for women and children, and protection of public drinking water supplies.

Improvements

Improving and maintaining the state's roads, natural resources, and parks claims the third-largest number of state dollars in fiscal 1988. Texas spent $3.3 billion on improvements for fiscal 1988, up 13.4 percent from fiscal 1987. Improvements accounted for 15.7 percent of state spending in fiscal 1988, up from 12.8 percent in fiscal 1982.

Administration

Running Texas state government claimed $770.6 million in fiscal 1988. This amount includes the cost of operating Texas' executive departments, business regulatory commissions, legislature, and judiciary. Administration accounted for 4 percent of state dollars spent in fiscal 1988.

Other Categories

There are a variety of other programs financed with state dollars, including grants to local governments and contributions to employee retirement systems. Spending on these other programs totaled $1.8 billion in fiscal 1988. These expenditures accounted for 9.6 percent of total net expenditures during the fiscal year. In fiscal 1982, these programs claimed 7.9 percent of state outlays.

Spending by Object

The state also spends money on a variety of items, or objects, that cut across the broad functions of state services. In fiscal 1988, for example, $3.9 billion was spent on salaries for the state's 175,000 employees, including faculty at state universities and colleges.

Consumable supplies and materials and operating expenses, the items needed to run state government on a day-to-day basis, totaled $1 billion for the fiscal year. And capital outlays for land, buildings and other purchases added up to $641.1 million for fiscal 1988.

Flow of Funds to Local Governments

Texas funnels billions of state and federal dollars each year to local governments for a variety of programs and services. In addition to the more than $6 billion in education funding, state and federal dollars also help local governments fund road, airport, and public transit projects and services.

Local law enforcement, traffic safety, civil defense, and disaster relief programs are supported by state and federal funds through public safety grants. Local governments receive help for local programs that serve the poor and elderly, improve parks and recreation areas, and support pollution control programs.

The comptroller also allocates local sales tax and mixed drinks gross receipts tax collections to local governments, and distributes metropolitan transit authority and city and metropolitan transit department taxes for local public transportation programs.

HOW DO THE BILLS GET PAID?

Money spent on state programs and services, or allocated to local governments, doesn't just appear where it's needed, when it's needed. It takes a great deal of effort and coordination to make sure the state pays its bills properly and on time and that all expenses meet legal requirements before they are paid.

Texas uses an intricate structure of more than 450 funds to keep track of state money. These funds are like checking accounts where state agencies can deposit money and pay expenses or make investments. The largest of these funds is the General Revenue Fund, where much of the state's revenue is deposited.

The Texas Comptroller of Public Accounts is the accountant for the state, writing more than seven million checks a year and monitoring state funds. Comptroller employees also work with state agencies to ensure that money has been spent properly and is within the guidelines and limits established by the legislature.

Maintaining state funds is sometimes like a juggling act—often money is transferred from one account to cover a temporary shortfall in another account. The comptroller must monitor all of the state's accounts to ensure that money is paid back when the lending account needs the funds.

SHIFTS IN SPENDING

How the state spends its money depends on a variety of factors, some of which are prescribed by law or by the state constitution. Some factors, such as the age makeup of the state's population and the strength of the economy, vary from year to year. As the school age population increases, more dollars must be spent on public schools. As the population ages, more money will be needed for services for the elderly. If the state economy worsens, more funds are needed for human services.

Within these general factors are numerous constitutional, state, and federal laws that earmark funds for a specific purpose or function. Some of these are referred to as "spending dedications" and include many of the constitutional and statutory provisions which determine how much state money is put into the public schools and into the retirement programs of public school teachers and state employees. Other examples of revenue dedications are the constitutional dedication of motor fuels taxes to highway spending, and the

statutory dedications of the cigarette tax to state and local parks.

The federal government requires that Medicaid money be spent on the poor. Federal programs often have a "matching" provision that requires the state to put up a certain amount of money before federal funds can be spent. For instance, federal law requires the state, like any other employer, to pay the employer's share of Social Security taxes for all state employees.

THE BUDGET PROCESS

Before any state revenue can be spent during a two-year budget period in Texas, a General Appropriation Bill, setting the guidelines for spending on all state programs, must be adopted. The starting point for writing the state budget is the comptroller, who submits to the legislature a formal estimate of revenue available for appropriation prior to each legislative session.

Each agency submits a formal budget request—a Legislative Appropriation Request—with the hope that these requests will be approved by the legislature as it sets the state's spending priorities and that the combined requests will fit within the framework of the comptroller's revenue estimate. These requests must follow state law and can include requests for funding above and beyond an agency's bare necessities. Requests for funding are almost always greater than the amount of revenue available; this is why the governor and the legislature have such an important role in determining the state's spending priorities over two years.

Budget requests are reviewed by both the governor and the Legislative Budget Board (LBB), a ten-member committee which is made up of the lieutenant governor, the Speaker of the House of Representatives, and eight other members of the Texas Senate and House of Representatives. After each budget is reviewed in a public hearing, the governor and the LBB develop separate appropriation recommendations for the legislature.

From these recommendations, the House Appropriations Committee and the Senate Finance Committee each write their own versions of the budget. When the separate House and Senate bills are complete, a joint conference committee of these two committees meets to iron out all the differences between the two budgets and to write one final state budget.

Once an Appropriations Bill is passed by the legislature, the comptroller must certify that the amount of money appropriated falls within the amount of revenue that has been estimated as available for spending. If the legislature decides to spend more money than that certified to be available by the comptroller at the beginning of the session, it must raise revenues.

The certified bill is then finally forwarded to the governor for signature. The governor has a **line-item veto** allowing the deletion of any item in the budget. The budget signed by the governor becomes the blueprint for state spending for the two-year budget period.

CONTENT QUESTIONS

1. Who determines how state revenue is spent?
2. List in order the four major expenditures of state government.
3. The permanent school fund distributes what income to the schools? How large is the fund?
4. The largest expenditure for human services is for what? Mental health, state homes, and corrections account for how much spending?
5. List the local government services that receive support from the state.
6. What is the line-item veto?

DISCUSSION QUESTIONS

1. Explain the "pay-as-you-go" provisions of the Texas budget.
2. Discuss the process for adopting the state budget. How could it be improved?

30
SCHOOL AID AND THE PROPERTY TAX

Janet Beinke[1]

In Texas today the average student's education costs about $3,200 a year, not counting the cost of school buildings. At that rate a student's kindergarten through twelfth grade career totals about $40,000.

That's just the cost of one student's education. Now, look at all the students around you; education adds up to lots of money. If you multiply the average education cost by the number of students in Texas schools, your calculator will show that public education is a $12 *billion* enterprise annually. In size, public education rivals major industries in the state. It has a workforce (teachers, administrators, and others) of over 365,000 and it has 3.2 million clients (students like you).

Yet during your school days you may not think about where the money comes from to pay for public education. Who pays for the teachers, counselors, bus drivers, and crossing guards? And what about funding of buildings and textbooks, or extracurricular activities? Those are the kinds of questions this chapter answers.

The check used to pay the public education bill comes from government (taxpayers). Though school districts do most of the spending, they only raise about 47 percent of public school expenses; the state of Texas pays for about 46 percent; and the federal government gives the other 7 percent.

THE PROPERTY TAX

Most local school revenues come from the **property tax** since it's the only tax that school districts can collect, according to the Texas Constitution. Property taxes are paid by property owners (your parents) on their land and buildings, and, in the case of businesses, on their equipment. (Renters do not pay a property tax directly, but they pay it indirectly since owners pass on their taxes within the rental fee.)

The first step in the property tax process is to determine the **market value** of all taxable property. The market value is what the property would sell for on the open market. Each county has an **appraisal** board that calculates the market value of property. All property is to be treated equally and uniformly, but exceptions are made for some types of property. For instance, farm land is evaluated based on its productivity rather than its market value. And even property that is *appraised* at 100 percent of its value is not all *taxed* at its full value. For purposes of school taxes, homeowners get a $5,000 reduction on the value of the house they occupy, while the exemption for the elderly and disabled totals $15,000. The **assessed value** of a property is the market value minus the exemption. The elderly (your grandparents) have their school tax bill frozen at the amount paid when they turned 65 years of age. Statewide in 1987 residential property accounted for 40 percent of assessed values, land for 12 percent, commercial or business property 41 percent, and oil and gas 7 percent.

[1]Research Analyst, Texas Research League, Austin, Texas.

Each school board uses the assessed value of property in its district (and what it expects to receive from the state) to set its tax rate. The rate is expressed in cents per $100 value. For example, if the tax rate is $1.00 per $100, the tax bill on a $50,000 house would be $500 and the tax on a $100,000 building would be $1,000. Every district sets an operating tax rate that cannot exceed $1.50 per $100 value. The money raised by this tax helps pay for things like salaries, building maintenance, and activities like football and choir. Any districts that have borrowed money to build facilities also adopt a debt-service tax rate. Added together these two rates equal the total tax rate.

Since property taxes are levied by 1,057 individual school districts throughout the state, the amount charged owners for properties of equal value varies depending on a district's total tax rate. In 1987, the owner of a $80,000 homestead would have paid between $74 and $1,084, with the average being $573, depending on which district the property is located in.

Another way to see the variations among districts is to compare the tax base per student, that is, the total assessed value of all taxable property divided by the number of students. The statewide average is about $210,000, but the extremes range from about $22,000 to nearly $6 million. In the district with the lowest values, a $1.00 per $100 valuation tax rate would produce only $220 per student from the average property, while the richest district would receive $60,000 for each student from the identical tax. These are the extremes, but they illustrate how local property values and tax revenues vary. (Remember the concepts of market value per student and the total property tax base, because they figure prominently in the allocation of state resources for education, which is discussed later.)

Cities, counties, and many special districts also assess property taxes to raise revenue, though school districts had the highest tax levy, collecting more than half of all property taxes in 1986. In fact, public school education is the most expensive of all nonfederal government programs. More than 30 percent of Texas state and local government expenditures went for elementary and secondary education in 1987.

Because so many governmental units depend upon property taxes to help pay for their opera-

tions, the total property taxes paid by property owners can be substantial. Taxpayers feeling the pinch have recourse to help check rising property taxes. Individuals can ask to have their property's true value reassessed if they feel the original appraisal was too high. Or, in instances where the amount raised by the property tax is more than 8 percent higher than the year before, voters may petition for a **rollback election**. If an election is held and approved, the tax rate is reduced in the following year to the level that would produce only an 8 percent increase in tax collections.

Think for a moment about the significance of property value variation among Texas school districts. The differences mean that in places with high property values even a low property tax rate results in substantial revenues, but that elsewhere a high property tax rate wouldn't produce much revenue because of low property values. As a consequence, if public education depended solely on local revenues, education expenditures (and perhaps quality) would differ greatly from district to district.

THE STATE'S SHARE

You'll recall, though, that local property taxes pay only 47 percent of the cost of education in Texas and state revenues pay 46 percent. So, taxpayers throughout the state—yes, even you—have a financial stake in your education.

Just as local school revenue comes from taxes, most state funds for education also come from taxes. The state does not levy a property tax, but it does assess a broad range of other taxes. For instance, portions of the state's 6 percent sales tax and 15 cents per gallon motor fuel tax go for public schools. When you buy a hamburger and shake, blue jeans, or gasoline for your car, you pay a state tax that in turn helps pay your teacher's salary.

Additional school monies come from earnings on state investments. Originally Texas funded public education through the Permanent School Fund (PSF). The PSF was given much of the public domain (state-owned lands) in the 1800s, and later Texas' off-shore lands. As the land was sold off or minerals were discovered, the revenues were invested in stocks and bonds. The PSF holdings cannot be spent, but the earnings can be. Textbooks are purchased indirectly by the PSF and remain state property even after they are distributed to school districts.

Distribution of The State's Education Monies:

A general diffusion of knowledge being essential to the preservation of liberties and rights of the people, it shall be the duty of the Legislature of the State to establish and make suitable provision for the support and maintenance of an efficient system of public free schools.

That's the way Article VII, Section 1 of the *Texas Constitution* words the state's basic doctrine on education. It expresses the state's interest in the education that *all* students receive. Since democracy depends on an educated and productive citizenry, the state wants all students to have equal access to a good education.

Formulas for calculating an individual district's share of state funds are quite complex. First, each district receives an equal per student amount from Permanent School Fund earnings, $266 in 1987-88. At one time, this would have been the state's entire annual contribution for a student's education. Today that amount covers only 8 percent of the $3,200 cost.

Next, an amount is adopted as the state's portion of the cost of providing basic classes to ordinary students. Because the actual cost differs among individual districts, the basic allotment is adjusted upward for factors affecting cost, such as the cost of living or a small student population.

Further adjustments seek to even out differences, not among districts, but among students. The basic allotment pertains to ordinary students, but not all pupils are ordinary. Some, such as handicapped, gifted, bilingual, and vocational education students, have special circumstances requiring smaller classes or specialized equipment. (The state itself operates schools for some students with special needs, particularly the blind, the deaf, and troubled youths.) Since the cost of accommodating these special needs is greater than the cost of the basic program, the basic allotment is adjusted for each category of special need. A district's allotment is calculated by multiplying the number of pupils in each category by the adjusted allotments. Other special allotments concern experienced teachers, prekindergarten programs for educationally dis-

advantaged children, and special preschool summer programs.

After the basic allotments for all districts have been calculated, the state takes responsibility for two-thirds of the total. But each district does not get an equal per-student share of the pot. Instead, allocations are based on a district's portion of total property values: the lower the property value per student the greater the amount of state support. In fact, some districts with high property values per student get no state aid for their basic program.

The reason for this unequal distribution of the state's school funds is the unequal ability of districts to pay for education. Each district's portion of the total statewide property values serves as a measure of its ability to raise revenues. In this manner, funding for the basic program is leveled out among school districts.

But after paying their local share of the basic program, some districts have little cash left for anything else, while others have plenty of funds. The state makes additional grants designed to further balance per-student resources. In this case, however, the state share is distributed only to districts with less than 110 percent of the average market value per student. A district's tax effort (that is, tax rate), as well as its market value per student, affects its allotment. Districts with per-student market value above 110 percent of the state average fund the rest of their program totally from local receipts. Districts above the 110 percent level may, however, receive enrichment funds designed to retain experienced teachers.

Even with a state funding formula designed to equalize per-student expenditures, the state's education finance system is being challenged in the courts. Most likely, 1989 will see alterations in the procedures discussed above or at least in the allocation formulas. Another probable change is in the area of facilities where the state may appropriate assistance for needy districts.

CONCLUSION

Local property tax revenues pay for half of public education expenditures statewide. But if a district's education expenditures depended solely on its own resources, or if the state handed out its education dollars on a strictly per-pupil basis, students in tax-rich districts would have an educational advantage over students in tax-poor districts. Thus, to help even out the differences in school districts' economic circumstances, the state's funds are not allocated equally per student.

Because of the way school finance is organized in Texas, people in your neighborhood, throughout your school district, and around the state are making financial contributions to see that you and your classmates have access to a good education. Taxpayers (including you) are willing to pay $40,000 for your education. You can skip classes, write graffiti on rest rooms walls, and throw spitwads in study hall, or you can try to get the most for your money. The opportunity only comes once.

CONTENT QUESTIONS

1. The annual cost of educating a student in Texas is _____, which means that the cost of putting a student through kindergarten to high school graduation is _____.

2. What percentage of the costs of education comes from local sources? From state sources? From federal government?

3. The local share of the costs of education is raised from a tax on _____. This tax is levied on the _____, which is market value less _____. When a property owner turns 65 this tax is _____.

4. The two principal sources for the state's share of education expenses are _____ and _____.

5. Why doesn't every school district receive the same amount of state aid?

6. How is the property tax for local schools calculated?

DISCUSSION QUESTIONS

1. Why are some school districts better able to support local schools than others?

2. Why does the state not make the same per-pupil grant to each school district?

3. Should education expenditures per pupil be equalized in Texas? If so, where should the money come from?

31

THE FEDERAL RESERVE BANK OF DALLAS

Sue Lynn Sasser, Ph.D.[1]

The **Federal Reserve Bank of Dallas** is one of twelve Federal Reserve Banks and twenty-five branches located throughout the United States (see Figure 31-1). As part of the Federal Reserve System, the Dallas Fed provides a wide variety of services to the federal government, financial institutions, and consumers. The Dallas Bank is headquarters for the Eleventh District of the Federal Reserve System, which covers the entire state of Texas, northern Louisiana, and southern New Mexico (see Figure 31-2). The Dallas Fed has branch offices in El Paso, Houston, and San Antonio.

THE FEDERAL RESERVE SYSTEM

Created by an Act of Congress in 1913, the **Federal Reserve System** serves as the nation's central bank. Daily operations at the Fed include holding reserves for depository financial institutions, making loans to financial institutions, providing fiscal services for the U.S. government, assisting in the transfer and collection of checks and electronic funds, supervising and regulating financial institutions, issuing consumer credit regulations, and managing the supply of money and credit in the economy.

All nationally-chartered banks and bank-holding companies are required to be members of the Federal Reserve System, while state-chartered banks can join at their own discretion. At the end of each year, member banks receive a 6 percent dividend on their investment in the Fed.

The Dallas Fed has approximately 1,000 member banks in its district. This figure represents about 40 percent of the banks in the three-state area and is similar to the national average of member banks. The number of member banks in the Eleventh District has decreased in recent years due to branching legislation in Texas and Louisiana, in-state mergers, and out-of-state acquisitions.

The system operates under the general supervision of the Board of Governors in Washington, D.C. The board consists of seven members appointed by the President of the United States and confirmed by the Senate. The fourteen-year terms are staggered, with one expiring every two years, to reduce the possibility of one President appointing a majority of the board members. To further insulate members from political pressures and private interests, individuals are limited to one full term on the board.

In addition to the board and the network of Reserve Banks, several committees meet regularly with board members to advise them on banking, consumer credit, and other economic issues. Committees, such as the Consumer Advisory Council, the Federal Advisory Council, and the Thrift Advisory Council, help the board deal with its varied responsibilities.

The **Federal Open Market Committee** (FOMC) is the most important committee in the

[1]Educational Specialist, Federal Reserve Bank of Dallas.

FIGURE 31-1
The Federal Reserve System

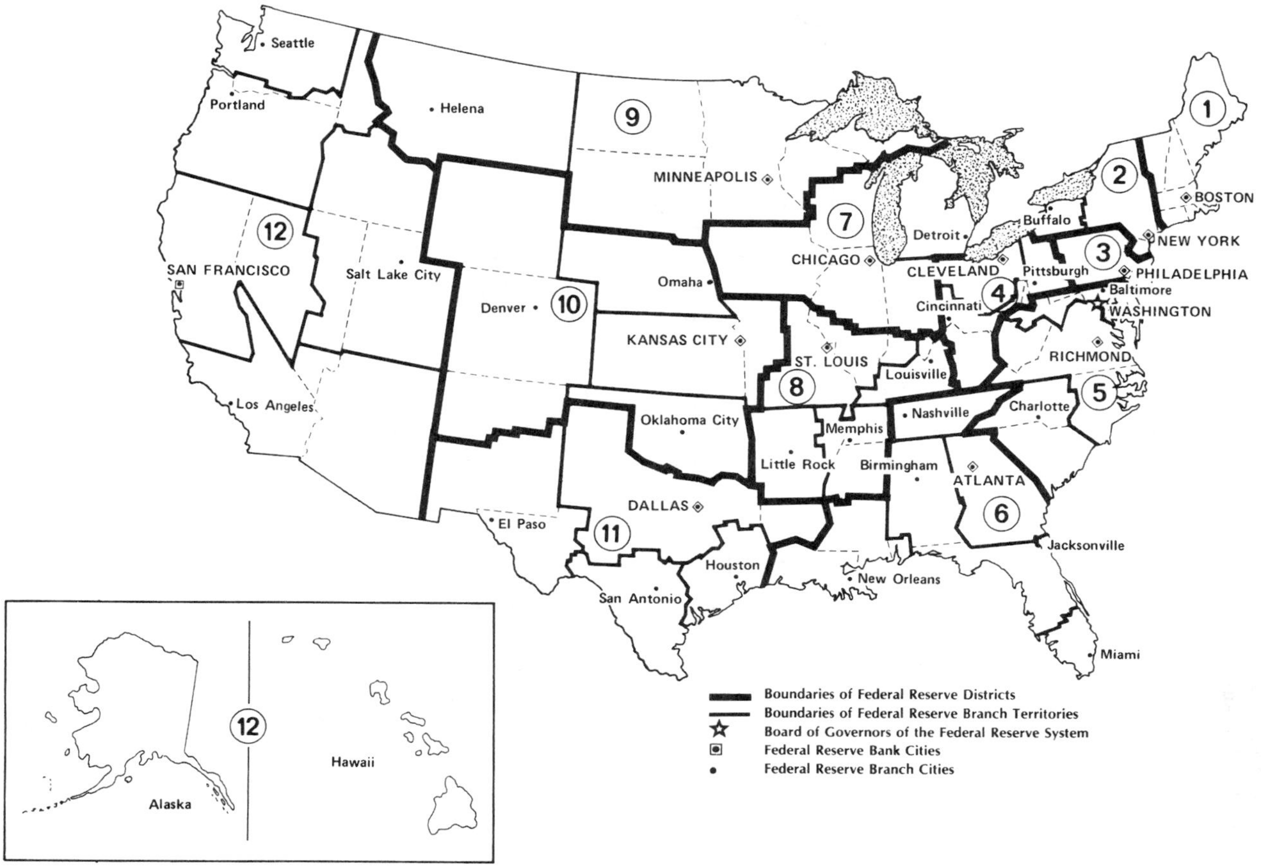

Source: Federal Reserve Bank of Dallas.

Fed structure because its actions mold the nation's monetary policy. The FOMC is composed of the seven members of the board and five Fed presidents who serve one-year terms on a rotating basis. The president of the Dallas Fed rotates on the committee with his counterparts in Atlanta and St. Louis.

Although created by congressional action, the Federal Reserve System is a self-supporting public institution. Since it receives no federal appropriations, Fed income is derived from three primary sources: interest on loans to financial institutions, fees for services provided to financial institutions, and interest on Treasury securities.

The Fed is a **not-for-profit organization** because its purpose is to serve the needs of the public, financial institutions, and the government. Therefore, after the Fed pays its operating expenses each year, the remaining earnings are transferred to the United States Treasury. The Fed usually returns more than 90 percent of its income to the federal government.

THE FED'S RESPONSIBILITIES

Perhaps the Fed's most important function is establishing the nation's **monetary policy** by managing the amount and availability of money and credit in the U.S. economy. Through its

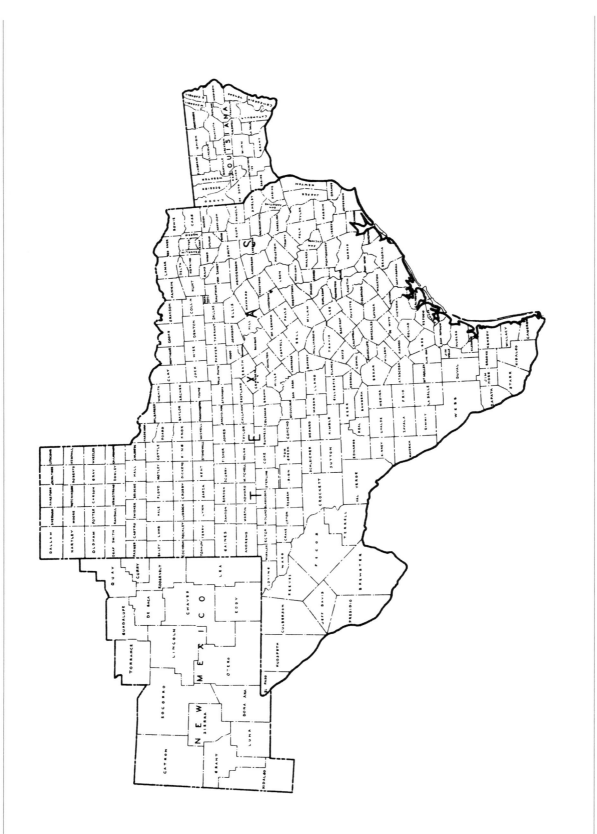

FIGURE 31-2
Eleventh Federal Reserve District

Source: Federal Reserve Bank of Dallas.

monetary policy actions, the Fed influences the price of goods and services, such as automobiles, stereos, and medical expenses. The Fed uses three instruments to implement its monetary policy: open market operations, the reserve requirement, and the discount rate.

Open market operations are the most powerful and most flexible tool of monetary policy. The FOMC directs the buying (or selling) of government securities at the New York Fed to increase (or decrease) the money supply. In addition, the Fed can raise or lower the percentage of funds that financial institutions must hold as reserves by adjusting the **reserve requirement**. It can also increase or decrease the **discount rate**, which is the interest charged to financial institutions that borrow money from the Fed.

Another important role of the Fed is maintaining a safe and sound financial system. The Fed's goal is to promote confidence in the nation's financial industry by implementing regulations for banks and bank-holding companies, reviewing and approving applications for banks to merge or acquire other holdings, examining state member banks, and reviewing those banks for compliance with laws and regulations.

Fed Banks are also depositories for currency and coin and **clearinghouses** for checks and **electronic fund transfers**. As part of this responsibility, the Fed distributes currency and coin to financial institutions, clears millions of checks and check-like items each day, and electronically transfers billions of dollars in funds and securities daily. Districtwide, the Dallas Fed processes about five million checks, conducts approximately 300,000 electronic transfers, and processes more than three million pieces of currency each day.

In addition, the Fed ensures the quality and integrity of the nation's currency by destroying unfit bills and identifying counterfeits. The Dallas Fed receives about two dozen counterfeit bills each week, which are turned over to the U.S. Secret Service for investigation. Furthermore, more than $160 million is shredded each day within the system.

The Fed also provides financial services for the federal government. It is "Uncle Sam's Bank," and the federal government utilizes District Banks much as businesses use financial institutions. The Fed holds deposits and issues checks for the Treasury Department as well as issuing, servicing, and redeeming **government securities**. Government securities are bonds issued by the government when it needs to borrow. In addition, Fed Banks process U.S. postal money orders and USDA Food Stamps. The Dallas Fed works closely with the Internal Revenue Service (IRS) Center in Austin to ensure prompt payment and refund of income tax payments.

In recent years, Congress has authorized the Fed to initiate several regulations to protect consumers' rights in credit and other financial transactions. The Fed, therefore, is responsible for writing and implementing regulations such as the Truth in Lending Act, the Fair Credit Reporting Act, the Fair Credit Billing Act, the Equal Credit Opportunity Act, and others.

THE ELEVENTH DISTRICT

Serving the Eleventh District of of the Federal Reserve System, the Dallas Fed employs about 1500 employees in its four offices. The District encompasses more than 350,000 square miles, making it one of the four largest in the system.

The Dallas Fed has a nine-member Board of Directors which oversees operations under the general guidance of the Board of Governors in Washington. The nine directors are divided into three categories, representing different segments of the banking, public, and business interest. The directors work closely with the Bank president to provide input regarding management of the local Bank and monetary policy decisions. Directors also vote on the Bank's discount rate, which is then approved by the Board of Governors.

Because of the Dallas Fed's commitment to the citizens of the Eleventh District, the Bank's Research Department focuses much of its attention on issues affecting the Southwest economy. Results from this research allow Bank staff members to actively participate in the formulation of public and private policies in order to promote the strength and stability of the Southwest economy.

Dallas was chosen as a Fed location in 1913, despite competition from Houston, Fort Worth, Oklahoma City, San Antonio, and El Paso. At that time, Dallas was rapidly expanding by developing new transportation facilities, commercial and cultural centers, and residential centers. The selection of Dallas for the Federal Reserve Bank reflected the city's cultural and economic growth and set its course as a leader in finance, trade, and commerce.

THE BRANCH OFFICES

The Dallas Fed's three branches in El Paso, Houston, and San Antonio play an equally important link in serving the Eleventh District. The branches are primarily regional centers for processing checks and distributing currency and coin in their territories.

El Paso, the smallest of the branches, has 100 employees. It serves southern New Mexico and far west Texas. Located about six blocks from the Rio Grande River and its sister city of Juarez, Mexico, the El Paso Branch is an important link with Mexico.

Houston, on the other hand, is the largest of the three Branches, with 200 employees. It serves financial institutions in southeast Texas and along the Gulf Coast. Houston serves as the official backup for the head office in case of any disasters or disruption of service from the Dallas office.

The San Antonio Branch is responsible for processing all government checks in the district and for handling tax payments sent to the IRS office in Austin. This branch, which has 150 employees, covers central Texas and the Rio Grande Valley.

Financial institutions in the remainder of the district—northern Louisiana, northern Texas, and the Panhandle—are serviced by the Dallas office.

COMMITMENT TO SERVICE

In its *Agenda for the 90's,* the Dallas Fed is committed to continually improve its service to financial institutions, business and industry, and the citizens of the Eleventh District. The Bank's mission for this decade is to provide leadership in solving the economic and financial problems of the business, government, and financial sectors of the Southwest.

Additionally, special emphasis has been placed on meeting the needs of financial institutions in the district and providing them with quality financial services. This commitment to the people of the Eleventh District must be achieved in a rapidly changing economic, legislative, regulatory, and technological environment.

CONTENT QUESTIONS

1. What territory does the Eleventh District of the Federal Reserve System include?
2. Which cities in Texas have branch offices of the Federal Reserve Bank of Dallas?
3. What are the functions of a Federal Reserve Bank?

DISCUSSION QUESTIONS

1. How do the services of the Fed differ from those of a commercial bank?
2. How has recent legislation permitting branch banking affected the Dallas Fed?
3. Discuss the importance of the Dallas Fed's Board of Directors.

32

FISCAL FEDERALISM IN TEXAS

Howard R. Yeargan[1]

In this country we satisfy most of our unlimited wants with voluntary exchanges between buyers and sellers—market transactions. However, there are some goods and services which cannot be transacted in this way. These are called **pure-public goods**. National defense is a good example of a pure-public good.

DEFENSE EXPENDITURES

It is silly to even consider that we might have national defense stores on every Main Street or in every shopping mall, where we could buy $500 worth of national defense, as we could buy a color television set. Defense just cannot be produced, packaged, and sold like private goods and services can. That means that the market system alone cannot provide for defense, or any other pure-public good or service. In fact, it doesn't make sense for even a city or state to try to provide its own defense in today's world. This must be done by the national government. We cannot each have a Polaris submarine cruising the world's oceans, or an air base in Turkey, or even a hand grenade. Only the political system, or government, can secure a satisfactory provision of these things. The federal government has always been the major provider of national defense.

Texans have benefited from the federal production of national defense in several ways. We have received protection, like all other U.S. citizens and our foreign allies. In addition to that, we

have received income from defense production. This comes in several forms. Some Texans are employed directly by the military services and thus receive their pay from them. In addition to that, the federal government purchases defense products and services from Texas companies.

Obviously, the Department of Defense (DOD) does not go to a company such as General Dynamics in Fort Worth and threaten to seize their plant if they don't produce military aircraft. The market system comes into play here. The DOD awards a contract to the company and buys airplanes from them. The manufacturer, in turn, hires people and other resources to do the physical work to build the airplanes, or other items. Many people earn income from this process. This is an example of what is called the **multiplier effect**.

Federal defense spending takes place over a large part of Texas. For example, San Antonio depends greatly upon five air bases and one army post in its metropolitan area. Corpus Christi has long had naval bases in its region. For many years military bases and defense manufacturers have been important sources of employment and income in the Dallas-Fort Worth metroplex. Many other cities such as Abilene, Big Spring, El Paso, Killeen, and Texarkana also depend upon military expenditures for a significant portion of their income and employment.

Consider how much is spent in Texas each year. In fiscal year 1986 the federal government spent a whopping $16.9 billion on defense in Texas. Of that amount $4.3 billion was paid to the military personnel stationed in Texas and to the

[1]Associate Professor of Economics; Director, Center for Economic Education, Southwest Texas State University, San Marcos, Texas.

civilian workers at military bases in Texas. In addition to that, Texas civilian contractors who sell things to the military also got contracts worth $10.8 billion. An additional $1.8 billion was spent by the Department of Defense in Texas during fiscal 1986. These figures do not count all of the income generated when people, like grocers, auto dealers, and filling station owners, sell their goods and services to people receiving federal money. If these expenditures are taken into consideration, the multiplied impact of federal defense expenditures in Texas would be more than $32 billion.

NONDEFENSE EXPENDITURES

Other federal agencies also spend a great deal of money in Texas, as they each produce their goods and services. In 1986 Federal Grant Awards in Texas totaled $5.8 billion. Nondefense salaries in Texas came to $3.2 billion. Retirement, disability, and other direct payments to individuals in Texas were $20.5 billion in 1986. Nondefense procurement contracts for Texas companies amounted to $1.9 billion. Other federal expenditures and obligations came to $1.1 billion.

Among the various nondefense activities which the federal government supports are direct payments to Texans such as social security, farm subsidies, welfare, and student loans. Federal dollars also support the activities of various federal agencies including agriculture, commerce, housing, transportation, and human services. Federal grants go to support research in science and medicine. Some of the more visible federally aided functions in the state include highways, immigration, and space. Control of illegal drugs and crime prevention have grown in importance, and the federal dollars have grown also. Cities receive federal dollars for streets, sewers, water, and urban development. Almost all aspects of the Texas economy are impacted by federal spending.

All of these direct expenditures add up to $47.343 billion. (If direct loans and loan guarantees are included, the total federal expenditures in Texas for fiscal 1986 would come to $72.8 billion.) Considering direct expenditures in 1986, Texas ranked third behind California ($100.9 billion) and New York ($59.4 billion). See Table 32-1. However, on a per person basis many states received much higher federal expenditures than Texas. In 1986 Texas received $2,838 per person, which ranked us fortieth.

FEDERAL TAX PAYMENTS

It is not a one-way street, of course. Federal expenditures come largely from taxes paid by U.S. citizens. Texans, as U.S. citizens, pay taxes to the federal government; "lots of taxes." Texas ranked third among all the states in the total amount of federal tax paid in 1986 (see Table 32-2). All federal taxes amounted to $53.6 billion. Of this amount, income and employment taxes came to a total of $48.9 billion. The total tax for 1986 was very close to the amount paid in 1985. Income and employment taxes for 1985

TABLE 32-1
Federal Expenditures by State
Fiscal 1986

Selected States	Total (billion $)	Per Person Amount ($)	Ranking
Total U.S.	830.3	3,392	
California	100.9	3,738	12
New York	59.4	3,345	20
Texas	47.3	2,838	40
Louisiana	12.4	2,749	43
Oklahoma	9.8	2,950	34
Arkansas	7.2	3,026	30
Alaska	2.7	5,091	1

Source: Author's calculations based on Tax Foundation, *Facts & Figures on Government Finance*, 1988–89 ed. (Baltimore: Johns Hopkins University Press) p. 102.

TABLE 32-2
Federal Tax Collections by State
Fiscal 1986

Selected States	Total (billion $)	Per Person Amount ($)	Per Person Ranking
Total U.S.	782.3	3,245	
California	89.6	3,321	1
New York	87.4	4,920	2
Texas	53.6	3,212	3
Louisiana	8.1	1,793	25
Oklahoma	10.0	3,041	24
Arkansas	3.3	1,385	34
Alaska	1.6	2,952	46

Source: Author's calculations based on Tax Foundation, *Facts & Figures on Government Finance*, 1988–89 ed. (Baltimore: Johns Hopkins University Press) p. 122–123.

totaled $44.1 billion, considerably less than in 1986. Added to these, corporate income taxes of $4.8 billion, excise (sales) taxes of $4.2 billion, estate taxes of $0.5 billion, and gift taxes of $35 million brought the total to $53.6 billion for the year 1985. This amounts to $3,270 per person in 1985, compared to $3,212 per person in 1986.

Clearly, the financial street between Texas and Washington, D.C., runs two ways. In 1986 Texans paid an excess of $6 billion more to the federal government than they received from it. That was $374 per person. In other years Texans received more income from the federal government than they paid in federal taxes. In 1986 the fiscal street simply had more financial "lanes" going to Washington than coming from it.

CONTENT QUESTIONS

1. What were the major categories of federal expenditures in Texas in fiscal 1986? How do these compare with total federal expenditures throughout the whole country?

2. What were the major categories of federal taxes paid by Texans in fiscal 1986?

3. Did Texans pay out more or less in federal taxes than they received in federal expenditures in 1986?

DISCUSSION QUESTIONS

1. What are "pure-public goods"? Give some examples. Why must the government provide these types of goods?

2. Why are tax payments not voluntary like private expenditures?

3. How would you justify the taxation of income?

6

ISSUES IN THE TEXAS ECONOMY

The Texas economy is not without its controversies. Throughout the next few decades, four major issues will influence the direction of our state. The first of these is the quality of education our students receive. Education is important because it allows a person to fully participate in the technologically advanced economy which will be the Texas of the future. Is the system of education in Texas up to the task?

Many of the chapters in this book suggest that Texas has been too dependent upon oil and gas for its prosperity. Economic diversification is seen as essential for the growth of the Texas economy. Development of new industries is the key to the future of Texas. How is this to be achieved?

Crucial to any state's economy is water. Without water most industrial and many recreational activities would be impossible. Without an adequate supply of good water the health of the people can be endangered. Texas is a hot, dry state that has taken water for granted. The result is a looming crisis that the state will have to meet.

The Texas economy is no longer isolated from the rest of the world. International trade is extremely important to Texas. Texas agricultural and manufactured products are sold throughout the world. The port of Houston is one of the world's most significant. Almost one out of every four Texans is dependent in some way or another upon international trade for his or her livelihood. As the world becomes smaller how will Texans respond?

Another problem facing the Texas economy is the continued availability of low-cost, yet reliable, electric power. Electric utilities are concerned that in the future they may not be able to meet the demands placed upon them. In their view, unwise policies are responsible for their present dilemma.

EDUCATION
W.N. Kirby, Ph.D.[1]

Texas has one of the largest systems of free public education in the nation, encompassing 1,090 independent school districts charged with educating some 3.2 million school children. More than $12 billion in state, federal, and local funds are spent on the public schools in Texas each year, making public education one of the biggest businesses in the state. But it is not the size of the public education system, or even the amount of money spent on it, that makes it the most important venture in Texas. Its importance lies in the impact education will have on the future of our state.

THE NEED FOR QUALITY EDUCATION

With ever-decreasing oil prices and the decline of the state's longtime agricultural economic base, the Texas economy must diversify. The need for a well-educated workforce becomes more critical as technological advances open doors to a future job market which depends upon a labor force that can think, create, and continue to learn. To meet the challenge of preparing a Texas workforce to meet the demands of the future, one must examine the changing complexities of the economy and the needs of the workforce. What changes must be made in the present to prepare for the demands of the future?

[1]Commissioner of Education, Texas Education Agency, Austin, Texas.

Several factors underscore the need for a world-class public education system in Texas, among them the fact that the composition of our workforce is changing. Forty years ago, clerical and professional workers comprised only 19 percent of all employed people in the United States. Today, these groups make up 35 percent of the American workforce. At the same time, the percentage of unskilled workers as part of the labor force has declined from 12 percent to 6 percent. Ten years ago in Texas, 25 percent of the workforce was involved in the oil and gas industries; today, that figure stands at less than 10 percent. The State Comptroller's office estimates that over the next decade and beyond, an estimated 75 percent of new Texas jobs will be in labor-intensive service industries. Even the lowest-level jobs in these areas, like clerk, salesperson, and cashier, will require reading, writing, and mathematics skills.

Changing demographics also will have an impact. The United States is expected to face a shortage of available workers as the twenty-first century approaches. By the turn of the century, the number of 16- to 24-year-olds entering the labor force will decline by more than 2 million while the number of available jobs will grow by 10 million. The Labor Department has already suggested that a massive importation of foreign labor may be necessary to fill the gap between the jobs that exist and the number of workers that will be available to fill them.

Another factor is that oil and agriculture, historically Texas' biggest economic industries, face stiff competition worldwide. Nations belonging to the Organization of Petroleum Exporting Countries (OPEC) account for 68 percent of the world's known oil reserves. This enables OPEC to virtually dictate events in the world oil market by either increasing or decreasing production.

The United States agricultural market also is declining, while the agricultural productivity of other countries is increasing. In the last seven years, American farm exports have decreased by approximately one-third, from $44 billion in 1981 to $28 billion in 1987. During that same time, America lost 625,000 family farms.

Increased agricultural competition from countries such as China and the Soviet Union means that Texas' ability to compete in the world agricultural market hinges on its ability to diversify. A report issued by Agriculture Commissioner Jim Hightower notes that the future for Texas farmers lies in a shift from grains and commodity items to fruits, vegetables, and specialty crops. Hightower's report estimates that these alternate crops, such as blueberries, nursery stock, pinto beans, crawfish, catfish, Christmas trees, wine grapes, and specialty vegetables, could contribute as much as $6.2 billion to the state's economy and create 75,000 new jobs.

Texas also needs to expand its food and fiber processing industries. The state is the nation's second largest producer of raw agricultural commodities, but processes only 6 percent of the nation's food. If that percentage were to increase by only 1 percentage point, the state could realize $3 billion in revenues and 90,000 new jobs.

EDUCATING FOR SUCCESS

Successful diversification depends upon education in agriculture as well as in other businesses and industries. Skills in marketing, planning, and creative problem-solving are essential for successful businesses and a successful economy. But research shows that the workforce is sorely lacking in the skills that are critical to success. Statistics show that 65 percent of new small businesses fail within their first year of operation. The Small Business Administration says that most of these failures are the result of the owners' lack of management skills. While most of these

owners have gained considerable technical skills and knowledge by working for someone else for many years, these technical skills are not enough to meet the daily demands of a business. These business owners need skills in buying and selling, pricing, marketing, public relations and advertising, creative problem-solving, research, and decision-making. They need planning skills to use when trying to attract partners, suppliers, and lenders. While experience can teach many valuable lessons, the foundation for these types of skills comes only through a solid, high-quality education.

TRENDS IN EDUCATION

Present indicators show that the state is making progress in its efforts to prepare today's school children to play key roles as future leaders. The most recent administration of the Texas Educational Assessment of Minimum Skills (TEAMS) tests showed marked improvement in the scores of students taking the reading, writing, and mathematics exams. Nearly 1 million students in grades 3, 5, 7 and 9 took the state-mandated basic skills tests during February 1988. Results showed that nearly three-fourths of the students in the third, fifth and seventh grades mastered the reading, writing, and math portions of the TEAMS test, compared to slightly more than half in 1986. An analysis of average TEAMS scores for school districts and campuses showed gains from 1986–87 to 1987–88 in more than 80 percent of Texas districts and nearly 70 percent of individual campuses.

The scores of Texas students on the Scholastic Aptitude Test (SAT), a major college entrance examination, also increased slightly from 1987 to 1988, while average national scores declined slightly. Some 80,107 high school graduates—or 44 percent of total graduates—took the SAT in 1988, an increase of 4,743 students over the previous year. Minority students accounted for approximately 50 percent of the increase. Texas students' mean score on the verbal section of the SAT was 417 this year, up from 416 in 1987, while the mean SAT math score rose three points from 459 in 1987 to 462 in 1988. The scores of minority students on the SAT are particularly encouraging. The verbal scores of Black students on the SAT increased 5 points from 341 to 346, while their math scores rose 12 points from 369 to 381, for an overall increase of 17 points. Mexican-American students' verbal scores increased from 371 to 372, and their math scores rose from 416 to 422, for an overall increase of 7 points. Since 1984, the first year that the education reforms were enacted, Texas' SAT scores have increased by 13 points, while the national average SAT score has increased by only 7 points during the same period. However, Texas students continue to perform below the national average on the SAT.

EDUCATION REFORM IN TEXAS

The education reform effort in Texas, which began in 1981 with the enactment of legislation establishing a standard statewide curriculum and a teacher testing program, culminated in 1984 with the passage of House Bill 72. This legislation brought major changes to the state's public education system, requiring a greater emphasis on academics for students and accountability for educators. Positive steps aimed at improving the academic achievement of Texas students included:

1. Reducing class sizes in kindergarten through fourth grade.
2. Establishing a prekindergarten program and language-intensive summer program for disadvantaged and limited English proficient students.
3. Requiring students to pass an exit-level exam in English language arts and mathematics before they receive a diploma.
4. Limiting participation in extracurricular activities to students who can pass all their courses.
5. Mandating annual classroom performance evaluations of all teachers.
6. Restructuring the state's school finance system to provide more funds to property-poor school districts.

Stronger high school graduation requirements were established for Texas students in the early 1980s. An advanced high school program was established with the college-bound student in mind. Foreign language study, courses in computer science, and other more stringent requirements are in place in the advanced program, with the regular program also being strengthened to require 21 units of credit for graduation.

In addition to improvements in the general instructional program in Texas public schools, the reform effort has resulted in significant changes to specific areas, including vocational education. The State Board of Education adopted the Master Plan for Vocational Education in Texas in 1986. The plan stresses a coordinated approach to vocational and academic education and is designed to redirect vocational education to provide students with strong academic foundations and broad occupational skills. Under this plan, sound academic foundations for all students in all grade levels are stressed, while career training is maintained as an integral part of the total educational process. Vocational education programs also are adaptable to the special needs of educationally disadvantaged students or for those who cannot meet standards for promotion.

THE FUTURE OF EDUCATION IN TEXAS

While these and other reforms have resulted in some measurable improvements in student performance, such as in the TEAMS results, they must be viewed as only the initial steps in the state's drive toward building a world-class education system. Significant improvement takes time, and critical challenges must be met in areas outside the instructional arena that also have a tremendous impact on the quality of public schools—areas such as educational equity, dropout prevention, family involvement, and drug abuse prevention.

With the importance that education plays in our state's economic development, Texans must be united in their desire for a world-class school system. We must develop a consensus for excellence, a strong and universal belief that high-quality education represents the road to economic diversification and future success. And we must act on those beliefs. The creation of an excellent education system to meet the needs of

Texas in the twenty-first century requires a philosophical and financial commitment on the part of all Texans. Educators, parents, business and industry, governments, churches, and communities all must be involved in education, and they all must be committed to excellence. The future of Texas and the nation depends on it.

CONTENT QUESTIONS

1. Why is education called one of Texas' biggest businesses?
2. By the twenty-first century, what will be the major problem regarding the American labor force?

3. Why do most new businesses fail?
4. What are some of the indications that the quality of education in Texas is improving?

DISCUSSION QUESTIONS

1. What are the changes that are affecting the Texas economy, and how will these have an impact on you?
2. Discuss recent reforms in the Texas education system. How have these improved (or not improved) the education you are receiving?

34

COMMONSENSE ECONOMIC DEVELOPMENT: THE NEW REALITIES

J. William Lauderback[1]
and
David R. Ellis[2]

The history of Texas is one of change and transition. We made our first fortunes by what we could graze on the land. Then, by what we could grow on it. Later, by what we found under it. World War II moved Texas into the manufacturing era. Then, in the late 1950s, a company in Dallas invented what we now call the microchip, and we moved into the electronics era. In the 1960s, as a result of the space program, we became the center of some of the most advanced scientific efforts the world had ever seen. The changes are still occurring today. Certainly, we moved through these various periods with different degrees of willingness; nevertheless, each represents a period of transition and change in our economic development history.

There have been other important changes as well. Perhaps one of the most important has been the increasing impact of external forces on our economy and the resulting need for internal planning strategies to adapt to them.

For example, in the 1940s, 1950s, and 1960s, Texas businesses grew primarily by concentrating on the Texas market and by exporting goods and services to other states. While local and national markets are still important today, ideas, products, capital, labor, and wealth cross international boundaries to a greater extent and at greater speed than at any time in our history.

While the degree of **globalization** varies by industry, most industries today operate in world markets. For example, in 1980, 50 percent of the U.S. economy was tied to international trade. By the year 2000, this percentage is expected to grow to 75 percent. In Texas, the impact is just as significant. Today, about one in every eight Texas workers is employed in an export-related field.

Another example comes readily to mind. As late as 1972, the Texas Railroad Commission, a three-member elected body, effectively set the world price of oil when they set the price for West Texas crude oil. Today, the price of oil is set by a small group of countries halfway around the globe, called OPEC (Organization of Petroleum Exporting Countries).

Still another aspect of the economic changes we are witnessing involves the significant challenges we face in terms of technology and innovation leadership.

Throughout our history, the Texas economy has relied on the development and application of new ideas to help spur our growth. For example, the railroad enabled commerce to flow east and west, not just toward the Gulf of Mexico. Improved drilling technology increased oil production. Medical breakthroughs discovered and developed here in Texas have extended the lives of

[1]Executive Director, Texas Department of Commerce.
[2]Director of Research, Texas Department of Commerce.

millions of people worldwide. These, of course, are just a few examples. But today, at a time when the competitive economic edge is increasingly derived from the application of technology, the superiority of the United States and Texas is eroding.

In the past, with a natural resource-based economy, we never had to worry that our oil and gas reserves would leave the state for a more attractive environment. They were here, and they would stay here, until we chose to mine and sell them. Human and technological resources, by comparison, are in constant demand and readily mobile. This is a fundamental concept of the global economy and a basic tenet of the environment in which we compete. Whether we like it or not, the reality of the global marketplace has had, and will continue to have, profound effects on our economy.

The fundamental result of these new changes to our economy has been in the form of a direct, substantial challenge to Texas. In simple terms, *we can accept our future as a matter of chance, or we can plan for our future as a matter of choice.* Texans have made a choice to compete.

A NEW FOCUS

Accepting the challenges of the new economy has brought renewed attention to the importance of sound state and local **economic development strategies**. For example, at the state level the Texas Department of Commerce was created in 1987 to initiate an aggressive statewide economic development effort. Additionally, the Texas legislature created the Strategic Economic Policy Commission to develop, for the first time, a long-range strategic economic development plan for the state. Much the same has been true at the local level as chambers of commerce, city councils, commissioner's courts, councils of government, and special-purpose economic development organizations have all felt the need to enhance and expand their development efforts.

Not surprisingly, there has been a corresponding increase in the number of economic development consultants and theoreticians ready and willing to meet the needs of these entities. Each one, of course, has a slightly different methodology, theory, or concept to solve the economic

problems of a community. To some, the answer is marketing. To others, business retention is the key. Still others say success is tied to indigenous job growth. What is the correct answer? Who do you believe?

FUNDAMENTAL STRATEGIES FOR ECONOMIC DEVELOPMENT

As confusing as it may seem, understanding what options are available and choosing a strategy that fits your community is probably easier than it appears.

Fundamentally, today's popular economic development strategies ultimately evolve into three main groups. For lack of other nomenclature, they could be termed the marketing strategy, the Petri dish strategy, and the greenhouse strategy.

The Marketing Strategy

The **marketing strategy** defines economic development as the process of marketing or "selling" a community's advantages and assets in order to attract new, major employers. One substrategy would suggest aggressively recruiting companies who are contemplating major plant relocations or expansions without regard to the type of company or its compatibility with the existing economic base. The other substrategy suggests targeting industry recruitment efforts based on a set of predetermined criteria designed to identify companies or industries which fill a particular economic niche or complement the existing economic base. In either case, this strategy involves a governmental or economic development entity picking "winners"—making decisions about what businesses or sets of businesses are to be pursued.

The Petri Dish Strategy

The **Petri dish strategy** defines economic development as a process of creating a total economic environment, the elements of which allow businesses and individuals to flourish. Those who subscribe to this theory would say that, in essence, the government and other economic development entities are not smart enough to follow the marketing strategy—that they are incapable of making decisions, which rightfully belong to the marketplace, regarding what industries should be brought into the community. Essentially, the Petri dish strategy is a noninterventionist strategy. It leaves the government responsible for only those things over which it has direct control. Proponents of the strategy would argue that if education, health care, infrastructure (streets, water, sewers), and other government-provided services are superior to those of the competition, economic growth and development will occur. Conversely, if these elements are deficient, growth will be slowed or nonexistent.

The Greenhouse Strategy

The **greenhouse strategy** defines economic development as a process of encouraging small business development formation and expansion. As opposed to the marketing strategy, and consistent with the Petri dish strategy, greenhouse proponents hold that it is not necessary to pick winners in the marketplace. Unlike the Petri dish proponents, however, they do feel that the government can do some things to insure higher business success rates. Small business incubators, loans, venture funds, combining private funds with public money, and technical support services are just a few of the techniques which proponents support. The greenhouse strategy, then, is somewhat of a blend of the two previous strategies, espousing the view that development is best left up to the marketplace, but with very targeted help from the government to fill specific voids.

FACTORS IN ECONOMIC DEVELOPMENT

Obviously, there are other factors which influence what particular economic development strategy is best for a particular community. For example, in any economy there is a mix of emerging businesses and mature business. They have different needs.

The food-processing and robotics industries provide examples at each end of the spectrum. The food-processing industry is mature. Absent any revolutionary innovative development, and none are foreseen in the short to medium term, much of what is going to occur will be a result of **economies of scale**, i.e., big companies buying out smaller companies to produce greater efficiencies through lower unit costs. The robotics industry, on the other hand, is in a different segment of the business-development cycle. Much of the development in that industry is yet to occur. New technologies will be created. New products will be developed. New markets will be discovered.

What does this mean for a community? A very simple analysis would show that the food-processing industry, because it is mature, would be looking for those characteristics in a community that would provide a **cost competitive advantage** in the manufacturing and marketing processes. Items falling into that category would include labor cost, labor availability, transportation infrastructure, and taxes.

A robotics company, however, being in an emerging industry, would be looking for different qualities in a community, qualities which could provide a **technological competitive advantage**. A technological competitive advantage exists when a firm has access to the latest and most advanced scientific knowledge. This knowledge may not be available to the firm's competitors. For example, access to a major research university would be important, as would the availability of specialized technical personnel and materials.

As we can see, in each instance, the potential and the needs of the industry are different. And, in each instance, different economic development strategies would be required for a particular company to find your town attractive as a potential home.

COMMUNITY ASSESSMENT

There is one final element critical to a sound economic development strategy: a candid self-assessment of the economic strengths, weaknesses, and trends of your community. It must be both a qualitative and a quantitative assessment.

For example, how do tax rates compare with those of other cities of like size in the state? In the nation? What about schools? What are the average SAT scores of graduating seniors? What is the utility capacity? Availability of water and sewer hookups? What about transportation? Availability of an airport nearby? Theaters? Shopping? Wages rates? What labor skills are available? What job-training programs are available? There are a myriad of questions that must be answered and an extensive amount of analysis that must be done. Without it, communities simply do not have the tools to make the necessary decisions, whatever economic development strategy they decide to pursue.

While this entire process is aimed at determining what strategies are best suited for an individual community, just as important is the sober realization that there are some strategies which simply will not work for some communities. Not all communities are destined to become the next Silicon Valley, nor are all equally likely to be prime candidates to land the next major expansion of a large, multinational petrochemical conglomerate. Consequently, an honest, objective appraisal of the assets of a community should not only identify particular strengths, but also help identify weaknesses and prohibiting factors which, taken together, help to narrow and sharpen the economic development focus.

Communities are becoming increasingly sophisticated and competitive in terms of economic development incentives and programs. Those that are most successful are those that decide on which strategy they will pursue and how they will pursue it, and arm themselves with the tools to do so. But, even then, it is important to realize that no one approach guarantees success. The ability of a community to remain flexible, to seize economic development opportunities when they are presented, is paramount.

CONCLUSION

Whether we wish it or not, Texas companies are now forced to compete in an international arena with companies from Japan, West Germany, the United Kingdom, Canada, Australia, South Korea, Mexico, and a host of other countries. *And so must Texas communities.* To remain competitive in terms of providing an attractive climate of opportunity for existing businesses to expand and for new businesses to be created, we need a concerted, planned, thoughtful, full-time effort at both the state and local level.

CONTENT QUESTIONS

1. The Texas economy is becoming more and more dependent on _____ trade.
2. Twenty years ago, who set the world price for oil? Who sets the price today?
3. What two state agencies were established to promote economic development in Texas?
4. What types of firms are looking for a cost competitive advantage? Which firms are looking for a technological competitive advantage?

DISCUSSION QUESTIONS

1. Discuss the three strategies a community can use to promote economic development. What is the best strategy for your community?
2. What are the strengths and weaknesses of your community in attracting new industry?
3. What type of business is your city likely to attract?

35

WATER
Herbert W. Grubb, Ph.D.[1]

Most of us know that we cannot survive for more than a few days without water. However, few of us are aware of it until our water supplies actually fail—either our wells go dry, our lakes are empty, or our plumbing collapses. Good, clean water is essential for human existence, for sanitation, for fire protection, to operate business and industry, to grow and process food and fiber for human uses, for the existence of fish and wildlife, for outdoor recreation, for urban landscaping, and for esthetics. The Texas climate ranges from humid in the east, with 56 inches of rainfall annually, to arid in the west, where annual precipitation is about 8 inches. How much water do we need, will there be enough to meet our needs in future years, and how do we insure that our future needs can continue to be met?

WATER FOR PEOPLE AND THE ECONOMY

The Texas population has grown rapidly. The population of Texas in 1900 was 3.0 million persons. In 1930, the population of the state had risen to 5.8 million, in 1960 to 9.6 million, in 1980 to 14.2 million, and in 1987 to 16.8 million. Population projections for the year 2000 range from 19.6 million persons to 21.2 million persons, and for 2030 between 28.2 million and 34.3 million. Well over 75 percent of these people are expected to reside in cities, where water will be needed in larger and larger quantities, and where pollution and the threat of pollution of water

supplies will become more and more serious. In our urbanized economy, between 10 percent and 15 percent of total water use is for direct use by people for drinking, cooking, sanitation, fire protection, urban landscaping, and recreation. Water use in households, commercial establishments, and for public requirements in 1980 was 2.8 million acre-feet (one acre-foot equals 325,851 gallons).

Our industrial and agricultural economies cannot function without adequate supplies of suitable quality water. For example, in the western part of the United States more than 70 percent of all water use is for growing crops, and in the traditionally "rain-fed" states of the East, irrigation is being increased each year to allow farmers to protect crop yields when droughts occur. Well over 25 percent of our nation's farm production and over 40 percent of Texas farm production depends upon irrigation.

In 1980, the total value of crop production in Texas was $4.3 billion. The availability of water for crop irrigation accounted for $1.7 billion of wages, salaries, rents, profits, and taxes. In 1980, agricultural water use was approximately 12.9 million acre-feet, 72 percent of the 17.9 million acre-feet total water use in the state.

Food processing, textile manufactures, energy refinement, electric power generation, metals, automobiles, paper, machinery, chemicals, wood products, plastics, electronics, and the many other products that we use every day require water somewhere in the production process. About 15 percent of our water use is for operating our industries.

[1]Director of Planning, Texas Water Development Board.

156

The value of shipments from manufacturing firms in Texas in 1980 was $160 billion and provided about 1.1 million direct jobs. The manufacturing sector paid $6.1 billion in direct taxes, excluding education taxes. After factoring in the indirect effects that flow from those amounts of direct manufacturing activity, the total value of output, direct and indirect, becomes $417.6 billion, with 4.2 million jobs, and $26.6 billion in taxes, excluding taxes to support education. Water use in manufacturing in 1980 in Texas was 1.5 million acre-feet. Without this water, manufacturing could not have taken place.

The value of steam-electric power generated in Texas in 1980 was about $7.1 billion, with residential use accounting for $2.7 billion, manufacturing $2.3 billion, and commercial uses $1.9 billion—almost all of the remainder. Direct employment in steam-electric power generation totaled about 43,000 jobs. Water use, mainly for cooling, during 1980 amounted to well over 16.5 million acre-feet, of which about 330,000 acre-feet were consumed, with the remainder being returned to the waterways for reuse.

There are benefits to society from public investment in water supply, water quality, and water transportation facilities. One of these is the continuous stream of products and services that flow into the economy and into the community from these capital items over their productive life span. Also, there is the value to society of jobs, incomes, and taxes that flow from the construction and maintenance of dams, reservoirs, water and wastewater treatment and conveyance works, and ports and harbors.

PROJECTIONS OF FUTURE WATER NEEDS

In order to meet the water needs of the future, it is necessary to develop long-range water plans. For planning purposes, population and water requirements projections have been made. In 1980, total water use was 17.85 million acre-feet. Projected water requirements range between 17.33 and 26.36 million acre-feet in the year 2000, and between 22.18 and 36.11 million acre-feet in 2030.

The economic base of Texas is being expanded from the historic foundations of petroleum, agriculture, and forestry into manufacturing of capital and consumer goods, trade, financing, services, and high technology. Recent planning projections indicate that the growth rates of basic, heavy, water-using industries such as petroleum refining, pulp and paper, chemicals, metals, and agriculture are leveling off in comparison to the rates of the past 20 years. In the immediate future there may not be any growth in some of these sectors, while the low water-using service sector and the high-technology sector are expected to grow at more rapid rates than in the past. This shifting of the structural base of the economy has significant implications for planning to meet the future water supply and water quality protection needs of the future. In the most recent projections for Texas, these trends have been taken into account.

PLANNING FOR FUTURE WATER SUPPLIES

Currently, the state's dependable surface water and ground-water supply is 16.3 million acre-feet per year. The dependable yield from the state's aquifers is approximately 5.3 million acre-feet per year and the firm yield from the state's seventy-one major reservoirs is about 11.0 million acre-feet per year. In 1985, aquifers supplied approximately 7.9 million acre-feet (56 percent) and surface water resources supplied approximately 6.2 million acre-feet (44 percent) of total water used. At the present rate of use, net annual ground-water "mining" is 2.6 million acre-feet per year. **Water mining** is the amount by which the yield of the aquifers is reduced each year due to usage in excess of the aquifer's ability to replenish itself. Estimated recoverable reserves of ground-water are about 418 million acre-feet. Of the 11.0 million acre-feet of dependable surface water, 56 percent is being used. Of the remaining 44 percent, 82 percent is committed to customers, with 18 percent available for growth. Without careful management and effective water conservation programs to eliminate waste and reduce the rate of growth in water use, there may not be enough clean water to meet projected future needs.

To meet our future water needs, we will have to improve our technology to:

1. Increase efficiency in all forms of water use;
2. reduce the rising costs of water supply, water treatment, wastewater reclamation, and flood protection functions;
3. develop acceptable water reuse methods;
4. lower the costs of desalting water;
5. find better ways to deal with hazardous and toxic wastes; and
6. modify our personal behavior insofar as water use and attitudes toward water are concerned.

In order to accomplish these goals it will be necessary for teachers, students, community leaders, civic clubs, and public officials to participate in efforts to increase public awareness and respect for water resources. After all, no amount of waterworks facilities or technology will adequately serve our needs if the resources are not properly understood and managed. We must find a way to effectively communicate about these matters with the general public. Water-resource sciences must be taught in our schools so that we have adequately informed graduates and sufficiently trained professionals to plan, manage, and maintain water-resource programs now and in the future.

CONTENT QUESTIONS

1. What are the main purposes for which water is used?
2. What percentage of Texas crop sales depends upon irrigation water?
3. Is total water use in Texas greater than long-term dependable supplies? If so, by how much?
4. Are basic industries such as agriculture and energy growing more or less rapidly than service industries and high technology? What does this mean for the Texas water supply?
5. What are the benefits to society from public investments in water resources?

DISCUSSION QUESTIONS

1. How can water conservation help solve water problems?
2. Can the people of Texas thrive and prosper if there is not enough water for business, industry, and agriculture?
3. Discuss how water for business and industry affects government services, including public education.

36

INTERNATIONAL TRADE
AND THE TEXAS ECONOMY

Thomas M. Stauffer, Ph.D.[1]

"Texas: Joining the World" was the headline of a feature article in a mid-1980s number of the *Washington Post*. It told the story of the wave of economic growth that had engulfed the state, beginning with the Arab oil embargo of 1973 and accelerating when President Ronald Reagan in 1981 lifted price controls on oil. When the end of the boom came in 1982-83, followed by an economic slump that characterized Texas throughout the decade, the *Post* article proclaimed an end to the state's "go it on your own" economic isolation.

FOREIGN INFLUENCES ON THE TEXAS ECONOMY

It took a long time for many Texans to realize that the rise and fall of the Texas economy in the 1970s and 1980s resulted, in large measure, from decisions made in Washington, D.C., or elsewhere in foreign nations, over which the state had little control. The economic isolation of Texas has always been more fiction than fact, but in earlier decades the state had a tendency toward insularity, and economic events outside the state had less significance for the state than for other parts of the nation. Some even suggested that Texans, if need be, could live by themselves and prosper, without trade abroad or even with other states. Such isolation never happened, but today it would amount to financial suicide even to try it.

[1]President and Professor of Public Policy, University of Houston-Clear Lake.

The Texas oil boom of the 1970s and early 1980s resulted not only from political decisions in Washington and other major capitals but also from actions of the Organization of Petroleum Exporting Countries (OPEC), mostly Middle East nations that benefit from keeping oil prices high. Coupled with Middle Eastern military and other intrigues, OPEC determined the price of oil and, in the process, had a big influence on the direction of the Texas economy. OPEC set prices at an artificially high level and the Texas economy boomed. When OPEC was no longer able to maintain the high prices, the Texas boom ended. While the Texas economy clearly joined the U.S. economy in the first quarter of this century, the Texas economy unmistakably joined the world economy in its last quarter.

FOREIGN TRADE

In 1987, Texas ranked second only to California in the total value of its exports. Table 36-1 shows the positions of the ten largest exporting states. In Texas, this export performance is the base for many jobs and much economic activity. Throughout the last two decades, the importance of foreign trade to the Texas economy has been steadily increasing.

In the early 1980s, as a result of national policies, the value of the dollar soared. The cost of U.S. products that foreigners wanted to buy also soared, while the cost of foreign products became lower for U.S. buyers. As a result, the nation was

TABLE 36-1
States Ranked in Order of 1987 Exports

Rank	State	Exports (billions of dollars)
1	California	27.5
2	TEXAS	19.7
3	New York	15.0
4	Michigan	13.0
5	Washington	10.6
6	Louisiana	9.8
7	Florida	7.6
8	Ohio	7.6
9	Massachusetts	7.0
10	Illinois	6.9

Source: U.S. Department of Commerce.

flooded by low-cost imports, led by Japanese electronics and automobiles, and American export markets dried up. The United States, which generally since World War I had sold more abroad than it bought, now found itself with a massive and stubborn **trade deficit**: it was now importing more than it exported. Economists lamented the loss of American jobs and the creation of a huge debt burden. But national leaders, led by James Baker, a Texan and Houstonian, who also was the U.S. Secretary of the Treasury, realized that the strong dollar came at too high a price.

Policy changes in 1985 lowered the dollar's value about 40 percent, and the U.S. trade deficit began to shrink. American exports surged; imported goods cost more. U.S. goods became bargains overseas, and the export boom helped fuel the diversification and expansion of the Texas economy. For example, as imported paper and clothing became more expensive, more of these goods were produced in this country, and job growth in Texas in those industries went up sharply. In fact, the vigor of export-related manufacturing helped lead the state out of the economic doldrums that began with the oil price collapse in 1982.

One-eighth of Texas manufacturing employment is tied directly to exports. Petrochemicals are the state's leading export, but other major exports include electronics, processed food, computers, lumber, and wood products. In agriculture, a quarter of the state's farm income derives from foreign sales. The value of exports shipped through the Port of Houston grew to $9.1

billion in 1987, and at Dallas–Fort Worth International Airport, the value was $1.5 billion, a threefold increase in seven years. By all estimates, the importance of foreign trade to the Texas economy will continue to grow steadily.

IMMIGRATION

In addition to goods and services, people of foreign birth have come to play a dominant role in the internationalization of Texas. In its history, looking back no more than two hundred years, the land that is Texas has been an international crossroads. Mexican involvement has always been strong, and many settlers in the last century came directly or indirectly from the nations and lands of Europe and Africa. Today, the growing number of Texas residents and citizens who were born in Latin America represents the fastest growing segment of the state's population. The number of Hispanic students enrolled in Texas colleges and universities, for example, is second only to California's total. Interestingly, the number of foreign students enrolled in Texas institutions of higher learning also ranks second only to that of California among the states. The influences brought by these and many other international groups to Texas, including a rapidly growing Asian segment and many foreign tourists, are fast altering the fabric of Texas art, culture, cuisine, economics, and politics.

A TEXAS WINDOW ON THE WORLD

No part of Texas is now immune from foreign influences, and Houston, at least in economic terms, leads the state as an international center. Ever since the opening of Houston's Ship Channel in 1912, the metropolitan area has grown in international importance as a crossroads for the world's people and commerce. Starting in World War II and continuing with the rapid expansion of the energy, space, construction, service, and medical industries in the 1960s and 1970s, the pace of international activity in Houston and its worldwide visibility has quickened appreciably.

Houston now has a distinctive international character, in terms of both business climate and demographics. In 1985, by conservative estimate, there were eight hundred banks, professional firms, enterprises, consulates, and public agencies in Houston with major international involvements, and another seven hundred had lesser but still significant global undertakings. Major communities of Hispanics, Asians, Middle Eastern and African peoples, and others, have taken root and are now flourishing in the region.

Texas is already more involved in the world's economy than most Texans realize. For example, Table 36-2 outlines some of the significant international activity in Houston.

A good part of Houston's long-term economic development strategy turns on attracting foreign companies, investment, and trade, and this applies to other parts of the state as well. The electronics industry in the Dallas—Fort Worth area has a major international thrust, and Dallas' huge World Trade Center, as well as very high-quality medical facilities, also make the Metroplex a major international center. Along the Texas-Mexico border, American companies have set up factories on the Mexican side to manufacture goods at low labor cost that are then sent back into Texas for shipment elsewhere.

In all of this activity, Texans are obliged to be a part of national policy decisions and international events. Foreign investment in the United States is growing faster than American investment abroad, and Texans must pursue those business opportunities.

TEXAS' PLACE IN WORLD MARKETS

Texans and their fellow Americans need to be concerned about their competitive position in world markets. Almost three-quarters of U.S. goods and services face competition from foreign suppliers compared with an estimated one-quarter only twenty years ago. Texas has joined the world economy, but so has the United States generally.

After World War II, the United States was unquestionably the dominant world economic power. Now, strong economies in Europe, Japan, nations along the rim of Asia, selected Third

---

TABLE 36-2
Houston as an International Center

1. The Port of Houston is one of the nation's largest, with ships from the world's seafaring nations calling regularly.

2. Houston has foreign consulates from fifty-four nations, in addition to dozens of foreign banks and forty-two international service agencies, through which commerce can be conducted.

3. As the nation's third-largest city, Houston is an ever-growing market itself and a principal gateway to the Sunbelt.

4. Houston is the international, national, or regional headquarters for important multinational corporations, and is Texas' principal international legal center. In 1984, the Texas Bar Association listed 592 attorneys as having special expertise in international law.

5. Major advanced-technology industries have been established in Houston with an unmistakable international orientation. These include operations in the fields of space, medicine, computers, construction, energy, and agribusiness.

6. Houston, served by several international airlines, has direct flights to and from Europe, Asia, Latin America, Canada, and Africa.

7. Houston's Texas Medical Center is widely praised internationally and routinely provides sophisticated medical treatment to thousands of foreign patients, including royalty and foreign leaders.

World nations, and even Communist nations mean that no one nation dominates, although the United States with its $5 trillion economy remains the world's leading economic power. Texas also is a formidable economic force. Its economy generates over $300 billion, and if Texas were an independent nation, it would rank tenth among the economies of the world.

Foreign interests have invested heavily in the U.S. and Texas economies. A large percentage of office buildings in downtown Dallas and Houston are foreign owned. Texas political leaders now travel to foreign capitals regularly seeking to attract economic activity to the state. Major Texas banks have developed international expertise. Sensitivity in Texas to international topics has increased enormously in just the last decade.

Frustration with this newly enlarged world role, however, is commonplace. For instance, the oil and gas industry remains important in Texas but control over the price of these commodities is no longer located in the state. In 1987, to illustrate, the United Nations passed Security Council Resolution 598, encouraging Iran and Iraq to cease eight years of war. When those nations finally heeded the resolution and implemented a cease-fire, both nations, having been large world oil suppliers before the war, wanted to normalize oil production for world markets. A fight broke out among OPEC members over each nation's rightful share of the market. The argument was further exacerbated by the fear of both Iran, a militant Islamic fundamentalist state, and Iraq, an advocate of Arab socialism. The governments in these nations conflicted with conservative monarchies on the western side of the Persian Gulf. Saudi Arabia, in order to keep and expand its own share of the world's oil market, increased its oil exports and drove down oil prices, including Texas prices. Texans had no role in the Iran-Iraq War or in the postwar maneuvering, but its economy was affected nonetheless. Knowing how to provide economic leadership amidst such great uncertainty has proved to be a tough challenge for the state's leadership.

THE FUTURE AGENDA ON THE INTERNATIONAL SCENE

Texans have developed considerable expertise in international commerce, yet rapid expansion of foreign trade requires still more. Foreign language skills, international business courses, and specialized seminars are all important, but remaining competitive in the world marketplace requires more. Texas must have a strong research and technological base to produce the products that the world will buy, and that in turn depends on the strength of the Texas schools and universities. It also requires capable management of resources, high-quality products, and a willingness to have a world view in conducting business abroad. The growth of the export sector in Texas demonstrates that Texans are learning rapidly what is required to be competitive.

Foreign trade is an important and growing portion of the Texas economy. Traditionally, Texans have often been able to ignore the rest of the world, and for a time, the rest of the United States, but those days are gone forever. The degree to which Texans respond to the world trade challenge and opportunities will be a leading factor in determining the state's future prosperity.

CONTENT QUESTIONS

1. List in order the three major states in terms of exports.
2. What was the major factor which caused Texas exports to decline in the early 1980s?
3. What is the fastest-growing segment of the Texas population?
4. If Texas was an independent nation, where would its economy rank among the nations of the world?

DISCUSSION QUESTIONS

1. What can Texas do to expand exports and remain competitive in world markets?
2. How has Texas been affected by recent immigration?

37

THE ELECTRIC UTILITY INDUSTRY: SAME CHARGE, NEW CHALLENGES

E. R. Brooks[1]

Since its beginnings in the late nineteenth century, the electric utility business has grown from small, isolated, entrepreneurial operations to a mature industry. In Texas alone, privately owned electric utilities have an investment of nearly $30 billion in plants and facilities.

But despite many other changes in its more than 100-year history, the electric utility industry's responsibility has remained constant: to provide reliable, economical electricity to everyone within the utility's service territory who is willing and able to buy it.

As the industry has grown, it has continually developed new and better ways to meet this responsibility. For instance, economies of scale (which result from large, very efficient electric plants) have reduced the cost per kilowatt-hour of electricity; and cooperative agreements among utilities, such as the Electric Reliability Council of Texas (ERCOT), have improved reliability. As a result, you probably never doubt that you will have affordable electric service a day, a year, or a decade from now. When you flip the switch on the wall, you probably never doubt that the lights will come on.

Today, the electric utility industry is in a period of rapid transition. Some of the challenges it

now faces could jeopardize its ability to execute its charge.

FUEL AND ITS IMPLICATIONS

Texas has been blessed with abundant natural gas and oil. This wealth of energy has, in many ways, defined the Texas economy. It has also shaped the Texas electric utility industry, which became heavily dependent on the state's ready source of inexpensive natural gas to fuel its power plants. In 1973, the oil embargo sent the price of oil and gas soaring and suddenly created such scarcity that Americans waited hours in line for the privilege of paying top dollar for a tank of gas.

To electric utilities in Texas, the oil embargo demonstrated the need for fuel diversification in their power plants. If natural gas was no longer either cheap or abundant, other fuel sources, such as coal and nuclear, would have to be developed. In addition, many new power plants began to be designed with the ability to use two different fuel sources. Such plants might burn natural gas as a primary fuel and burn coal when natural gas was not available or was too expensive.

A natural gas-fired power plant takes about three years to build; coal- and nuclear-powered plants take much longer and cost much more. Today, a coal-burning plant takes an average of eight to ten years to build. Nuclear power plants

[1]Executive Vice-President, Electrical Operations, Central and South West Corporation, Dallas, Texas.

take even longer to complete, and their cost can run into billions of dollars.

Fuel diversification is imperative to guarantee the nation's energy security. But with generating plants requiring many years to build, fuel diversification makes the need for long-range planning even more critical. It also means that power companies must be willing and able to undertake expensive construction projects, such as building coal and nuclear plants.

NEW COMPETITORS

Operating on the assumption that increased competition in producing electricity would result in lower costs, the federal government passed the Public Utility Regulatory Policies Act (PURPA) in 1978. This act provides financial incentives to encourage large industrial facilities and independent power producers to generate power from their own plants. It also requires electric utilities to buy that power at their "avoided cost," that is, what it would cost the utility to produce the power itself.

Some of these nonutility power producers are large commercial or industrial facilities, such as hospitals and manufacturing plants, known as cogenerators. Cogenerators produce *electricity* at the same time they produce *heat* to run their plant or to provide a comfortable environment for their staff and patients. The name "cogenerator" comes from this ability to produce both power and useful heat at the same time.

Electric utility companies question the wisdom of having cogenerators. Encouraging such competition in power production seems, at least on the surface, to make good common sense. However, most of these nonutility producers are neither willing nor financially able to build the more efficient, but also most costly and time-consuming, coal and nuclear plants. With the price of natural gas again low, they prefer to build lower-cost gas plants, a trend which threatens to increase our dependence on a single source of energy once again.

Utilities are obligated to serve anyone in their service territory who wants to buy electricity and is able to pay for it. Independent power producers have no such obligation. If a market is unprofitable, they can leave it and move on. So, will customers find themselves without electricity,

because a power producer left the market? Or is the local electric utility still obligated to have the capacity to serve everyone in its territory, just in case an alternative power source becomes unavailable? And, if so, who pays for the utility's additional generating capacity?

All of this brings up the question of planning. In a system where nonutility power producers move in and out of the market at will, how can we do the planning that will guarantee reliable, economical electricity for you, your children, and your grandchildren? And, as we have already seen, far-sighted planning becomes especially important when plants take from several years to more than a decade to build.

ACCESS TO THE TRANSMISSION SYSTEM

When independent power producers and cogenerators produce electricity, they still have to find a way to move that electricity from the plant to their customer. Since electric utilities have already built the transmission system to do just that, it does not make good economic sense to duplicate the system. The alternative is to allow nonutilities to transmit their electricity over the utility-owned transmission system.

That access to the transmission system, called **wheeling,** does, in fact, make good economic sense, provided utilities are not *required* to provide the service on demand. Requiring that service is called **mandatory wheeling**. If such complete, open access to the transmission system is ever required in Texas, it could seriously undercut the reliability—and even the economy—of electric service.

What's wrong with mandatory wheeling? For starters, mandatory wheeling enables large industrial customers such as manufacturing plants to buy cheap electricity from a distant source and wheel it to their facility. Then the plant is no longer a customer of the utility. And that means higher rates for the other customers, because the utility built its power plants and lines, in part, to serve that large manufacturer. When the manufacturer is gone, the plants and lines still must be paid for. As you can see, mandatory wheeling also raises planning problems similar to those we discussed above.

Finally, mandatory wheeling could seriously hurt the reliability of electric service. An electric transmission and distribution system is designed to carry certain amounts of power. If the utility is not permitted to control how much power flows on the line, the result may be damage to the system or "brownouts." Brownouts occur when electric current supplied to consumers is reduced. Often this results in lights dimming and machinery running more slowly. We may even reach the point where we will no longer be certain the lights will come on when we flip the switch.

THE UTILITY RESPONSE TO A CHANGING ENVIRONMENT

Clearly, electric utilities operate in a rapidly changing business environment. Their own response includes new ways to hold down costs without sacrificing reliability. For instance, some electric utilities have diversified their operations, adding other products or services that may or may not be related to the electric utility business. Still others have chosen to gain economies of scale by merging their operations or acquiring another utility. No matter what form this response takes,

it illustrates the electric utility industry's commitment to provide low-cost, high-quality service to all who want it.

CONTENT QUESTIONS

1. The electric utilities industry in Texas became dependent on what inexpensive source of fuel? The rising price of this fuel after 1973 caused Texas utilities to look to what two other fuels?
2. What is PURPA and what does it provide?
3. What is "avoided cost," and what are "cogenerators"?
4. What is "wheeling"?

DISCUSSION QUESTIONS

1. Why are electric utilities opposed to cogenerators?
2. What problems are created by mandatory wheeling?

7

THE ECONOMIC HISTORY OF TEXAS

Texas has a rich and colorful history. We are the only state that has been a colony of two other nations (Spain and Mexico) and an independent nation before statehood. Often the history of our state is told in terms of its generals and politicians. Yet, Texans are the way they are due more to economic events than to political occurrences.

These chapters trace the development of the Texas economy from a poor, underdeveloped land under Spanish rule to the prosperous state of today. It is often difficult for Texans to remember that for most of the state's history we were an impoverished and struggling people dependent upon what the harsh earth yielded for our prosperity.

The history of Texas is an economic story. It was the economic policies of Spain that caused Texas not to grow in its early years. Economic issues ignited the Texas desire for independence. It was the failed economic policies of the Texas Republic that forced Texas into statehood.

The Civil War was not as cruel to Texas as it was to the other states in the south. Because Texas was never occupied by Union forces, the destruction of farms and factories which took place elsewhere did not occur here. But the problems of reconstruction after the Civil War did leave a negative impact, and dictated the state's political and economic life for seventy-five years.

In the last 125 years the three Cs—cotton, cattle, and crude oil—shaped the Texas economy. Most Texans earned their living by producing one of these three commodities. The prices of these were set by forces beyond the control of Texans. When these forces were kind, Texans prospered.

The Great Depression was a turning point for Texas. The attitude of Texans towards their economy and towards the role of government as a participant in that economy changed dramatically. A new set of values eroded the old. Life and politics in Texas were never quite the same.

The Texas economy during the 1940s and 1950s was a time of tremendous growth sparked not only by the expansion of the petroleum industry, but also by defense contracts and government spending within the state. Led by petrochemicals, this was the period in which Texas' economy began to industrialize and diversify.

The last two decades have seen the period of Texas' greatest prosperity, followed by a crash. The action of the oil exporting nations in the early 1970s drove up the price of oil. Texans benefited greatly and the economy boomed. But at the same time, Texans became more and more dependent upon this one industry for their income. In the early 1980s when oil prices collapsed, Texans realized that their economy had failed to diversify and that they were vulnerable to forces over which they had no control.

What does the future of the Texas economy hold? Will we be able to diversify, attracting the new industries and creating the new jobs which are vital? What policies must be pursued by business and by government if this is to be accomplished? It will not happen automatically. Are Texans up to the challenge?

38

THE ECONOMY OF TEXAS UNDER SPAIN

Nita Sue Kent[1]

The early economy of Texas was controlled by politics. Natural resources, geography, and inhabitants all played their roles, but they were not as important as the area's political status. The economy of Texas went through three distinct phases before statehood. The colonial system of Spain, the Republic of Mexico, and finally independence as a republic all imposed certain limitations and expectations on the economy.

GEOGRAPHY AND THE ECONOMY

While the geography of the region never changed, its function in the creation of Texas varied because of the different needs of these governments. Spain saw Texas as part of a vast empire, and tried to stabilize the area to protect Spanish interests to the south and west. The long gulf coastline, instead of the positive feature it later became, was seen as a threat that had to be guarded to prevent unregulated trade. The wide stretches of arid wasteland made communication with the more fertile parts of the area difficult. Control by Mexico was also complicated by these same features. Once Texas was independent, however, the coastline made transportation to the port of New Orleans easy, and the desert served as a protective buffer between the Republic and Mexico.

Although the geography of the area was a major influence, it never was as vital to the economy as the political considerations of the governments that controlled the area, or as the character of the people—both native Indians and immigrants—who lived in the land.

The first economic development in Texas began in 1598 when a trail was blazed from Chihuahua, in Mexico, northwards to cross the Rio Grande at the location of today's El Paso. Not until 1681, with the establishment of Ysleta, was a permanent settlement located there. It is the oldest European community in Texas. For the next two hundred years, this was the major supply route from the interior of Mexico to the northern colonies.

THE MISSION ECONOMY

Spanish imperial policy developed three major goals: to maintain territorial claims, to settle the land with soldiers and colonists loyal to Spain, and to stop Anglo-American infiltration. The mission system was developed as part of that policy. The missions were under government control. Mission expenses were paid out of state funds, and the missionaries were approved by the viceroy, the Spanish governor in Mexico City. The missions were established to convert the native Indians to Christianity, make them into productive workers in the Spanish colonies, and strengthen Spanish claims to the land. Spanish missions were successful in California, Mexico,

[1]Author and historian.

and other parts of the empire. In Texas the missions were not successful. Disease, danger, and distance crippled them; trade restrictions killed them.

This early economic system was not based on the principles of a free market economy. The government believed its goals were more important than economic prosperity for the people in the region. The traditional economy of the American Indians had been one based on self-sufficient agriculture or hunting.

Through the missions, the Spanish tried to impose a command economy on the Native Americans. Some of the Texas Indians, like those in California and Mexico, had been settled in one area for many years, growing corn, melons, and squash and hunting deer and small animals for their food. Others, such as the fiercely independent Comanches and Apaches, followed the buffalo herds and often raided the agricultural Indians.

The farming Indians were willing to move to the missions. The Spanish gathered them together in settlements that combined military defense with an agricultural and religious center. In return for protection and instruction, the mission Indians were expected to grow enough crops to trade as well as live. The mission Indians also began to raise cattle. This foundation of livestock and farming, which formed the economic system of Spanish Texas, continued into the twentieth century. Since the land was fertile, and water and game were abundant, the Indians and the few immigrants who joined them tended to be relaxed about growing more food than they needed.

PROBLEMS OF THE MISSION ECONOMY

Even more limiting were the trade restrictions that Spain imposed. Spanish colonists were forced to trade only with Spain. Hundreds of miles of mountains and deserts—as well as the Apaches and Comanches—lay between the Spanish authorities in Mexico City and the Texas missions. The tribes and settlements in Louisiana were much closer to the farmers. But since Louisiana was controlled by the French, mission trade with any of the French-held territory was forbidden. If the trade with Louisiana had been

allowed to develop, the mission economy might have survived.

Other major problems hurt the Texas missions. The mission Indians were under constant threat from the nomadic, warlike Comanches and Apaches. There was little incentive to store up extra crops and livestock if the predatory Indians would probably raid, destroying what they did not take.

Disease was the last difficulty that completely ruined some missions. Because they had not developed immunities, the Indians died from illnesses that, to the Spanish, were minor. When conversion to Christianity seemed to lead to death and disease, many Indians went back to their old ways of life. But basic to the failure of the missions were the economic restrictions placed on trade.

SPANISH COLONIES IN TEXAS

In addition to the missions, Spain tried to colonize the area, but with little success. Spain had strict rules about who could be a colonist. Only law-abiding Catholics loyal to Spain were welcome. As with the missions, colonists were not allowed to trade with Louisiana. Only three communities took lasting form under the long years of Spanish domination: San Antonio, Goliad, and Nacogdoches. San Antonio and Goliad were both located on the San Antonio River, with Goliad closer to the coast, in the rolling grasslands of the prairie. They formed the bottom two points of a triangle which had its top point at Nacogdoches, located in the piney woods of East Texas.

Spanish colonists did not like the damp forest areas of East Texas as much as the grasslands closer to Mexico. The immigrants who settled Nacogdoches were, for the most part, from Louisiana. Many were adventurers who were escaping trouble in the more civilized parts of the United States. Since Nacogdoches was in the sparsely settled and unregulated border area, they tended to gather there. But, in general, Spanish efforts to settle the Texas area failed because of the severe regulations about who could colonize and how the colonists could conduct trade.

Another Spanish trade regulation forbade any shipments from the coast. All traffic was required to move along a route that paralleled the coast but never came closer than a hundred miles or so.

Even local shipments, from one part of Texas to another, were forbidden. All trade from Texas, as well as from Mexico, was supposed to move through the seaport of Vera Cruz. These limitations on trade only encouraged piracy and smuggling in the sparsely settled areas.

THE END OF THE EMPIRE

Eventually, as their empire weakened, the Spanish had two choices. Spain could pull back to hold the area bordered by San Antonio and Goliad and protect the prime ranch country of South Texas, or it could allow more flexibility by accepting Anglos as immigrants. After France sold the Louisiana Territory to the United States in 1803, the situation was even worse. Spain faced the difficulties of having Texas on the borders of a growing and land-hungry nation. Spain tried to improve the situation by accepting Anglo settlers to serve as a buffer between the rapidly expanding United States and the raids of Indians, to protect the more heavily Spanish populations of San Antonio and northern Mexico.

But at the end of the long years of Spanish domination, the non-Indian population of Texas had only risen to a few thousand individuals. Spain left a legacy of little more than some Spanish place-names and a tradition of property rights for women.

CONTENT QUESTIONS

1. The first European community in Texas was _____, which was established in _____. The first economic development in Texas was a trail between _____, in _____, and _____.
2. What were the three goals of Spanish imperial policy toward Mexico?
3. What type of economic system did Spain try to impose on Texas?
4. What were the problems of the mission economy?
5. List the three lasting communities established in Texas under Spain.

DISCUSSION QUESTIONS

1. How did geography affect the Spanish domination of Texas?
2. Discuss the mission economy as it was established by Spain in Texas.
3. Why did Spain fail to establish more permanent communities in Texas?

39

THE ECONOMY OF TEXAS UNDER MEXICO AND AS A REPUBLIC

Nita Sue Kent[1]

Not until Mexico broke free from Spain in 1822 did the population of Texas rise dramatically. Mexico expanded and improved the **empresario system** created by the Spanish. The major features of the empresario system had been proposed in Spain in 1813, but the system was not put into effect until 1820 when the Spanish broke precedent and invited foreigners to settle on New Spain's northern frontier.

An empresario was an entrepreneur who contracted with the government to recruit and supervise colonists. The empresario was assigned a large area of land to be settled by a specific number of families. As an agent of the government, the empresario selected the colonists, divided and assigned the land, and made sure the colonists obeyed the regulations of citizenship.

STEPHEN F. AUSTIN

By far the most successful of the empresarios was Stephen F. Austin, who built on a foundation laid by his father, Moses Austin. In 1798, Moses Austin obtained a grant of land to settle thirty families in Missouri, then a part of Spanish territory in America. He was successful and remained a loyal Spanish subject until the United States took control of the territory in 1804.

Moses Austin stayed in Missouri, prospering in lead mining and banking until 1818, when the first great national bank failures hit the United States. Banks had made loans to land speculators with only the land as collateral. This was fine until inflated prices made the market collapse. Banks across the country closed, and depositors lost their money. The bank failures ruined Moses Austin financially. To rebuild his wealth, he decided to organize a colony once again, but this time in Texas. The long, dangerous trek to Mexico and back to obtain the permit to colonize ruined his health. He died before the plan could be accomplished.

His son Stephen, then 27 years old, took over the leadership of the colonists. In 1821, he received approval from the Spanish government for the colony, but then Mexico gained its independence. After Austin renegotiated the contract with the new Mexican government in 1822, the new colony was established on the banks of the Brazos River. Austin's grant was unique in that he was the first empresario allowed to recruit Anglo settlers.

The lands Austin was given in his grant were some of the best in Texas, with fertile soil covered by grass and trees and watered by good rivers and streams. Each family could obtain a grant of almost 4,500 acres, much more land at a much lower cost than good land could be bought for in the United States.

[1]Author and historian.

THE PERIOD OF SETTLEMENT

Under the colonization law of 1824, new settlers were exempted from taxes and customs for seven years. By 1830, this period of grace was ending for many colonists. One of the Mexican government's problems was a lack of money to pay for the frontier defense and education system demanded by Anglo-Texans. In 1830, the government tried to tighten up on tax collections to raise money. The colonists protested and avoided paying their taxes.

Between 1830 and 1834, Mexico suspended immigration because of the unsettling influence of the Anglo settlers who resisted Mexico's domination and even argued over the amount of money due the empresario. When immigration was resumed, the pressure of individuals from the north seeking land and opportunity made the Anglo population grow even faster.

Settlers both legal and illegal continued to pour in. The empty area of Texas was vast, and publicity helped. Colonists bragged that they could only prosper in an area where land was cheap, and where they paid no taxes, performed no public service, and were generally free from government supervision. Most of the Anglos clung to the civil rights they had grown up with under the Anglo-Saxon system of justice instead of accepting the Mexican system. The two systems were different in many respects. In Mexico's eyes, Anglo attitudes about the rights of citizens to gather and protest were treasonous. An individual could be arrested and held without trial. The Mexican system regarded slavery very differently, too. Under Mexican law, a slave's labor, but not the slave as an individual, was controlled by the slavemaster. Slaves had rights as human beings. Under the Anglo system, the slave was a piece of property to be used or disposed of at the will of the owner. Mexico passed laws regulating slavery in Texas, but the laws were not enforced.

In spite of the turmoil over legal and economic rights, Texas was prospering. By the mid-1830s, Texas exports, including cotton and beaver, otter, and deer skins, amounted to $500,000. There was a trade imbalance, however, since Texans imported over $600,000 in manufactured goods. There was little currency in Texas. Ninety percent of the business transactions in the area were conducted through barter or credit. Rules were established to determine the value of items of barter. For example, a cow with a calf was determined to be worth $10 credit.

THE REVOLUTION AND REPUBLIC

Eventually the combination of the Anglos' dissatisfaction with Mexican rule and Mexico's suspicions about Anglo intentions set in motion the events that led to the Texas revolution in 1836. With independence, the empresario system came to an end. The population had grown to over twenty-five thousand people, with about four-fifths Anglo.

Citizens of the new republic were full of optimistic plans for a far-flung empire of their own that would stretch from Louisiana to Santa Fe. In reality, the Republic of Texas never controlled any area beyond the Nueces River. These visionaries believed the United States would lend them money to consolidate the new government, but political and economic considerations within the United States prevented that. From the beginning, some Texans favored joining the United States. The slavery issue was gaining strength and U.S. congressmen who opposed the creation of another slave state blocked that move.

Other problems plagued the new republic. Although many rivers emptied into the Gulf of Mexico, few of the waterways in Texas proved navigable. The rivers were shallow, wandering, and clogged with sandbars. Only the Brazos and Trinity rivers carried much shipping.

Transportation inland, almost impossible by boat, was difficult by land because of Indians. Most of the inhabitants of Texas lived within two hundred miles of the gulf coast.

The bays were shallow and unprotected from storms. The area's major seaports, Galveston and Houston, were hit by repeated yellow fever epidemics, beginning in 1839, which inhibited their development.

ECONOMIC PROBLEMS OF THE REPUBLIC

In spite of the constant military threat from Mexico, which was trying to regain its territory, and from hostile Indians, who were under increasing pressure as more settlers arrived, the most troublesome problem of the Republic of Texas was its economy. Most Texans still lived in a subsistence economy, raising only enough crops to feed themselves, but independence attracted land speculators. There was still very little currency in Texas. After barter, the principal medium of exchange was bank notes from the United States. Only the strength of the bank from which they were issued guaranteed the value of these notes.

In 1837, the United States had another major financial crisis. New York banks stopped backing their notes with gold and silver. Hundreds of banks failed, triggering the worst economic depression in United States history. It lasted five years. At first, Texas was not affected, but when the depression finally hit the new Republic, it was devastating.

The first president of the Republic of Texas, Sam Houston, was very conservative with the Republic's money. He spent only $2 million for public expenses in his first term. A lack of revenue, however, prevented expenditures even he thought necessary. At its beginning, the new republic was $1,250,000 in debt. The new Secretary of the Treasury did not have any stationery on which to write official letters. Local officials were paid in kind, with livestock or goods, or they served without pay.

During his first administration, Houston issued $650,000 in interest-bearing notes, called **star money** because the star of Texas was printed on the back. These notes held their value when redeemed in late 1836. Paid off before the panic of 1837 reached Texas, star money was the only specie ever issued by the republic that did not devalue immediately.

Land was Texas' only asset, and conflicting policies were adopted for land use. Land was to be used to back notes issued by the government, but also vast amounts of land were being given away, which devalued the land and the money.

In the sparsely settled republic, Texans could easily evade the few direct taxes their congress did levy. Because there was so little hard cash in Texas, the taxes were difficult to collect. Customs collections were the only real source of revenue for the republic. These taxes ranged from 1 percent on necessities such as breadstuffs to 50 percent on luxury items like silk. Throughout the life of the republic, customs revenue

accounted for between 50 and 80 percent of the government's income.

Bleak enough at the beginning, the financial affairs of the Republic of Texas only grew worse after Houston left office. The second president, Mirabeau B. Lamar, was much more extravagant with money. Already low, tariff duties were cut almost to a free-trade basis. Direct taxes and license taxes were levied, but were difficult to collect and brought small returns. In three years, the government took in a total of $1,083,661, but spent $4,855,213.

As soon as it achieved independence, the republic tried to stabilize its financial position by seeking a loan of $5 million. Finally it secured a meager loan of $457,380 from the Bank of the United States. Lamar wanted to create a gigantic Texas bank, owned and operated by the government, but never could get it established or funded by anyone.

Like many other governments that were broke, the republic decided to print money. Texas had more than $800,000 of treasury notes still in circulation that had already depreciated by 15 to 50 percent. The Texas Congress authorized government noninterest-bearing notes, known as **red backs**, because of the color on one side of each bill. Over $3,500,000 was issued. No limits were placed on the number that could be issued other than the amount of appropriations that the Texas Congress might vote. By the end of 1841 they were worth only 12 to 15 cents on the dollar.

THE COMING OF STATEHOOD

Pressures within the republic from Anglos with strong ties to the United States, the financial struggles of the small impoverished government, the constant threat from Mexico's attempts to recapture Texas, and pressure from expansionists within the United States all led to Texas joining the Union in 1846 after ten years of independence.

CONTENT QUESTIONS

1. What was an "empresario"?
2. Stephen F. Austin obtained a contract from the government of _____ to establish

a colony on _____ in _____.
This was the first _____ settlement in
Texas.

3. What three things did the Anglo colonists in
   Texas see as necessary for their survival?
4. Texas gained its independence in
   _____. At that time, its population
   was _____ Anglo and totaled
   _____.
5. What was "star money"?
6. The major source of tax revenue for the
   republic was _____.

DISCUSSION QUESTIONS

1. What were the differences between the
   Anglo-Saxon and Spanish systems of
   justice?
2. What were the financial problems of the
   Texas Republic?
3. What would Texas be like if the state had
   remained a republic?

40

THE CIVIL WAR AND RECONSTRUCTION IN TEXAS

Jo Ann Sweeney, Ph.D.[1]
and
Alan Garrett[2]

More Americans were killed in the Civil War than in any other war before or since. The Civil War has been called the first "modern" or "total" war in which not only armies were targeted for destruction, but also any civilian property of value to the war effort. The hardships faced by many, especially those in the South, are almost beyond modern comprehension.

From the ashes of the war arose the United States you know today, a more unified nation in which the supremacy of the federal government is never seriously questioned. The Civil War accelerated the United States' movement from an agrarian nation, composed primarily of small farmers, to the industrial giant and world leader it is today. Although Texas did not bear the brunt of the fighting, as did the Southern states east of the Mississippi River and the border states, it too was radically and forever changed by the Civil War and Reconstruction.

TEXAS BEFORE THE WAR

The decade before the Civil War was a period of great growth in Texas as people moved to the state seeking to improve their lives. Most of these new settlers were from the South. They brought from there their ideas concerning the proper relationship between federal and state governments, the correct organization of society, and the necessity of slavery. During this time, the state's population nearly tripled to over 600,000, approximately one-third of whom were slaves.

Despite the widespread acceptance of slavery, the vast majority of Texans did not own any slaves. Fewer than 25 percent of the citizens were slaveholders. Many Texans, however, saw slave ownership as their key to economic advancement. During the 1850s, land was relatively cheap. Slaves enabled a farmer or planter to work more land. With more land in production, and hence a greater income, the farmer could acquire more slaves, enabling him to obtain still more land. This process was generally accepted as a quick road to not only wealth, but also power. Between 1850 and 1860, the percentage of state offices held by slave owners increased from approximately 40 percent to over 50 percent. Slave owners also controlled about two-thirds of the state's wealth and were responsible for over 90 percent of its cotton production.

Settlers expanded the frontier northwestward into the plans during the same decade. As they moved further from established areas, they began to encounter an increasing number of Indian raids. The army proved to be generally ineffective in protecting the settlers from the Indians. Also during the 1850s, Mexican bandits captured

[1]Assistant Dean, School of Education; Director, Center for the Advancement of Economic Education, University of Texas at Austin.
[2]Graduate Assistant, Center for the Advancement of Economic Education, University of Texas at Austin.

and briefly held Brownsville. No help was provided by the federal government.

As 1860 neared, Texans became increasingly disenchanted with the government in Washington. Most accepted the Southern view of states' rights. Failure to provide needed military assistance accelerated the federal government's fall from favor in Texas. The national government was also beginning to be viewed as an enemy of slavery, believed by many to be a necessary basis of the Southern and Texan economies and ways of life.

SECESSION

After Lincoln was elected president in 1860, Southern states, starting with South Carolina, began to secede from the Union. With their ties to the Southern states and long-standing dissatisfaction with the federal government, Texas secessionists began their attempts to remove the state from the Union.

At first the governor, Sam Houston, refused to call the legislature into special session to consider secession. Secessionists then had counties send delegates to a convention to consider the matter. Ninety-two of the 122 counties then in existence sent delegates. Houston called the legislature into session to have them declare the convention illegal, but instead they sanctioned it.

The convention passed an Ordinance of Secession on February 1, 1861, with 166 delegates voting for it and 8 against. A statewide election was held on February 23, 1861, to approve or reject the ordinance. Over three-quarters of the voters approved, and Texas withdrew from the Union on March 2, 1861, the twenty-fifth anniversary of independence from Mexico.

Texas then joined the Confederate States of America. Houston, the hero of San Jacinto and twice president of the Republic of Texas, refused to take an oath of loyalty to the Confederacy. He was removed from office and replaced with a secessionist. The stage was set for the great struggle to determine the destiny of the nation.

TEXAS AND THE WAR

Very few military engagements took place in Texas during the Civil War. Most of the fighting was confined to the coastal areas as the Union attempted to close Confederate ports and eliminate foreign trade. Federal troops captured and briefly held Galveston and Brownsville before being expelled by Confederate forces. A Union invasion force of over 5,000 men was defeated at Sabine Pass by 47 Texans, preventing the capture of Houston and Beaumont. Texans thwarted an attempted invasion of the northeastern part of the state during the Red River campaign in Louisiana. The last battle of the war was fought at Palmito Ranch near Brownsville on May 11, 1865, more than a month after Lee's surrender at Appomattox, Virginia.

While no fighting of any significance to the outcome of the war occurred in Texas, the state's contribution to the Confederacy was significant. An estimated 60,000 to 90,000 Texans served in the Confederate armed forces, approximately one-third of them east of the Mississippi River. The others defended the coasts and frontiers of the state, took part in engagements in Louisiana and Arkansas, and attempted to capture California (this endeavor failed at the Battle of Glorietta Pass, in northern New Mexico). Texans were involved in every major campaign of the war and were highly valued by Confederate leaders.

Texas' economic support was vital to the Confederate war effort. Since Texas, the "backdoor of the Confederacy," was relatively undisturbed by invaders, many planters were able to maintain production of cotton for export and farmers continued to grow food crops. The long border with Mexico provided a trade route which could not be closed by Union blockade. Cotton could be shipped across the border and overland to Mexican ports, where it was sold to raise much needed funds. Imports to the Confederacy likewise came through Mexico and across the Rio Grande to Texas. Such trade, however, was unable to keep up with demand, and severe shortages of consumer goods developed in Texas and throughout the South.

In addition to the shortages, inflation, lack of manpower, and other problems prevalent throughout the Confederacy, Texans were in the unique position of facing three enemies simultaneously. Union troops blockaded the Gulf ports and occasionally attempted to invade these cities. A genuine fear of a Mexican invasion across the Rio Grande existed in the state. The Texas revolution had occurred only a quarter of a century earlier, and for many the old hostilities had not ended at San Jacinto. The greatest threat was that from Indians along the northwestern frontier. The withdrawal of federal troops at the onset of the war left this entire region unprotected for a while. Many Texas troops were required to try to keep the Indians in check. During the Civil War years, Indian attacks on settlers increased greatly, and the settlers were in many cases forced to move back to more established areas. Many of those who remained banded together and built private forts for protection. In some places, Indians forced the frontier back by about one hundred miles. More damage during the years 1861–65 in Texas resulted from Indian attacks than from the actual hostilities of the war.

Texans suffered many fewer hardships than did those in Confederate states east of the Mississippi River. The state was spared the destruction that others endured. The Civil War did, however, halt and to some extent reverse the progress the state had been making since its entry into the Union in 1845. The state and its people survived to face the uncertainties of Reconstruction.

RECONSTRUCTION

Reconstruction began when 1,800 federal troops arrived at Galveston on June 19, 1865. The emancipation of all slaves and the appointment by President Andrew Johnson of a new governor were announced. Johnson sought to follow Lincoln's policy of quick assimilation of the former Confederate States back into the Union. The state held a constitutional convention in February 1866 and produced a document very similar to that written in 1845. The convention included in its new constitution the abolition of slavery and limited civil rights for blacks. Johnson approved the constitution in 1866 and declared the rebellion in Texas to be over.

Many Texans assumed that, since the war and Reconstruction were finished, life would soon return to what it was prior to 1861. The next legislature passed several laws curtailing the rights of blacks and appointed two secessionists to serve in the United States Senate. During this

time, Johnson's power had been greatly reduced and the Radical Republicans in Congress sought to impose their rule upon the nation and punish the South. In March 1867, they divided the former Confederacy into five military districts, each ruled by an army officer wielding virtual dictatorial powers. Elected state officials were removed from office, and Radical Republicans and those holding similar views were appointed. Voting requirements were rewritten to exclude most of the white males of the state.

A new constitution was written in 1869 which gave full rights to black citizens. The Radical Republican-controlled legislature passed a number of unpopular laws in 1870. State militia and police forces under the direct control of the governor were formed, the elections of 1870 were postponed until 1872, and the governor was given the power to appoint over 8,500 local officials. These laws were so despised by Texans that they became known (along with several others) as the **Obnoxious Acts**. Violence, corruption, rising taxes, and the harshness of Radical Republican rule angered many Texans. The Radicals lost control of the legislature to moderates and Democrats in 1872, and executive powers began to be reduced. Democrats regained the governorship in 1874. Radical pleas to Washington for help were unanswered, and Reconstruction was over.

THE AFTERMATH

Another constitution, the one we have today, was written in 1876. This document severely limits executive powers, for it was written by men who had suffered the abuses which can occur when too much power is centered in the hands of one individual. Agriculture rebounded during and after Reconstruction. The cattle industry began at this time and grew rapidly. The value of manufactured goods produced in Texas in 1870 was almost double that of 1860. United States Army units began to protect the frontier again. The battle against the Indians culminated in the Red River War of 1874, during which Col. Ranald S. Mackenzie, the ablest Indian fighter of his time, defeated the last "wild" Indians in Texas at Palo Duro Canyon and forced them to withdraw to reservations.

Thus by 1876 Texas was free of Indian threats and was once again ruled according to the wishes of its citizens. The economy had been rebuilt and was improving, and the hardships of the Civil War and Reconstruction were gone and the way paved for the state's transition into the modern age.

CONTENT QUESTIONS

1. Why was Texas spared the destruction endured in most of the rest of the South during the Civil War?
2. Who were the three major enemies faced by the Texans during the Civil War years?
3. Why was most fighting in Texas confined to the coastal areas?
4. What were three major contributions Texas made to the Confederate war effort?

5. Describe how the content of the 1876 Texas constitution reflected the Reconstruction years.

DISCUSSION QUESTIONS

1. How did President Johnson's plan for Reconstruction differ from that of the Radical Republicans?
2. Discuss how daily life in Texas was affected by the Civil War.
3. Using what you know about Texas and United States history, describe why the cattle industry did not develop in Texas until after the Civil War and why it did so quickly after that conflict.

41

COTTON, CATTLE, AND CRUDE OIL: TEXAS 1870–1910

Calvin A. Kent, Ph.D.[1]

Despite the romantic picture portrayed in novels and movies and on television shows, in the period between the Civil War and the turn of the century the overwhelming majority of Texans were poor—dirt poor. The Civil War had left a shattered state economy. Well over 90 percent of all Texans were subsistence farmers barely eking out enough from the land to feed themselves and their families. They lived in the most abject poverty, hoping only to be able to grow enough to sustain themselves and those who were dear to them until the next harvest. Theirs was the life of self-sufficient subsistence farming. The wheat they grew became their bread. Their animals supplied them with meat and milk. They grew cotton for their own clothes. Farmers produced for themselves and not for the market.

AGRICULTURE

There was very little commercial agriculture. With the exception of West Texas, where cattle was raised for the market, most farmers were self-sufficient in 1870. But the next thirty years would see all that change. Slowly, the self-sufficient farm would give way to commercial farming where the farmer specialized in a single farm product produced mainly for the market and not for home consumption. By 1900, the Texas econ-omy had undergone an incredible transformation from self-sufficiency to commercial agriculture. In 1870 less than half of Texas was settled, with only 61,125 farms. By the turn of the century the number of farms had grown to 352,190 and the entire state was populated.

Cotton

While cattle receives most of the attention in the movies and novels, it was not nearly as important to Texas as was cotton. Cotton was the dominant source of income for Texas farmers and for the state until the coming of the twentieth century. Cotton was an extremely demanding crop to grow. It required a large number of man-hours of back-breaking labor spent in the blistering Texas sun; first planting, then hoeing, and, last, picking the cotton. Despite this, cotton was popular for two reasons. First, there was always a market. Although gluts on the market from time to time would drive prices down, farmers could always sell what they produced at some price. The second reason for cotton's popularity was that it was a sure bet. No matter how bad the weather, the cotton crop always came through. Some years yields would be greater and other years much less. But cotton never failed the farmer. By the turn of the century cotton was produced over the entire state of Texas.

Second to cotton in terms of importance to the farmer was the production of wheat. Originally,

[1]Herman W. Lay Professor of Private Enterprise; Director, Center for Private Enterprise, Baylor University, Waco, Texas.

wheat was grown in Texas merely to provide bread for the farmer's family, but as the rest of the nation became urbanized and city stomachs needed bread, wheat production as a commercial crop slowly grew across the state. By the turn of the century wheat production was concentrated in the high plains of western Texas competing with cattle for the available land.

Cattle

All this is not to say that cattle ranching was not important, but its contribution to Texas folklore is greater than its contribution to the Texas economy. Nevertheless, this period gave Texas its most enduring symbol—the cowboy. Before cattle raising could be a serious occupation the Indians had to be subdued, the frontier secured, and the buffalo removed from the land suitable for cattle grazing. This was accomplished during the 1870s by the Texas Rangers who not only pacified the Indians, but eliminated the marauding Mexican bandits whose livelihood consisted of stealing Texas cattle. The buffalo were extinguished from the landscape by massive hunts. The hides were valuable, but hunters from the east flocked to Texas just for the opportunity to shoot a buffalo.

Cattle prices rose steadily during the 1870s and early 1880s. Rising incomes and increased industrialization in the eastern United States created a strong demand. These high prices caused a flood of new entrants into ranching. European investors were attracted to put their money into Texas cattle. Economic history repeated itself. The supply of beef grew so quickly that the demand was unable to keep up. Prices collapsed, and most of the large ranches went broke and were sold in smaller pieces to cotton and wheat farmers.

RAILROADS

During the 1870s and 1880s cattle was allowed to roam freely and was rounded up twice a year to be driven to markets. The long cattle drives were a relatively short-lived phenomenon and had practically ended by the middle of the 1880s. What brought about their demise was the rapid spread of the railroads across Texas. Track mileage dou-

bled between 1880 and 1890. The money that could be made in shipping both Texas cotton and cattle to markets in the eastern United States and Europe led to a tremendous boom in railroad development. Unfortunately, the boom brought with it corruption, and railroads soon became the object of the Texas agrarian movement.

Railroads made an important contribution to the Texas economy. Many of Texas' current cities were railheads established to service railroad equipment and their crews. Cities like Fort Worth, El Paso, Abilene, Laredo and Amarillo owed their growth to the railroads. The railroads changed the trade patterns of the state. Prior to their arrival, trade had gone to the river cities or overland to the gulf ports such as Galveston. The railroads reversed the flow. Now crops, cattle, and other products could be transported overland through the northeast at a significant savings in both time and money.

THE AGRARIAN REVOLT

To understand the agrarian revolt one must first understand the conditions under which Texas farmers labored. After the Civil War there were very few banks in Texas, and farmers needed to borrow money to put in their crops and buy the necessary equipment and supplies their operations demanded.

The Crop Lien System

The result was the **crop lien system,** in which the so-called **furnishing merchant** would supply the farmer with the needed essentials (tools, seed, clothes, and food) and would hold a lien on his crop as security or collateral until the loan was repaid. Furnishing merchants were the object of much ridicule and condemnation as they often charged farmers high rates of interest and high prices for the merchandise. The farmer often found himself perpetually in debt to the furnishing merchant, since the income from his crop was insufficient to repay the debt owed. In defense of the furnishing merchant, it must be pointed out that the business was highly risky because there was no assurance that the farmer would ever be able to pay. The cost to the merchant of transporting goods from the east and supplying them to farmers was high.

Despite the crop lien system, Texas agriculture did evolve from self-sufficiency to commercial production. This was accomplished by larger and larger spreads which could be farmed or ranched more efficiently. Charles Goodnight established the JA Ranch in the Texas panhandle in the 1870s as the first large-scale commercial cattle operation in the state, and others soon followed his example.

The Range Wars

Inevitably, conflict resulted. The cotton and wheat farmers sought to prevent the free-roaming cattle from destroying their crops. In the late 1870s barbed wire was introduced by John W. "Bet-a-million" Gates, and farmers flocked to buy the product to fence off their land to keep the "critters" out. Range wars soon developed between the open-range cattlemen and the settled farmers. The farmers would fence the cattle off from water and place fences across the trails used to move the herds. In retaliation, the cattlemen would cut the fences of the farmers. The news of the violence which accompanied these wars gave bad publicity to the state and discouraged immigration and settlement. It required a special session of the Texas legislature to end the practice.

Political Action by Farmers

The range wars were not the primary concern of most farmers. As commercial agriculture increased the supply of cotton, wheat, and cattle, the prices of these products fell. Farmers faced poverty in the midst of plenty. The better their production of crops or cattle, the lower the prices they would receive. Lacking a sophisticated understanding of economics, farmers blamed their problems on the banks and merchants that charged high interest rates and prices. Later, the railroads would feel the farmers' fury, since the railroads paid low prices to the farmers for the grain and cattle which they bought for shipment out of state, and charged high rates to the farmers for their transportation. Groups such as the National Grange, The Knights of Labor, The Farmers Alliance, the Greenback Party, and the

Populists all claimed the allegiance of the farmers by demanding easier credit and regulation of the railroads.

The Texas constitution had prohibited state-chartered banks. The farmers felt that the banks with national charters could only loan their money at high rates of interest because the national banks had to back their loans with reserves of gold and silver. During this period many farmers supported the Greenback Party, which championed an expanded money supply not based on either gold or silver.

But farmers were even more upset about the railroads. The owners of railroads colluded to pay the farmers low prices when their crops or livestock arrived at the terminal. Most towns had service from only one railroad. The costs of transport many miles to the next railhead were prohibitive. So the farmers had no choice but to accept the price. In addition, the railroads exercised their monopoly power by exacting high shipping rates, further angering the farmers. While overproduction may have been the major cause of the Texas farmers' poverty, the railroad companies contributed to the farmers' plight.

The Grange, the Farmers' Alliance, and the Populists were the organizations which led the agrarian revolt. In 1891 the legislature created a Railroad Commission whose job was to regulate all aspects of railroad transportation in the state. The powers of the Railroad Commission were increased in the following decades to include the oil industry, oil pipelines, and trucking.

THE BEGINNINGS OF THE OIL INDUSTRY

In 1901 Texas history changed. On January 10, which is the most important date in Texas economic history, Anthony Lucas brought in the Spindletop oil well three miles north of Beaumont. Spindletop was not the first oil well in Texas. Over 300 wells in Corsicana were producing 500,000 barrels a year by the turn of the century and total state production was 836,000 barrels a year. But the production at Spindletop exceeded that amount within a few days. Its first year of production saw an output of 3.2 million barrels of oil. By the following year oil production across the state was up to 21 million barrels per year.

What followed was an oil boom with hundreds, even thousands of new wells being drilled each year. This growth in the oil industry created an explosion of demand for related business. Steel had to be secured for pipes and derricks. Railroad track and pipelines had to be built. Banking was needed as the new firms sought credit. As new oil companies were started they issued stock to be sold to the public which created jobs for brokers. All of this in turn created demands for retail stores and warehousing. Carpenters were needed to build the boom towns as were doctors and barbers to service them. By the time of the First World War, the oilman had replaced the cowboy as the source of Texas legends.

Supply quickly exceeded demand and the price dropped to 3 cents a barrel. Prior to this time, oil had been used principally as a lubricant, or refined to produce kerosene for household lighting. The low price encouraged railroads, factories, and steamships to switch from coal boilers to engines that used oil as a fuel. This conversion from coal to oil supported the Texas oil industry until Henry Ford produced a car after World War I that was affordable for most Americans.

Spindletop was the end of the agricultural era in Texas. After 1901, oil and related industries dominated the Texas economy for over eighty years. Farming slipped into a distant second place. Oil boom towns sprang up across the state and the interests of the oilmen replaced the interests of the farmer as the prime concern of politicians.

CONTENT QUESTIONS

1. Describe Texas farmers in 1870.
2. For Texas agriculture the dominant source of income was _____. Why was this product popular?
3. Before cattle ranching could be established in Texas what three things had to happen?
4. What event caused the end of the cattle drives?
5. What started the range wars?
6. What regulatory agency was created in 1891? What industries does it now regulate?

DISCUSSION QUESTIONS

1. Explain how the crop lien system worked.
2. Why were farmers unhappy during this period? What did the farmers want done about their problems?
3. How has the oil industry affected Texas?

42

THE GREAT DEPRESSION
George Green, Ph.D.[1]

The **Great Depression** of the 1930s was the most serious economic crisis in the history of the United States and of Texas. Some sections of the nation and the state were hit harder than others, but no area escaped the hard times. Texas was still mainly rural, and many Texans thought the state would not suffer from downturns in the business cycle. Like many Americans during the first two or three years of the Depression, they tried to deny the existence and the seriousness of the crash. Texas newspaper editors in 1930 and 1931, for instance, proclaimed prosperity. By 1932, however, hard reality could not be ignored, and most Texans admitted that there was an economic emergency that might last for a long time.

Actually, many Texans had been living in depressed conditions since World War I. The tremendous demand for agricultural products during the conflict generated prosperity for Texas farmers, but overproduction afterwards caused prices to drop. In the 1920s as well as the early 1930s farmers often hauled cotton to the gin and discovered that they would not receive enough for it to pay ginning costs. Many farmers would then dump the cotton along the roads to rot. Sometimes corn fetched such a low price that it was burned for fuel instead of sold. By 1931 or 1932 most Texas farmers realized that overproduction was the basic agricultural problem and that only the federal government could do much about it. Many abandoned farming altogether. Forty per-

cent of the state's population lived on farms in 1930, but only a third did so by 1940.

IMPACT AND EXTENT

Meanwhile, as a pitiful indicator of the hard times, tramps and other transients wandered through Texas' farms and cities. Looking for work, whole families were often reduced to begging from house to house. Some were children, traveling alone. Because of its warmer climate and major east-west highways and railroads, Texas attracted many transients from out of state. Many towns and private agencies, overwhelmed by the volume of poverty and joblessness, refused to help transients, and some could not even help local citizens.

Texans still adhered to the rugged individualism philosophy of frontier times, and some considered it so humiliating to seek assistance from others that they preferred to endure cold and hunger. Texans were also reluctant to support relief activities because it might create a segment of the population that would refuse to work in the future. Others thought that public relief was an error because people should face the consequences of their refusal to prepare for hard times. Public opinion gradually changed, though, as people realized that they were the victims of political and economic forces beyond their control.

City charities and private agencies, including churches and the Salvation Army, attempted to render assistance through soup kitchens and

[1]Professor of History, University of Texas at Arlington.

commissaries, but their efforts were hopelessly inadequate and disorganized. These attempts were also sometimes humiliating, requiring answers to personal questions in exchange for miniscule amounts of very plain provisions. In the depth of the Depression in 1932 there may have been 400,000 Texans unemployed, 100,000 of whom were penniless. Swarms of indigents sought protection in abandoned buildings, shanties made of discarded boxes, and caves. Houston announced that there were no longer enough relief funds available for whites, and that Negroes and Mexicans were no longer eligible for relief and were being told to shift for themselves. Most Texans and Americans gradually came to believe that the federal government would have to provide the necessary relief.

Local institutions were hit hard. In 1934 Beaumont cut school expenditures by almost one-half and turned off the street lights. In San Antonio, school teachers whose husbands earned $2,000 per year or more were not rehired. Even many churches were forced to close.

THE GOVERNMENT'S RESPONSE

Organized groups took up the call for federal responsibility. Farmers clamored for federal help. The Texas Municipal League predicted bankruptcy for many of the state's cities unless the federal government took action immediately. Texas labor unions called on Congress to lower unemployment. Bankers, who had never before favored intervention from Washington or Austin, demanded congressional and state aid.

Speaker of the House John Garner and Senators Morris Sheppard and Tom Connally, all of whom were Democrats from Texas, helped push a public works bill through Congress. It would have provided work relief for hundreds of thousands of the unemployed. Republican President Herbert Hoover clung to the belief that charity should remain a private, local matter and vetoed the bill. The President, however, did establish the Reconstruction Finance Corporation in 1932 to provide loans to banks, insurance companies, and other businesses. Through 1938 it loaned over $114 million in Texas, greatly stimulating the state's economy.

Hoover and the Republican party had taken credit for prosperity since 1921, and in the early 1930s were forced to accept the political blame for the hard times. Hobo shacks became known as "Hoover Hotels," while jackrabbits were "Hoover Hogs." Texans also became more resentful of banks and businesses for such problems as high interest rates and the maldistribution of wealth. As unemployment became more widespread, criticism of foreign groups increased, aimed especially at migrants from Mexico who would work for lower wages and accept lower living standards than legal residents.

To cope with the Depression, a majority of Texans embraced ideas and programs that indicated a change in their thinking. The old ideas of extreme self-reliance, business dominance of the economy, and small inactive governments were abandoned. Demonstrations of the unemployed occurred in Texas' major cities, and a number of Texans were highly critical of the capitalist system, but most of the criticism was channeled into support of the Democratic party and Franklin Roosevelt in 1932. Roosevelt and his Texas running mate John Garner received 89 percent of the votes cast in the state.

OIL AND TIMBER

Of all the state's industries, petroleum notably defied the sluggish economy. In the autumn of 1930 veteran wildcatter C. M. ("Dad") Joiner hit oil near Overton, tapping into the immense East Texas field, and triggered a boom. Thousands of successful wells soon led to overproduction, with oil dumped on the market for as little as ten cents a barrel. The Texas Railroad Commission tried to conserve the resource and stabilize prices by limiting production, but it was hindered for several years by court suits filed by irate small producers and the running of illegal "hot oil." For a time, state troopers shut down the field and suppressed violence. Gradually the situation was brought under control, and the East Texas field proved to be the greatest private sector stimulus in the state. Indeed, oil and oil refining became a mainstay of the Texas economy.

The forest products industry—particularly the new commercial utilization of yellow pine—was also centered in East Texas and was prosperous.

THE NEW DEAL AND TEXAS

Roosevelt's New Deal instituted work relief programs. The **Civilian Conservation Corps** enlisted young men to plant trees, build bridges and roads, and devise flood and erosion controls. By the spring of 1936 some 63,000 Texans were enrolled in 77 Texas camps, and $50 million had been injected into the state's economy through this program. Even larger appropriations were expended by the **Federal Emergency Relief Administration**, which helped migrants, rural students, and many others. By March 1939 the **Public Works Administration** had completed over six hundred projects in Texas, had another three hundred underway, and had spent over $100 million in the state. The **Works Progress Administration** launched thousands of projects and had spent about $180 million by the summer of 1939 on the construction of Texas streets and highways, public buildings, city and roadside parks, and airports.

The state government shared in relief efforts. In 1933 the state adopted a constitutional amendment authorizing up to $20 million in bonds for relief of unemployment. The **bread bonds** were sold during the administrations of Miriam A. ("Ma") Ferguson and Jimmie Allred.

Business recovery in 1933 was promoted by the **National Industrial Recovery Administration** (NIRA), which set aside antitrust legislation and allowed industries to come together and write codes of conduct, that is, to set prices. The price codes helped stabilize many businesses by insuring a profit. The law also helped workers by establishing a 35-hour-maximum work week, forty cents an hour minimum wage, and the right of collective bargaining through unions. Most Texas employers soon opposed the law because they believed the business emergency was over by 1934. The NIRA was struck down by the U.S. Supreme Court in 1935.

Scores of banks in Texas had failed since 1929, wiping out millions of dollars in savings. Banking recovery was brought about largely by the **Federal Deposit Insurance Corporation**, which guaranteed individual deposits up to $5,000. Recovery on the farms was affected by a federal program which paid farmers to reduce their output. In 1935 Texas farmers withheld about 5.5 million acres from the production of cotton,

wheat, and corn, and their income was 58 percent higher than in 1932. The **Federal Surplus Relief Corporation** distributed agricultural surpluses to impoverished families, including 26 million pounds of food in Texas in 1938. The combined efforts of all the relief and recovery agencies, however, did not always reach the destitute family in the street. The editor of the Fort Worth *Union Banner* wrote in 1938 that as he looked out of his office window he saw men, women, and children prowling through garbage cans in the alley looking for food.

New Deal reform measures also had an impact on the Texas economy. The **National Labor Relations Act** prohibited employers from discriminating against union members in hiring and firing, allowed workers to join unions, and required companies to engage in collective bargaining with them. The new **Congress of Industrial Organizations** (CIO) attempted to organize workers in basic industries. Perhaps their most spectacular success in Texas during the Depression was among San Antonio's pecan shellers, who earned an average of $2.50 per week! This industry was so depressed that it was the only one in the nation that was forced to mechanize by the passage of another reform measure, the Fair Labor Standards Act in 1938, which set 25 cents an hour as the minimum wage.

The craft unions in the Texas State Federation of Labor showed how organized labor coped with the hard times. The plumbers' and printers' unions in Austin rented a building downtown, installed beds and baths, and provided a free night's lodging and clothes wash to unemployed craftsmen who were seeking work or passing through. Dallas Southwestern Bell Telephone operators agreed to work only three or four days a week for over two years so that jobs could be spread out among more people.

THE NEW DEAL: AN EVALUATION

Altogether, Texas received $717 million from the federal government between March 4, 1933, and January 1, 1938. The receipt of nearly $3 million per week gave purchasing power to desperate Texans. It directly benefited the state's businesses. The conservative *Texas Weekly* noted that there was a close correlation between relief funds and retail sales, because those on relief spent almost all of the money just to survive. Another boon to Texas was the tremendous improvement of the infrastructure, that is, the dams, roads, parks, and public buildings that touched every county in the state.

Conservative critics at the time asserted that the New Deal had gone too far, that it had foisted off a permanent welfare system that sapped people's incentive to work, vastly increased the national debt, and failed to restore the nation to prosperity at the end of the 1930s. Some critics of more recent times, on the other hand, argue that the New Deal programs were half-measures that did not go far enough, that they delivered no permanent solutions for such problems as corporate power and unemployment. Most Texans at the time believed that no programs would have worked any better and that federal relief, recovery, and reform steps were necessary before the nation could come to grips with the harshest economic era since Reconstruction.

CONTENT QUESTIONS

1. What caused the farm problem in Texas after World War I?

2. Why did Texas attract transients during the Great Depression? What problem did this create?

3. What agency did President Hoover create during the depression, and how did it help Texas?

4. Which two Texas industries prospered during the depression?

5. How did the Public Works Administration help Texas?

6. Which agency restored confidence in Texas banks, and how did it do this?

DISCUSSION QUESTIONS

1. How did public opinion in Texas change over the course of the Great Depression?

2. What happened to the Texas labor movement during the Great Depression?

3. How possible is another great depression today?

43
THE TEXAS ECONOMY DURING THE 1940s AND 1950s

Calvin A. Kent, Ph.D.[1]

As was true for the rest of the nation, the Great Depression did not end in Texas until the coming of the Second World War. While the entire nation was affected by the conflict, no single state was more heavily impacted than the state of Texas. Texas sent the highest percentage of its population into military service. Almost 750,000 men and 12,000 women served their country. Although Texas represented only 5 percent of the nation's population in 1940, it provided 7 percent of its soldiers and an equally high percentage of its war casualties.

WORLD WAR II

The war was good for the Texas economy. Texas was home for 15 major military posts, which saw 1.25 million soldiers trained. In addition, several prisoner-of-war camps were located within the state. Texas became the center for the Army Air Corps. The state's clear skies and vast open spaces made it an ideal training site for airmen. Randolph Field, Kelly Field, and Brooks Field, all at San Antonio, were enlarged and expanded. Ellington Field near Houston was rebuilt, and new facilities were established at Wichita Falls, San Angelo, Lubbock, Midland, San Marcos, Amarillo, Waco, and elsewhere. It was not surprising that the Air Force training command was located in Fort Worth.

[1]Herman W. Lay Professor of Private Enterprise; Director, Center for Private Enterprise, Baylor University, Waco, Texas.

The economic impact was not limited to military facilities. The Texas oil industry expanded spectacularly and by the war's end Texas was supplying 50 percent of the nation's demand for petroleum, and over 80 percent of the nation's oil was being refined in the state. Manufacturing employment grew by 250 percent. This period saw the beginning of the Texas aircraft industry. Shipbuilding along the Texas coast also grew dramatically and the Bay area became the center for the United States' petrochemical industry.

The combined effects of 750,000 Texans in the armed services and the growth of industry led to a shortage of workers and to rising wages. That shortage was principally alleviated by the entry of women into the workforce taking industrial jobs previously performed by men, and the migration of Mexican workers to work in nonsensitive jobs throughout Texas.

It was widely anticipated that when World War II was over that the economy would slide into another depression without the stimulus of defense spending. This was not the case for the nation as a whole, and it certainly was not the case for the state of Texas. World War II had transformed Texas into an industrial giant and had created the conditions which would lead to a period of unprecedented prosperity. In the late 1940s the wartime industries continued to expand to meet the demands of the postwar growth brought on by the returning servicemen.

A major factor explaining the economic growth of Texas during the latter part of the 1940s and

188

throughout the fifties and sixties was the power of the Texas congressional delegation. During the Depression Texans had elected a strong slate of pro-Roosevelt Democrats. Many of them enjoyed long tenures and became chairmen of important committees. Texas' Sam Rayburn became Speaker of the House of Representatives and Lyndon Johnson became the Senate majority leader, the vice-president and, later, the President of the United States. The Texas delegation never forgot who sent them to Washington. A steady stream of federal money, not only for defense, but also for agriculture, highways, commerce, and industry nourished the Texas economy.

The growth of the Texas economy caused growth in state government. In 1949 the fifty-first Texas Legislature enacted a variety of new laws designed to remedy many of the social ills of the state. It provided for improvements in the institutions for the mentally ill and the modernization of the state prison system. It also provided for the reorganization of the state public school system by requiring that school districts provide a twelfth year in their high schools, that teachers meet certain minimum standards, and that students stay in class for at least nine months of each calendar year. To pay the price, the Texas legislature passed its first billion dollar budget.

THE 1950s

Demands for even better state services for prisons, education, highways, and hospitals continued into the 1950s. The legislature then, as now, was eager to pass expenditure bills, but was reluctant to raise additional taxes to pay for them. As a result, the state continually looked for new ways to raise revenue. One method was the collection of oil royalties from the drilling on state lands. During the 1940s the Texas oil industry had gone offshore into the Gulf of Mexico. Texans claimed that the state's land extended twelve miles out into the Gulf and that all oil extracted from these **tidelands** was subject to a royalty payable to the state treasury. By 1950 over $10 million a year in lease money for these oil wells was coming to the Texas Treasury.

The U.S. Supreme Court ruled that Texas did not have claim to the tidelands oil. The strength of the Texas delegation in Congress made it possible for legislation to pass both houses to reverse that Supreme Court decision, but the legislation was vetoed by President Truman in both 1946 and 1952.

During his campaign for the presidency, native son Dwight Eisenhower promised to sign such legislation if it were presented to him. Because of this, many Texas Democrats led by Governor Allen Shivers refused to support the Democratic nominee for President, Adlai Stevenson, who supported Truman's position. As a result, Texans voted for General Eisenhower. One of Eisenhower's first acts as President was to deed the tidelands to Texas, securing to the state this lucrative source of revenue to fund education.

This election began a political trend that has persisted until the current day. No Democrat has ever won the presidency without carrying Texas.

The 1950s saw a continued expansion of the state's industrial base. Petroleum remained the state's economic cornerstone. Cheap and abundant electricity attracted the aluminum industry to Texas. The cold war assured a high level of defense spending which Texas firms were already equipped to handle. Perhaps the most significant event was in 1959 when researchers at Texas Instruments developed the first usable microchip. This invention was to propel Texas to the forefront of the nation's high-tech states in future years.

During the 1950s, despite drought and oil gluts, the state grew increasingly prosperous. The middle and upper income groups grew richer, but the underclass, including many Blacks and Hispanics, remained unaffected by the growing prosperity.

Political corruption and economics were tied together in the 1950s by two major scandals. A significant number of Texas insurance companies failed, leaving the holders of their policies without recourse. During the subsequent investigation it was found that several Texas legislators had been on the payrolls of these insurance companies and had used their influence to pass lax laws and to prevent adequate enforcement of the laws. In another notable incident the Texas Land Commissioner, who previously had been elected to nine consecutive terms, was convicted of taking bribes and sent to the penitentiary.

The industrialization of Texas during this period was uneven. It was primarily based on the exploitation of the state's natural resources—lumber, oil, gas, minerals, aluminum, and land. The large size of the state, its sparse population, its inferior transportation system, and the shortages of water and iron did not allow for the development of a diversified industrial base, as was the case in the midwestern states and the eastern part of the nation. As a result, the prosperity of Texas was highly dependent upon forces over which Texans had no control. Like the underdeveloped countries of today, Texans were at the mercy of the market forces which set the price for these natural resources. When demand was high (as was the case for oil, lumber, and food products), the state prospered. But when demand fell off, the state floundered. This was particularly true in the oil industry where many poor Texas farmers and ranchers became millionaires overnight when oil was discovered on their land. By the mid-1950s, over $0.5 billion in oil royalties was going to Texas landowners.

A LOOK AT THE 1960s

The 1960s saw some diversification in Texas' economy. But there was a continued reliance in Texas upon extractive industries for its prosperity. High-tech firms were beginning to grow, but their major contribution was to come in later decades. Following the assassination of President John Kennedy on November 22, 1963, Lyndon Johnson ascended to the presidency. Having a Texan in the White House insured the continuing flow of federal money to the state. The prime example was the establishment of the National Aeronautics and Space Administration's manned spacecraft center in Harris County south of Houston. That facility is now named the Lyndon B. Johnson Space Center in honor of the President who made it possible. The result was to move Texas to the forefront of the space age and to further strengthen its claim as being a high-tech leader.

Rising demand in the United States and worldwide for oil and lumber products during the 1950s and 1960s continued to support the prosperity of the state. But as was the case in the 1940s, this growth did not benefit everyone. The oil industry is one which employs a relatively

small number of people in relatively high-paying jobs. Economists say the oil and petrochemical industries are not "labor intensive," but "capital intensive": they rely extensively on high-tech drilling and refining equipment and plants. As a result, the oil and petrochemical boom brought great wealth to landowners fortunate enough to have "black gold" on their farms, to the highly skilled workers in the oil and petrochemical industries, and to the investors wise enough to put their money into this boom industry.

Fueled by rising revenues from the taxation of oil and gas, Texas politicians during the 1940s and 1950s lived in the best of all possible worlds. They were able to expand government services without having to significantly raise taxes. The growth of state spending exceeded the growth in state income. In 1961 the legislature was forced to pass the state's first sales tax to pay for the increased costs of education. That tax has now become the major source of state revenue.

Agriculture also changed dramatically during this period. By the 1960s, the **tenant farmer system** had almost disappeared. Under this system landowners did not work their property, but instead leased it to tenants. The tenants paid rent to the landowners by giving them a percentage or share of the crop that was raised on the land. Many of the tenant farmers were very poor and could lease only a few acres of land. By 1960, the size of Texas farms had more than doubled and mechanization had forced most of the tenant farmers off the land. Those who remained were themselves highly skilled and recognized operators. The result was that while farming became more prosperous, many tenant farmers were forced off the land and driven to the cities, where they became part of the urban poor. Faced with racial discrimination, many of the Blacks began a migration out of Texas to the northern industrial areas where they hoped to find jobs.

CONCLUSION

In 1973 when the Organization of Petroleum Exporting Countries (OPEC) imposed a world oil boycott, oil prices skyrocketed. Texas was the chief beneficiary of OPEC's action. The decade of the 1970s until the collapse of oil prices in 1981 became the most prosperous in Texas' history. Events of the 1980s have demonstrated the weakness of the Texas economy during the forties, fifties, and sixties. Its overreliance upon the extraction of a single commodity for its prosperity left it extremely vulnerable to forces over which it had no control. Much effort will have to be expended in the years to come to diversify the state's industrial base.

CONTENT QUESTIONS

1. How did the Texas congressional delegation help the state during the 1940s and 1950s?

2. What industries were the base of the state's economy during this period?

3. What two scandals occurred in the 1950s?

DISCUSSION QUESTIONS

1. In what ways did World War II affect the Texas economy?

2. What was the tidelands dispute, and how would Texas have been affected if the election of 1952 had gone differently?

3. During this period, why was Texas like an underdeveloped country of today?

44

BOOM AND BUST: THE TEXAS ECONOMY IN RECENT DECADES

Patrick Kelso, Ph.D.,[1]
and
Barry L. Duman, Ph.D.[2]

The last thirty years of Texas' history have been characterized by growth that was far greater than that experienced in the nation as a whole. But this growth was to come to an abrupt end by the early 1980s. The cause of the boom and the cause of the bust were the same: the oil industry. The forces of supply and demand in world markets set the price of oil and the prosperity of the state.

THE 1960s

Texas in 1960 was a populous, urbanized, and rather prosperous state. Its almost ten million people made it the nation's tenth largest state. Seventy-five percent of this population lived in urban places (cities of more than 2,500 population). Personal income per person was $1,880 in 1960 prices, which would be about $5,000 in 1988 prices.

A look at the basic economic structure provides an insight into the state's economic situation. The structure of an economy indicates to what extent it is specializing in the various types of economic activity, such as agriculture or manu-facturing. The structure of a state's economy is determined to a great extent by the structure of the nation's economy. Insight into the unique character of a state's economy can be obtained by comparing state economic specialization with national economic specialization.

Table 44-1 presents 1960 Texas employment by economic sector as a percentage of total employment. It indicates that most Texas workers were employed in manufacturing (16 percent), retail and wholesale trade (21 percent) and services (22 percent). Agriculture, construction, and transportation together employed a further 24 percent of Texas workers.

The second column of Table 44-1 indicates how closely the Texas economic structure mirrors the United States economic structure. The percentage of Texans employed in each sector is divided by the percentage of the U.S. workforce employed in the same sector. If the Texas structure were identical to the U.S. structure, all the numbers would be 1.00—meaning that the same percentage of the labor force worked in those sectors in Texas as in the United States. Numbers ranging between 0.90 and 1.10 may be regarded as approximately equal to 1.00. Numbers greater than 1.10 mean that Texas employment is more heavily concentrated in that line of production than is United States employment. Numbers less than 0.90 mean that Texas is less

[1]Associate Professor of Economics, West Texas State University, Canyon, Texas.
[2]Professor of Economics; Head of the Departments of Accounting, Economics, and Finance, West Texas State University, Canyon, Texas.

TABLE 44-1
Texas Economic Structure
1960

Sector	Texas % of Total Employment	Texas % of Employment divided by U.S. % of Employment	Texas % of state income divided by U.S. % of nat. income
Agriculture	8.8%	1.31	1.28
Mining (oil & gas)	3.0%	2.86	5.25
Construction	7.6%	1.27	0.98
Manufacturing	16.2%	0.64	0.65
Transportation and Utilities	7.4%	1.13	1.09
Wholesale and Retail Trade	21.2%	1.23	1.03
Finance and Real Estate	4.2%	0.94	0.89
Services	22.2%	1.10	0.88
Government	4.7%	1.00	1.07

Sources: U.S. Department of Commerce, Bureau of the Census, *Social and Economic Characteristics of Texas* (Washington, D.C.: U.S. Government Printing Office, 1960); Office of the Governor of Texas, Texas 2000 Commission, *Texas Past and Future: A Survey* (1981).

concentrated in that line of production. The third column of Table 44-1 provides the same comparison between sources of Texas income and sources of U.S. income.

Columns 2 and 3 of Table 44-1 lead to these conclusions about the structure of the 1960 Texas economy: Texas was more heavily specialized in agriculture and mining (oil and gas) and much less specialized in manufacturing than was the nation; construction, trade, transportation, and public utilities were relatively important sources of jobs but not so important as sources of income.

The decade of the 1960s saw impressive growth in the Texas economy. The U.S. economy enjoyed an unusually long and strong recovery between 1962 and 1969, and Texas participated fully in the nation's prosperity. Texas population grew by 17 percent, making it the fourth-largest state. Personal income for the state grew 67 percent, which raised income per person to $3,600 in 1970 prices (about $8,500 in 1988 prices). Total employment in the state grew about 26 percent during the decade.

The growth in Texas employment did not take place at the same rate for all sectors of the economy. Employment grew most rapidly in manufacturing, financial services, and government. Employment actually dropped in agriculture and mining (which is mostly oil and gas). Employment grew slowly in the other sectors of the Texas economy.

By comparing Tables 44-1 and 44-2 these changes can be seen. It also is apparent that the structure of the Texas economy began to be more like the structure of the U.S. economy. This is represented by the ratios moving closer to 1.00 in 1970 than they were in 1960.

The Texas economy grew along with the U.S. economy. Its structure reflected the structure of the U.S. economy. This structural change represents a continuation of a trend that began in the 1940s. In 1940, one-third of Texas labor was employed in agriculture and oil and gas extraction. By 1970 less than one-tenth of the labor force was employed in these sectors. Over the same period, employment in manufacturing, construction, finance, and professional services grew from less than one-fourth to more than one-third of the labor force.

THE 1970s

Table 44-3 shows the structure of the Texas economy in 1980. A comparison of this table with Tables 44-1 and 44-2 reveals that there was a reversal of the trend toward less dependence on mining (oil and gas). Texas also became relatively more dependent on construction, transportation,

TABLE 44-2
Texas Economic Structure
1970

Sector	Texas % of total employment	Texas % of employment divided by U.S. % of employment	Texas % of state income divided by U.S. % of nat. income
Agriculture	4.4%	1.26	1.28
Mining (oil & gas)	2.4%	2.67	4.59
Construction	7.0%	1.27	1.07
Manufacturing	17.4%	0.74	0.80
Transportation and Utilities	6.5%	1.00	0.98
Wholesale and Retail Trade	20.9%	1.34	0.99
Finance and Real Estate	4.9%	0.97	0.94
Services	25.1%	1.02	0.92
Government	5.4%	1.02	1.02

Sources: U.S. Department of Commerce, Bureau of the Census, *Social and Economic Characteristics of Texas* (Washington, D.C.: U.S. Government Printing Office, 1970); Office of the Governor of Texas, Texas 2000 Commission, *Texas Past and Future: A Survey* (1981).

TABLE 44-3
Texas Economic Structure
1980

Sector	Texas % of total employment	Texas % of employment divided by U.S. % of employment	Texas % of state income divided by U.S. % of nat. income
Agriculture	3.3%	1.21	.82
Mining (oil & gas)	3.3%	3.33	4.20
Construction	8.6%	1.57	1.33
Manufacturing	17.9%	0.78	0.82
Transportation and Utilities	7.5%	1.22	1.01
Wholesale and Retail Trade	21.8%	0.94	1.11
Finance and Real Estate	6.0%	1.06	0.97
Services	27.3%	0.93	0.88
Government	4.5%	1.03	0.89

Sources: U.S. Department of Commerce, Bureau of the Census, *Social and Economic Characteristics of Texas* (Washington, D.C.: U.S. Government Printing Office, 1980); Office of the Governor of Texas, Texas 2000 Commission, *Texas Past and Future: A Survey* (1981).

and public utilities. The Texas economic structure became less like that of the United States in every sector except agriculture, manufacturing, and trade.

Since the 1960s, the Texas economy has been on a roller coaster ride. First came the explosive growth and prosperity of the 1970s. Things were going well, and the Texas economy seemed to be invincible. Starting in 1981, the economy took a dramatic turn for the worse, and Texans were astounded and ill-prepared to cope with the new challenge.

Perhaps a good starting point in analyzing the events of the more recent past is the Arab oil embargo of 1973. This was an embargo on oil sales to the United States which was imposed in reaction to the U.S. support of Israel in its conflict with the Moslem states of the Middle East.

The actual embargo was brief, but it was followed by an enormous boost in petroleum prices by the Arabs and their allies in the new world oil cartel called the **Organization of Petroleum Exporting Countries** (OPEC). (A **cartel** is an agreement among producers to raise prices and cut output.) As far as Texas was concerned, the embargo was a real blessing. For the first time in modern memory there was a real U.S. oil shortage. The U.S. demand for Texas crude oil shot up meteorically. Prices actually doubled in a two-year period.

The oil boom period lasted from 1974 to 1982. Table 44-4 shows the contrast between the economic growth trend of the oil boom and the trend of the 1960s. Total employment grew more than twice as fast in the eight years of the oil boom as it had in the decade between 1960 and 1970. Employment in construction grew more than three times as fast; employment in retail trade grew two and one-half times as fast; and services employment grew almost twice as fast. The most dramatic contrast is in the oil and gas extraction industry (which is 90 percent of Texas' mining sector). In the 1960s, employment in mining declined slightly each year. But between 1974 and 1982, employment increased by almost 20 percent per year. This means that the total number of people employed in this industry more than doubled in eight years.

Of course, rising employment meant rising prosperity. Income from construction increased at an annual rate of 7.5 percent whereas the United States saw a 1 percent growth. Texas manufactur-

ing output increased at 3.9 percent per year, while U.S. manufacturing increased at a rate of only 0.1 percent. Personal income in Texas increased at an annual average rate of 17 percent as compared to the United States average of 12 percent.

The result of all this prosperity was a rise in retail spending that reached boom proportions. Small businesses in Texas were the direct beneficiary. In 1975, 16,725 new firms went into business; in 1979, the number of new businesses started was 41,130.

Banking and financial activity also reached record levels. For example, in 1960 the total banking resources in the state amounted to $13.5 trillion. By 1980, this total had reached $111 trillion, and by 1982 had risen to $153 trillion.

THE 1980s

The oil boom began to turn into the oil bust in 1981. Oil prices passed their peak in early 1981, and the feeling that the Texas economy was invincible went out the window. There was a growing glut of oil and gas in the world markets because the members of the oil cartel could not restrain themselves from overproducing. The Middle Eastern members of OPEC were at odds over Lebanon and the Iran-Iraq conflict. Many governments felt that their countries needed all the revenues they could get from oil sales.

World oil demand had also declined. This was partly the result of energy conservation programs that had been introduced in the United States

TABLE 44-4
Rates of Change of Texas Employment by Economic Sector 1960-1985
annual percentage change in employment

Sector	1960–70	1974–82	1982–85
Oil and Gas	− 0.3	19.4	− 6.3
Construction	1.6	5.0	− 1.7
Manufacturing	3.5	3.5	− 2.3
Trades	2.4	5.9	2.0
Services	3.9	7.1	3.7
Government	3.9	4.0	3.0
Other	7.8	5.0	2.7
Total	2.6	5.6	1.3

Sources: Texas Comptroller of Public Accounts, *Special Financial Report: The Texas Economy in 1984*, pp. 1–6; "The Texas Economy in 1985," *Fiscal Notes* 85, no. 2 (February 1985), pp. 1–3; "The Texas Economy in 1987," *Fiscal Notes* 87, no. 2 (February 1987), pp. 1–3.

and major oil-importing nations. The recession that began to affect the United States and the world in 1981 was partly responsible also.

Figure 44-1 shows some of the dimensions of the turnaround in the Texas economy. The drop in oil prices were accompanied by an increase in office-space vacancy rates, a drop in spending for new construction, an increase in unemployment, a soaring rate of business failures and a slowing down of increase in income per person.

Employment in oil and gas, construction, and manufacturing fell from 1982 through 1985. The oil industry was hit the hardest. It suffered drops of employment equalling over 6 percent per year. Employment grew slowly in the rest of the economy.

Real estate suffered severely also. Not only did new construction spending experience a sharp drop, but corporations and individuals vacated existing properties in droves. Many of the business vacancies were the result of bankruptcies; many individual homeowners lost their homes due to unemployment.

The impact on Texas banks and savings and loan institutions was drastic. Banks dependent on real estate and oil-related loans floundered and, in many cases, failed. The severity of the problem increased to the point where all but two of the ten largest banks in Texas have been involved in some form of rescue or takeover. Also, many savings and loan institutions were reorganized by the federal government to save them from collapse.

Currently, the state economy is showing many signs of recovery, although the end of the fighting between Iran and Iraq has set off further drops in oil prices. The impact of the oil boom on the state's economy was at best a mixed blessing. Although it brought great prosperity for some eight years, it also caused the severest recession in the state since the Great Depression of the 1930s. The oil boom of the 1970s interrupted the diversification of the Texas economic structure into areas other than agriculture and oil and gas extraction which had happened in the 1960s.

The significance of the lack of diversification is illustrated by the contrasting fates of the Texas economy and the national economy in the 1981 recession. Unemployment started rising in the United States and Texas at the same time. The rising interest rates that caused the national recession also hurt the state economy. But national recovery began in 1983, assisted by falling oil and gas prices in the petroleum-consuming states. At that time, Texas was plunging further into recession because its economy was heavily dependent on the falling oil and gas industry. The fate of Texas now depends on how rapidly the state's economic structure can be diversified to meet the challenges of the future.

CONTENT QUESTIONS

1. When compared to the nation as a whole, the Texas economy was more specialized in _____ and _____, and less specialized in _____.
2. What happened to Texas' population, personal income, and employment between 1962 and 1969?
3. What is a cartel? What is OPEC?

DISCUSSION QUESTIONS

1. How was the growth of the Texas economy affected by the oil boom of the 1970s? What changes did this bring?
2. How was the impact of the 1981 oil bust felt in Texas?
3. If you were advisor to the governor of Texas what would you tell the governor to do to prevent another problem like the oil bust of the 1980s?

FIGURE 44-1
How Hard Times Hit the Texas Economy

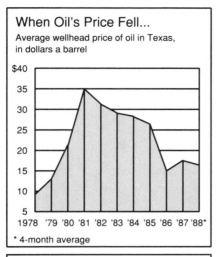

When Oil's Price Fell...
Average wellhead price of oil in Texas, in dollars a barrel

* 4-month average

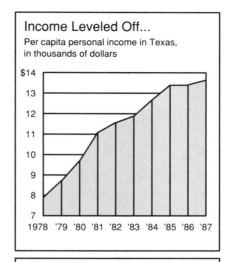

Income Leveled Off...
Per capita personal income in Texas, in thousands of dollars

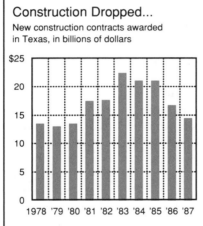

Construction Dropped...
New construction contracts awarded in Texas, in billions of dollars

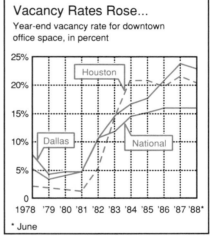

Vacancy Rates Rose...
Year-end vacancy rate for downtown office space, in percent

* June

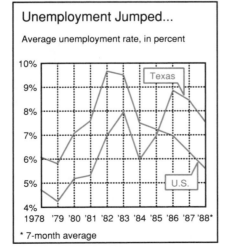

Unemployment Jumped...
Average unemployment rate, in percent

* 7-month average

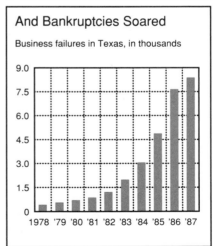

And Bankruptcies Soared
Business failures in Texas, in thousands

Source: "Texas Sees First Signs of Recovery, But It Faces Painful Changes," *Wall Street Journal*, 22 August 1988, p. 1.

45

THE FUTURE OF THE TEXAS ECONOMY

M. Ray Perryman, Ph.D.[1]

Despite many ups and downs, Texas has managed to carve out an impressive record of long-term economic prosperity. The eras of cattle, cotton, and oil have left indelible imprints on the business complex. They have, without exception, fostered a fiercely independent spirit, a penchant for risk-taking, and a can-do attitude which will be essential in meeting the competitive challenge of the future.

At the present time, the Texas economy stands at the most fundamental crossroads that it has ever faced as a republic or a state. While the past has certainly been characterized by colorful and fascinating periods of tremendous disparity, there has been a consistent theme running through the entire march of time. As Texas has moved from wagons to automobiles to airplanes and from rural dominance to vast urban concentrations, it has managed to build its prosperity on the foundation of a rich endowment of natural resources. Be it livestock or crops or the extraction of "black gold" from the depths of the Permian Basin, Texas has always derived its engine of growth from agriculture and mining. While many new factors have surfaced in the state over the years, none has yet managed to displace a basic dependency on natural resources.

THE NEW TEXAS ECONOMY

The future must, however, be a substantial departure from the past. Texas faces a new economic environment in which it must seek new and more diversified avenues for business expansion and individual prosperity. Agriculture will continue to be important, but is no longer in a position to drive the economy forward in a sustained manner. Petroleum will be a vital part of the overall picture, but the days of rapidly rising and dependable prices are probably over. In fact, the geological properties of the oil fields in Texas virtually assure declining levels of extraction. There will be less oil available. To the best of anyone's knowledge, there is no new crop or mineral that is likely to emerge as a resource sufficiently large and stable to assure continued prosperity. Thus, the new Texas economy must not only diversify, but must also achieve its destiny more with its human endowments and less with natural ones.

TEXAS AND THE U.S. ECONOMY

In order to examine the primary forces which will shape the future of Texas, it is necessary to briefly explore some critical events of the recent past. The decision by the Organization of Petroleum Exporting Countries (OPEC) to impose an embargo on oil shipments to the United States

[1]Herman Brown Professor of Economics; Director, Baylor University Forecasting Service, Waco, Texas.

brought substantial changes to both Texas and the country as a whole. The resulting energy crisis helped to plunge the United States into a lengthy recession. Subsequent rises in oil prices also contributed to national contractions in 1979 and 1980-81. The period from 1973 to 1981 was extremely sluggish for the domestic economy, and from 1978 to 1981 performance was highly volatile with virtually no growth at all.

During this difficult era for national business activity, Texas experienced incredible prosperity. Because the state is blessed with substantial petroleum reserves, rapid increases in energy prices led to an economic boom of enormous proportions. The real gross state product (GSP) estimates prepared by Baylor University Forecasting Service reveal that Texas grew at a compounded annual rate of more than 6% from 1973 to 1981. In those turbulent years between 1978 and 1981, when the United States as a whole did not expand at all, Texas rode higher oil prices to a total gain in real output of more than 23 percent. The state not only extracted its own oil, but also manufactured rigs, pipes, and other types of equipment for international drilling activity.

The extraordinary growth in a single state in the midst of deterioration in the surrounding country did not go unnoticed. The late 1970s and early 1980s saw Texas become an obsession for much of the world, largely because of its amazing economic performance. Southwestern art, the "Austin" sound, the "Urban Cowboy" movie, the "Dallas" television show, boots, hats, jeans, and the Dallas Cowboys became international phenomena. At the height of this euphoria, Texas got another shot in the arm when the Microelectronics and Computer Technology Corporation (MCC), a major electronics and computer "think tank," announced its decision to locate in Austin. The future could not have been brighter than it seemed in 1981.

THE CRISIS OF THE 1980s

At the peak of its success, the foundations of the Texas economy began to crumble. In early 1981, the globe found itself with enormous excess supplies of petroleum, and prices began to slip. With the weakness in oil markets, the state began a dramatic contraction in which tens of thousands of manufacturing and mining (extraction) jobs were lost. A modest recovery followed, but 1986 brought another plunge in oil prices and a second severe recession in Texas. The need for a much greater degree of economics diversification became readily apparent, and numerous initiatives began to surface.

Because of a unique set of circumstances, Texas found itself with a dramatic surge in construction activity at the same time that its basic economy was reeling from the cumulative effects of repeated oil price shocks. The **supply-side policies** of the Reagan Administration in the early 1980s resulted in a tax bill which contained several provisions that encouraged real estate development. (In general, supply-side policies seek to create a favorable business climate which will help businesses produce goods and services more efficiently.) Major changes in the regulatory structure of the financial system made a lot of money available to fund new building activity. These factors, coupled with the widespread belief that oil prices would continue to rise and that Texas would continue to prosper, led to a period of rapid build-up in all types of space (offices, apartments, retail centers, industrial buildings, houses, etc.) throughout the state. Thus, construction soared in 1982 and for several years thereafter. Although the underlying business complex remained weak, Texas continued to add new structures.

The situation came full circle in 1986 and 1987 with a collapse in oil prices, enormous excess supplies of real estate, a new federal tax law which eliminated many of the incentives to purchase buildings, and a set of financial institutions which were severely weakened by the loans which provided the funds for much of this development. Texas finds itself with an imperative need to bring new forces to bear in shaping its economic future. At the same time, it clearly possesses the resources needed to ensure prosperity over an extended period of time.

FACTORS IN THE NEW TEXAS ECONOMY

The future of Texas will be determined by many complex factors. The next few decades present a challenge to achieve a more balanced and diverse economy. The traditional reliance on natural resources must give way to products which are higher on the **value-added** chain. (The term *value-added* indicates the amount by which the worth of an item is increased by having additional processing done to it, such as when a manufacturer takes a raw material and processes it into a product.) Agriculture must be supplemented by expansion of food processing. Despite the fact that the state has long been a dominant producer of farm commodities, Texas processes only a small fraction of what it grows. In a similar manner, the extraction of oil must be supplemented by the generation of new products which use petroleum as an input through biotechnological research.

The new Texas economy will focus on aircraft, electronics, communications, and other emerging growth industries. Reflecting a widely chronicled global trend, the state will see the ever-increasing importance of the service sector. Information, business, and medical services are likely to be especially significant in the next several years. Many of the new jobs in Texas will be generated by small businesses and new companies. Programs to encourage the creation and expansion of these types of concerns will become a more and more vital component of economic development efforts.

The competition for business activity is extremely intense at present. More than 10,000 communities in the United States are aggressively seeking to expand employment opportunities. Indeed, the efforts to attract new industry extend throughout the world. Cities and regions all across Texas are now mobilizing with programs to foster new development. They are studying their labor resources and existing businesses in order to identify target industries for potential locations to the area. They are establishing small-business development programs to aid in the creation, financing, and expansion of local concerns. Regional agencies to promote growth are being formed throughout the state. Programs aimed at international cooperation are greatly accelerating. Individuals, communities, and agencies are working diligently to meet the challenges of the new economic reality.

The long-term future of Texas should be extremely bright. The aging of persons born in the "baby boom" era, i.e., between 1945 and 1964, is bringing fundamental change in the demographic and economic structure of the United States. The rate of expansion in the labor force will be reduced considerably over the next two decades. This situation is quite positive in that it assures the nation of an older, better educated, and more experienced group of workers than at any time in history. On the other hand, this emerging pattern also leads to a significant labor shortage over an extended period of time.

While Texas certainly will be impacted by this population trend, the age composition of the state is considerably younger than that of the nation as a whole. Hence, there will be a substantial relative advantage for Texas. The work force within the state is younger than that of the rest of the nation and, more importantly, the natural rate of growth in the number of potential employees will be much higher. Consequently, there will be strong incentive for all types of production to locate in areas with relatively abundant supplies of workers. When this advantage is joined to the continuing migration toward the Sun Belt, the ongoing efforts by the state officials to stimulate growth by enhancing the business climate, the activity by local and regional groups, the tremendous natural resource endowments, new programs at the major universities within the state, and the efforts to rapidly absorb new technology into production processes, the outlook for Texas becomes quite encouraging.

CONCLUSION

Because of the factors noted above, the Texas economy is predicted to expand at rates well above those anticipated for the nation as a whole. The Texas Econometric Model, which was developed and is maintained at Baylor University Forecasting Service, projects that Texas will experience higher rates of increase in gross product, employment, income, population, and other indicators of overall prosperity than will the nation as a whole over the next twenty years. While the performance is not likely to match that of the oil boom, the next two decades will nonetheless be a period of substantial overall prosperity. The new Texas economy will be different in structure. It will be more diversified, will rely somewhat less on natural resources for its strength, and will be largely built by relatively small businesses. It will be less susceptible to fluctuations in the price of a single commodity, but more sensitive to movements in national activity. Texas is indeed on the threshold of major economic changes and is experiencing a transition that is interesting to observe and in which it is even more exciting to be a participant.

CONTENT QUESTIONS

1. Throughout Texas' history the state's economy has been based on _____. The key to the state's economic future will be _____.

2. For the United States economy between 1973 and 1981 there was _____ economic growth. But for Texas there was _____ in the economy.

3. What caused the boom in Texas construction during the decline in the oil industry?

4. For Texas to grow in the future, what are some of the industries which must be developed?

5. What has been the population trend in the United States, and what does this mean for the economy?

DISCUSSION QUESTIONS

1. Why will Texas not be able to depend on oil as the basis for its economy in the future?

2. What can be done to promote economic diversification?

3. How do you feel about the future of the Texas economy?

GLOSSARY

★

Aid to Families with Dependent Children (AFDC). Aid to Families with Dependent Children is a government welfare program established by Congress to provide money to poor parents to assist them in providing food and other necessities for their children. To be eligible, parents must meet certain conditions and must demonstrate the need for the money.

accelerator effect. The accelerator effect refers to the investment which results from the multiplier effect. When money is spent, this creates income and jobs. This growth creates the demand for new factories and facilities to be built. For example, when tourists come to Texas and spend their money this creates a demand for new hotels, restaurants, and attractions to be built. Investment in these new facilities is what is being referred to when economists talk about the accelerator effect. *See* multiplier effect.

access charges. An access charge is levied by a local telephone company against a long distance telephone company. The long-distance telephone company must use the local phone company's switching services to connect callers. When an individual dials a long-distance phone call, the call begins with a local exchange and then is transferred to a long-distance company. The long-distance company must connect the call through another local exchange. The access charge is levied by local phone companies for use of their exchanges.

acquisition. An acquisition occurs when one firm buys out or acquires another firm. This is usually done through a merger. Under the process of acquisition the buying firm purchases the outstanding stock or shares of the firm being acquired. *See* merger.

agrarian society. An agrarian society is one characterized by small, basically self-sufficient farms. While these farms may produce some items for sale on the market, the vast majority of what they produce is for home consumption.

agribusiness. Agribusiness refers to those firms involved in the processing and distribution of farm products. For example, firms which export grain, butcher beef, or provide insurance and banking services to farmers are involved in agribusiness.

allocative efficiency. *See* efficiency.

applied research. Applied research addresses a particular problem to see what scientific knowledge can be used in the problem's solution. Applied research is directed towards taking new technologies and finding some practical use for them. For example, much of the basic research now being done in superconductivity has yet to be applied to any new product or service. This will be the responsibility of applied researchers in the future. *See* superconductivity; basic research.

appraisal. When an estimate is made by an expert of the market value of a property (like a house, farm or business) that is called an appraisal.

apprenticeship program. An apprenticeship program exists when a worker serves a period of time under the close supervision of a master workman, who teaches the apprentice the skills of a particular trade. Unions make extensive use of apprenticeship programs where new workers are taught the necessary skills to perform their jobs by seasoned and highly skilled workers.

appropriation. An appropriation is the amount authorized by a legislative body to be spent on a particular governmental function.

aquifer. An aquifer is an underground river or lake found in a rock or sand formation. By drilling a well into the aquifer, water can be obtained for municipal use or for irrigation of farm land. When the amount of water taken out of an aquifer is greater than the amount of water which seeps into it the aquifer falls and water mining has resulted. Aquifers are also referred to as subsurface water. *See* water mining.

arithmetic mean.   *See* mean.

assessed value.   The value of property against which the property tax is levied is called the assessed value. To get assessed value the total market value of all property in a local government's jurisdiction is determined. Assessed value is market value minus deductions for exemptions given to certain groups such as the aged. *See* property tax; market value.

assets.   Assets are items of value that an individual or a business firm owns. For example, the assets of a typical business firm would consist of any land, buildings, equipment, and inventory the firm owns plus any cash it has in the bank.

avoided cost.   Avoided cost is the price that an electric utility must pay to a cogenerator for the electricity produced by the cogenerator. Avoided cost is calculated by figuring what the expense would have been to the utility if it had generated the electricity from its own plant rather than buying it from the cogenerator. *See* cogeneration.

backdoor of the Confederacy.   Backdoor of the Confederacy is a term that historians apply to the state of Texas. Since Texas was not invaded by Union troops, economic activity was not disrupted by the Civil War. In addition, the long Texas coastline was never effectively blockaded by the Union, so trade could continue.

bank account.   A bank account is the amount an individual or firm has on deposit with a bank or other financial institution. Individuals may make withdrawals from their bank accounts by writing checks. This transfers the money in their bank accounts to other individuals' accounts.

bank note.   Bank notes are money issued by commercial banks. These notes are supposed to be backed by the bank holding either precious metals such as gold and silver or government bonds. One problem with bank notes was that banks tended to issue more notes than they should have based on the precious metals and bonds they held. This caused them to devalue. *See* commercial banks; government securities; devaluation.

barter.   When one product is traded for another, this is barter. No money is necessary, since products are directly exchanged for each other.

basic allotment.   The basic allotment is the cost of providing education to a typical student in Texas schools. The basic allotment which a school gets depends not only on the number of pupils, but on the characteristics of the pupils. The basic allotment goes up for students who are handicapped, gifted, bilingual, or enrolled in vocational education programs. The state pays for two-thirds of the basic allotment for each school district.

basic research.   Basic research occurs when an individual explores some new idea without knowing what the practical applications of that idea will be in the marketplace. Basic research is the foundation upon which applied research is based. *See* applied research.

bill.   A bill is a proposed piece of legislation that has not yet been enacted. A bill becomes a law when a legislative body passes it and it is signed by the chief executive of the government.

biotechnology.   Broadly defined, biotechnology is any technique that uses living organisms to make or modify products, to improve plants or animals, or to develop microorganisms for specific uses. Biotechnology is not new, but recent years have seen the acceleration of biotechnology to improve the yields of various crops in Texas and other states. One of the most widely used biotechnologies is genetic selection, which is designed to create plants that are more productive while being increasingly resistant to drought and disease.

bonds.   Bonds are issued by a government as a means of borrowing. They are promises to repay the lender at some future date. Since the government promises or guarantees that the bonds will be repaid they are also referred to as government securities.

Border Industrialization Program (BIP).   The Border Industrialization Program was designed to encourage manufacturing plants to be established along the Mexican border with the United States; plants would operate in both countries. The United States and Mexican governments each make concessions to the other to allow the Border Industrialization Program to work. The United States allows products assembled in plants on the Mexican side to be imported to the U.S. side without restrictions or tariffs. The Mexican government allows the twin plants on the Mexican side to be wholly owned by American companies. *See* twin plant program; maquiladora program.

boycott.   A boycott is an organized refusal by a group of people to do something. Sometimes a group of individuals may refuse to buy a certain product, in which case it is said that they are boycotting it. Boycotts are a form of protest.

Bracero Program. The bracero program began during World War II to help alleviate worker shortages in the United States. It consists of allowing Mexican migrant farm labor to work in the United States. Since the 1960s the bracero program has been reduced and the use of undocumented Mexican migrant workers in the United States is now illegal.

bread bond. Bread bonds were issued in Texas during the early years of the Great Depression. The purpose of the bread bonds was to raise money for relief of the unemployed.

budget/balanced budget. A budget is a statement of income and outgo for a government or business. When a government's or business' income is equal to its outgo, then its budget is said to be balanced.

business cycle. A business cycle is a recurring phenomenon in a free enterprise economy. It consists of a period of prosperity followed by a period of recession followed by a period of recovery. Some industries are very sensitive to the business cycle. When times are good they prosper and when times are bad they do not. Other industries are less sensitive to what phase of the business cycle the economy is in. See free enterprise system; recession.

by-product. When one product is produced as a result of manufacturing another product, it is referred to as a by-product. For example, leather is a by-product of the meat-packing industry.

capital. Something used to produce something else is called capital. One form of capital is tools. Another form of capital is the skills and education of the labor force, which is called human capital. In economics, the term *capital* may also refer to money which is available to invest in a project. When used this way it is referred to as financial capital. See capital goods; human resources.

capital goods. Capital goods are the tools that we use to produce goods and services. For example, a hammer is a capital good because it is the tool used by a carpenter to build a house. In the same way, an airplane is a capital good because it is used to transport people and to produce air service. See capital.

capital-intensive. A capital-intensive industry is one that primarily uses machinery rather than labor to produce a good or service. For example, petroleum refining is a capital-intensive industry. Only a few workers are needed in the vast refining complexes. Capital intensive industries require large amounts of investment to get started. Gas and electric utilities are other examples of capital-intensive industries. See capital.

cartel. A cartel is an agreement among producers of a product to set prices and to allocate the market among themselves. Under a cartel each producer agrees to allow the cartel to determine how much they can produce and at what price their product can be sold. The objective of a cartel is to maintain high prices by limiting the supply, and by coordinating the production activities. Cartels are illegal in the United States, but not always in other countries. The best example of a cartel today is OPEC (See Organization of Petroleum Exporting Countries).

certified bill. The certified bill is one in which the State Comptroller for Texas has certified that there is a sufficient amount of revenue available to pay for the expenses covered by the legislation. If there is not sufficient revenue available, the Comptroller cannot certify the bill and the bill is void. See revenue.

chemical revolution. The chemical revolution occurred between 1940 and 1960 in agriculture. It refers to the use of vaccines, medicines, fertilizers, pesticides, and herbicides to grow more and better crops. Currently, the chemical revolution is giving way to the biotechnological revolution in Texas agriculture. See biotechnology.

Chamber of Commerce. A Chamber of Commerce is a group of businesspersons and other citizens who organize for the purpose of promoting trade and economic development in their community. Members of the Chamber of Commerce pay dues. Chambers of Commerce work to improve the business climate in their communities and to attract new industry.

check clearing. Check clearing is the process by which a check written on one bank is accepted by another bank. When individuals write checks on their bank accounts and give them to other individuals who have bank accounts at other banks, it will be necessary for the other banks to clear the checks by presenting them for payment at the originating banks. In the United States, the Federal Reserve System is responsible for clearing checks among banks and certain other financial institutions.

Civilian Conservation Corps. The Civilian Conservation Corps was a New Deal program established by the Roosevelt Administration which enlisted young men to plant trees, build bridges and roads, and construct flood and erosion controls. *See* New Deal.

clearinghouse operation.   When the Federal Reserve clears a check written by the payor on one bank and adds it to the account of the payee whose account is in another bank. *See* Federal Reserve System.

cogeneration.   Cogeneration refers to the process whereby electricity is generated using the heat created by a large industrial or commercial business. The excess heat, instead of being wasted, is used to fuel an electrical generator and to produce electricity. Under the terms of the Public Regulatory Practices Act this cogenerated power is to be made available to electric utilities to serve their customers. *See* public utility.

collateral.   Collateral is property used to secure a loan. For example, when a person takes out a loan to buy a house, the house serves as collateral for the loan. If the individual cannot pay off the loan, the collateral is sold to satisfy the debt.

colonization.   Colonization is the economic control of one country by another. Colonists rarely possess the full political or economic freedoms that are granted citizens in the home country. The idea behind colonization is to operate the colonies for the benefit of the home country rather than for the prosperity of the people living in the colonial territory.

command economic system.   A command economic system places the authority to direct and control economic activity in the hands of a central group of governmental planners. These planners decide the needs of the people and the country. Most economic questions are answered for the people by these economic planners, who decide what will be produced, how it will be produced, and who will get it after it is produced. The Soviet Union, Eastern Europe and mainland China are examples of economies that are basically command.

commercial agriculture.   Production of livestock and crops to be sold on the market rather than to be used for home consumption is called commercial agriculture. Commercial agriculture developed in Texas after the Civil War when the small subsistence farmers began to expand and to produce cotton, wheat, and, later, livestock to be sold nationwide. *See* agrarian society.

commercial bank.   Commercial banks accept deposits from individuals, businesses, and governments, and make loans. Commercial banks are different from other financial institutions in that they only have to hold a small fraction of their deposits as reserves. The rest they can loan out. *See* financial institutions; reserve requirement.

commodity.   Commodities are products produced for sale in a market. The term is often used in relation to agricultural output. Crops such as wheat, cotton, timber, and peaches are all examples of commodities.

community.   Community is the desire to live in harmony with others in the economic society. Community is achieved when the majority of people share the same economic goals and values. Community can also refer to a city. It can also mean a group of people who share common values.

comparative advantage.   Comparative advantage explains why it is profitable for either people or nations to specialize and to trade with other individuals or nations who specialize. For example, the United States may be four times more efficient in the production of beef and twice as efficient in the production of bananas as is some other country. Comparative advantage teaches that the United States should specialize in the production of beef because that is where its greatest advantage or comparative advantage lies and allow the other nation to produce the bananas. The United States would then trade beef for bananas.

competition.   Competition is the disciplinary force in the marketplace. It refers to a situation where no single individual can control the market. Competition exists when there are many buyers and sellers. If a prospective customer is unhappy with the price or quality of the product supplied by one producer, he or she can always turn to a competitor. Without competition the market economy does not work. *See* market economic system.

competitive position.   The ability of a region, state or country to compete against other regions, states, or countries is known as its competitive position. The more favorable a location is for a particular type of business or economic activity, the greater its competitive position will be. For example, because of the large number of high-tech firms located in Texas and because the state system of higher education stresses high technology, Texas' competitive position in all high-tech fields is considered to be excellent. *See* competition.

comptroller.   A comptroller (pronounced like "controller") is an official in either a government or business who is responsible for keeping track of the income and outgo of funds. The state of Texas has a comptroller who is responsible for the collection of all state taxes and other amounts due the state.

Congress of Industrial Organizations (CIO).   The Congress of Industrial Organizations was a confederation of industrial unions whose members all worked in a specific industry. Examples of industrial unions were those for the steel workers, mine workers, or auto workers. Unlike craft unions, industrial unions allowed all workers, skilled or unskilled, to join. *See* craft union.

consumer control.   Sometimes called consumer sovereignty, consumer control refers to the fact that in a market economy it is consumers, rather than governmental planners, who dictate what will be produced. *See* market economic system; command economic system.

Consumer Price Index (CPI).   The Consumer Price Index is one measure of inflation. It tells us how much the cost of living has gone up. It is calculated by looking at what happens to the prices of over 400 items typically consumed by American families. *See* inflation.

contract.   A contract is an agreement to do or not to do something. Any time you agree to buy a product or to sell your labor services you have entered into a contract. Under all contracts one person gives up something to the other person in order to get something from that other person.

corporate franchise tax.   The corporate franchise tax is levied on the privilege of doing business in the state of Texas. It is based on the taxable capital of the firm, which is the value of the firm's assets and includes their plant, equipment, inventory and money. *See* capital.

corporation.   A corporation has all the legal rights of an individual. When people buy shares they are buying ownership in the corporation. A corporation differs from a proprietorship and a partnership since those who own the corporation are not responsible for the corporation's bills. The individuals who own proprietorships and partnerships must pay the debts of their businesses. Corporations finance themselves by selling shares to the public and operate under charters or grants of permission issued to them by the government.

cost competitive advantage.   A cost competitive advantage is one that a particular city or area has over other areas. It means that the cost of production in that area is lower than what it would be elsewhere. Such cost advantages can arise from lower costs of labor and transportation and lower taxes. *See* competitive position; *compare* technological competitive advantage.

cow-calf operation.   A cow-calf operation is one where a herd of cows is kept year-round for the production of calves. When the calves are taken from their mothers they are put on pasture for several months and then shipped to a feedlot (where they are known as feeders) before they are shipped to the slaughterhouse.

CPI.   *See* Consumer Price Index.

craft union.   A craft union is formed by highly skilled workers who work in a particular craft or profession. Unions of carpenters, electricians, and plumbers are examples of craft unions. *Compare* industrial union.

credit.   Credit allows someone to buy now and pay later. Credit is extended or given to individuals when they are allowed to purchase products and pay for the products at a later date.

crop lien system.   The crop lien system was the method used by small farmers in Texas and in other states to finance their operations. The farmer would obtain his supplies from the furnishing merchant. The furnishing merchant would extend the farmer credit with the farmer's crop being held as collateral. When the farmer's crop came in and was sold, the farmer was expected to pay off the furnishing merchant. *See* furnishing merchant; collateral.

currency.   Currency is another term used to describe paper money. In the United States, currency consists of $1, $5, $10, $20, $50, $100 and $1,000 bills. Currency is used as a means of assisting trade.

customs collections.   Tariffs and import fees are examples of customs collections. These are duties imposed on the importation of goods into one country from another. These were a principal source of revenue for the government of Texas while it was a republic. *See* revenue.

data.   Data is a set of statistics or numbers arranged or presented in such a way as to explain something. Data may be presented as either a table of numbers or as a graph which is a pictorial representation.

dedicated revenue.   Under the Texas Constitution and state laws, much of the state's revenue is dedicated for specific purposes. For example, the gasoline tax is dedicated for the building of state roads and bridges. Most state revenue in Texas is dedicated to a specific function. *See* revenue.

demand.   Demand refers to the amount that consumers are willing to buy. As a general rule, as the price goes down consumers are willing to purchase more. *Compare* supply.

demographics.   Demographics is the study of population change and movement within a region. Demographics seeks to answer questions such as, "Is the population getting older, better educated, more urbanized and healthier?"; "Where do people live?"; and "What do they do?"

deposit. A deposit is an amount of money placed in a bank or other financial institution. People make deposits into their bank accounts so that the money will be there when they need it in the future.

deregulation. When a government removes restrictions and guidelines that it has placed upon a particular industry the government is engaging in deregulation. Deregulation has taken place recently in many industries, including oil and natural gas. Government no longer establishes the prices at which oil and gas can be sold. Deregulation has also occurred in other industries such as airlines, trucking, and finance.

devaluation. *See* devaluation of currency.

devaluation of currency. Devaluation occurs when money (currency) loses its purchasing power. Devaluation has taken place when a dollar buys less due to rising prices. *See* inflation. Devaluation can also occur between currencies used in different countries. For example, in recent years the peso has devalued relative to the U.S. dollar. This means that the peso buys fewer U.S. products because it takes more pesos to purchase the dollars that are needed to obtain U.S. goods.

development agency. A development agency is a part of government that has as its function promoting economic growth in a city, state or region. The purpose of the development agency is to attract new business to an area and to promote the growth of businesses already located in that area.

discount rate. The discount rate is what the Federal Reserve Bank (The Fed) charges member banks for the loans it makes to them. When the Fed wants banks to make loans and increase the amount of money in the economy, it lowers the discount rate to encourage the banks to borrow so they can in turn lend money to their customers. When the Fed raises the discount rate it discourages banks from borrowing money to make loans. *See* Federal Reserve System; commercial bank.

displacement. Displacement refers to the substitution of a machine or a skilled worker for an unskilled or less skilled worker. Displaced workers are a problem in the Texas economy, as they often lack the skills and training to take other jobs. Displacement can also happen when an industry declines and people lose their jobs. This was the case with the Texas oil industry during the 1980s.

diversification. Diversification occurs when an economy becomes less dependent on one or a few industries for jobs and income. One of the problems of the Texas economy has been the lack of diversification and its overdependence upon the oil industry.

divestiture. Divestiture is a legal process by which a large firm is broken up into many smaller firms. This took place when AT&T was broken up into regional telephone companies. This was done in the belief that increased competition would serve the public better. *See* competition.

dividends. Dividends are the income that shareholders receive out of the profits of the corporations in which they own stock. Not all corporate profits are paid out to shareholders in the form of dividends. Some are reinvested in the company to allow the company to expand and grow. The state also receives dividends on the corporate stock it owns.

duty. A duty is another word for a tax levied on a particular product. The term is often used to refer to taxes which must be paid on products brought into one country from another country. *See* tariff.

economic base. The economic base refers to those products and services that provide the primary sources of employment and income within an economic region or market area. For example, the economic base of the Houston area is petroleum and petrochemicals, while the economic base of the high plains in West Texas is agriculture. *See* market area.

economic development strategy. Economic development strategies are the various plans and proposals used to attract new industries and jobs into a region. These may include such things as giving tax breaks to new industries, upgrading the quality of education, advertising and promotion of the community, or improving a city's streets, water, and sewer system. *See* greenhouse strategy; marketing strategy; Petri dish strategy.

economic freedom. Economic freedom refers to the ability of producers and consumers to do as they please with the resources and products they own. While perfect economic freedom does not exist, a market economy provides more of it than any other economic system. *See* market economic system.

economic growth. Economic growth refers to an increase of per capita income in an economy. For economic growth to take place, total output of goods and services must increase faster than the population does. *See* per capita.

economic isolation. Economic isolation is an attempt by a city, region, or state to be entirely self-sufficient. Under this idea, the city, region, or state would produce virtually all that was consumed within its territory. There would be relatively little trade, if any, with other cities, regions, or states.

economic problem. The economic problem refers to the conflict between scarce resources and the almost unlimited demands for those resources. Because resources are scarce, not everything we want can be produced. We are therefore forced to make choices.

economy of scale. Economies of scale exist when a single firm provides a service more efficiently than multiple firms could. In many cases, the technology is such that a large firm can be more efficient than many smaller ones could be. A local telephone exchange exemplifies the idea of economies of scale. *See* natural monopoly.

economize/maximize. This refers to the process of making economic choices so as to gain the greatest possible benefit from those choices. When we select one alternative over another, we select the one that will give us the greatest pleasure or satisfaction. For example, when we choose a hot dog over a bowl of chili (assuming both cost the same) we are saying that the hot dog gives us more satisfaction or pleasure than the bowl of chili would.

efficiency. Economic efficiency means getting the greatest amount of output out of a given amount of resources. This is sometimes referred to as technical efficiency. Another view of efficiency is what is called allocative efficiency, which means that resources are allocated in accordance to the goals of society. For example, if society would like more to be spent on national defense and less on highways than is actually being spent, then allocative efficiency has not been achieved.

electronic fund transfer. When money is moved from one bank account to another by use of computers, this is called electronic funds transfer. When people use automatic teller machines to withdraw money from their checking accounts this is an example of electronic funds transfer.

Eleventh District. The Dallas Federal Reserve Bank serves the Eleventh Federal Reserve District, which includes Texas and parts of Louisiana and New Mexico. *See* Federal Reserve System.

emancipation. Emancipation refers to the freeing of the slaves ordered by President Lincoln during the Civil War. The Emancipation Proclamation ended slavery in Texas and the rest of the Southern states.

embargo. An embargo occurs when one nation prevents the importation of a product into another nation. In 1972 the Organization of Petroleum Exporting Nations (OPEC) put an embargo on oil shipments to Europe and the United States. The result was the oil boom of the 1970s. *See* OPEC; oil boom/bust.

emerging growth industry. Emerging growth industries are those that will supply the jobs and incomes for Texans in the future. Among the emerging growth industries are aircraft, electronics, communications, and other high-tech services.

employment. Employment refers to the job a worker holds. It can also mean the number of people working in an industry or a region.

empresario. An empresario was an entrepreneur who contracted with the Spanish government to recruit and supervise colonists brought into Texas. The empresario was given a large area of land and the right to divide and assign the land among the colonists. He was also responsible for making sure the colonists obeyed the laws of the land. *See* colonization.

energy crisis. The energy crisis developed in the 1970s, when the Organization of Petroleum Exporting Countries (OPEC) cut off the flow of oil into world markets. As a result, there was not enough oil or natural gas available to supply the energy the American economy needed. *See* OPEC.

entrepreneur. Entrepreneurs are the innovative risk takers in an economy. They are the people that produce new products, services, and technologies and place them on the market. Entrepreneurship is often associated with individuals owning their own businesses, but this is not always the case. Entrepreneurs see what others have overlooked and act on their insights by taking the risks associated with bringing their ideas to the marketplace.

entrepreneurship. Entrepreneurship is what entrepreneurs do. It refers to the process of having an idea and bringing that idea to the marketplace. *See* entrepreneurs.

equilibrium. Equilibrium refers to the price and output that result when supply and demand are equal to each other in a market. If a price is too high for equilibrium, more will be produced than what consumers want and the price will fall to equilibrium. If the price is too low in a market, then prices will be bid up until the market is cleared. *See* supply; demand.

equity. In economics, equity concerns the distribution of income. It involves a value judgment as to what is a fair or just distribution of income.

exchange rate. The exchange rate refers to how much one nation's currency is worth in terms of another. For example, if the exchange rate between pesos and dollars is 200 to 1 it will take 200 pesos to buy one dollar.

exemption. An exemption allows an individual to avoid paying all or a portion of a tax. For example, in Texas, food products have received an exemption from state sales tax.

exhaustible resource.   Exhaustible resources are those that can be used up and will not be replaced. For example, oil is an exhaustible resource. We are currently taking large amounts of oil out of the ground, which cannot be replaced. This means that in the future, Texas will run out of oil because the state will have exhausted this resource.

expenditure.   An expenditure is a cash outlay for a specific purpose. Government budgets always include these outlays.

export.   Exports are goods produced in one country and sold in another. For example, farm products grown in Texas are often exported to other countries.

factors of production.   The factors of production are the resources available to produce goods and services. These include land, labor, capital, and entrepreneurship. All factors of production are scarce. That is why not everything that everybody wants can be produced.

farrow-to-finish operations.   This is a term used by pork producers. It means that the hog is born and raised to market weight on the same farm. Not all pork producers are farrow-to-finish operators. Many sell young pigs to others to fatten them for market.

Federal Deposit Insurance Corporation (FDIC).   It is responsible for insuring (up to $100,000) the deposits of individuals and businesses in commercial banks. Commercial banks pay an insurance fee to the FDIC. In recent years, the rash of bank failures in Texas and elsewhere has seriously depleted the FDIC's insurance funds. See commercial bank.

Federal Emergency Relief Administration.   The Federal Emergency Relief Administration was a program established by the Roosevelt Administration under the New Deal to help migrants and rural students. See New Deal.

Federal Home Loan Bank Board.   The Federal Home Loan Bank Board was established for enforcing the laws and regulations pertaining to savings and loan institutions. It performs the same function for thrift institutions that the Office of the Comptroller of the Currency does for national banks. See savings and loan association.

Federal Open Market Committee (FOMC).   The Federal Open Market Committee is a branch of the Federal Reserve System. It has the responsibility for buying and selling government bonds on the open market to influence the money supply. See Federal Reserve System.

Federal Reserve Bank of Dallas.   The Federal Reserve System operates through 12 regional banks, one of which is located in Dallas. The Dallas Federal Reserve is responsible for executing Federal Reserve policy throughout the territory of the Eleventh Federal Reserve District, for which it is responsible. It handles check clearing and regulates the member banks within its district. See Federal Reserve System; Eleventh District.

Federal Reserve System.   Established in 1914, the Federal Reserve System regulates the commercial banks that are members and seeks to control the supply of money in the economy. The Federal Reserve System consists of 12 regional banks, one of which is located in Dallas. All national banks must become members of the Federal Reserve System and state banks may become members if they agree to be regulated by the Federal Reserve. See commercial banks.

Federal Savings and Loan Insurance Corporation (FSLIC).   The FSLIC or Federal Savings and Loan Insurance Corporation insures the deposits of savings and loan associations. Currently, individuals and businesses have insurance up to $100,000 on their accounts. During the mid and late 1980s a large number of depositors found that their savings and loan associations were being closed, but none of them lost any money, due to the insurance provided by the FSLIC. See savings and loan association.

Federal Surplus Relief Corporation.   The Federal Surplus Relief Corporation distributed agricultural surpluses to impoverished families during the Great Depression.

financial institution.   A financial institution receives money from savers and makes it available to investors. This process is known as intermediation. Examples of financial institutions are commercial banks and savings and loan associations. See commercial bank; savings and loan association.

fiscal year.   For a government or business the fiscal year is the 12-month period for which they budget. It may not correspond to the calendar year which runs from January to December. The federal government's fiscal year runs from October to September.

foreign investment.   When individuals and businesses located in foreign countries invest their financial capital in Texas or anywhere else in the United States this is called foreign investment. When people living in Texas or other parts of the United States build factories or invest in other countries, this is also foreign investment. Foreign investment is good for a country because it attracts money, which in turn creates jobs and employment opportunities. *See* capital.

free enterprise system.   *See* market economy.

free exchange.   Free exchange, also called voluntary exchange, refers to the fact that in a market economy no one is coerced into either buying or selling. Transactions in a market economy take place because both the buyer and the seller gain from the transaction and neither is being forced to make it. *See* market economy.

full employment.   Full employment exists when everyone who is looking for a job is able to find one. It is impossible for this to be achieved, so as a general rule economists say that full employment exists when 94-96 percent of the labor force has found jobs. There is always a small percentage of the labor force that is between jobs and for this reason are not employed.

furnishing merchant.   The furnishing merchant is the businessperson who supplies farmers with the seeds, fertilizers, and other supplies they need to put in their crops. In the past, since most farmers were unable to pay for these at the time of purchase, the furnishing merchant extended them credit through the crop lien system. *See* crop lien system.

General Agreement on Tariffs and Trade (GATT). The General Agreement on Tariffs and Trade is an international arrangement in which most of the nations of the world have agreed to work together to lower trade restrictions on the goods that flow between these nations. GATT has established rules and regulations that the member nations agree not to violate. The United States is a member of GATT.

General Revenue Fund.   The General Revenue Fund is where all monies collected by the state of Texas, not specifically dedicated by law or by the constitution, are deposited. The legislature then appropriates the money in the General Revenue Fund to perform the various functions of state government such as building highways, providing for education, or building prisons. *See* dedicated revenue.

globalization.   Globalization refers to the trend which has developed in the 1970s and 1980s for Texans to sell their goods and services, not just in Texas or the United States, but in other countries as well.

GNP.   *See* Gross National Product.

government securities.   Bonds and other debt issued by federal, state, or local governments are called government securities. Governments issue bonds when they need additional revenue to pay their expenses. These are called government securities because the government guarantees or promises that the bonds will be repaid out of future revenues. This promise makes the bonds secure.

Great Depression.   The Great Depression began in 1928 and continued until the outbreak of the Second World War. It was the longest period of recession in the history of the United States. Businesses and banks failed, while unemployment spread to record numbers of Texans and other Americans. *See* recession.

greenhouse strategy.   The greenhouse strategy is one method which local development agencies have used to try to increase the number of jobs in their community. Under this approach, local governments and other community groups work with small businesses that are already located there, encouraging their development and expansion. This is done by establishing incubators for small businesses, by making loans or venture funds available, or by providing technical support services. *See* economic development strategy; incubators; venture capital.

Gross National Product (GNP).   The Gross National Product is the most widely used measure of economic activity. It refers to the total value of all the goods and services produced in the nation during a given time period.

Gross State Product.   The Gross State Product is the total value of goods and services produced within the boundaries of a state during a single year. Gross State Product is determined by adding together the market value of all final goods and services produced in the state. Gross State Product does not include the value of goods produced in other states and brought into the state of Texas for sale, but it does include products produced in Texas and sold in other states.

growth.   *See* economic growth.

House Bill 72.   House Bill 72 was a law passed in 1984. Its purpose was to reform Texas education by requiring a greater emphasis on academics for students and accountability for educators.

human resources.   Another term for labor is human resources. It refers to the quantity and quality of the labor force. Human resources refers to the human element in production.

illiteracy.   The inability to read and write is described as illiteracy. While most people can read and write at least a little, many cannot read and write well enough to hold jobs in the economy.

This type of illiteracy is a major problem in the economy.

imperial policy. The economic control used by Spain to restrict its colonies is known as imperial policy. *See* Spanish colonial system.

import. Imports are goods produced in a foreign country and purchased in this country. For example, the United States now imports large amounts of petroleum from other nations.

income. Income is the amount of money received by an individual, a business, or a government. When an individual is paid wages, when a business sells its product, or when a government collects taxes, they have received income.

incubators. Incubators are governmentally sponsored programs to encourage the formation of small businesses within a community. Usually, they take the form of having the local government or development agency acquire a building in which, at low cost, it leases space to many small businesses just getting started. In addition to providing low-cost space, the business incubator also provides secretarial, receptionist, and bookkeeping services to these small firms. When the firm reaches a predetermined size it leaves the incubator and proceeds on its own.

independent power producers. Independent power producers are companies that generate electricity, but are not subject to public utility regulation. Independent producers do not operate under the same restrictions or requirements that electric utilities do. They do not have to serve all customers who request service. Independent power producers are also called nonutility power producers. *See* public utility.

index number. An index number is a statistical measure which allows for adjustments in a series of figures. For example, the Consumer Price Index is an index number used to measure inflation. It indicates how much the prices consumers pay have gone up over a given year. *See* Consumer Price Index; inflation.

industrial union. An industrial union organizes all workers whose jobs are in a particular industry. For example, the United Auto Workers is an industrial union to which all workers in the automobile industry may belong regardless of what their specific jobs are in automobile production. *Compare* craft union.

industrialization. Industrialization is the conversion of an economy from farming to manufacturing. The history of Texas has been one of industrialization. In the beginning, our economy was principally dependent upon agriculture and has slowly evolved into one primarily dependent upon manufacturing in major industries.

industry. An industry is a group of businesses which are involved in the production of a single type of product. For example, tourism is an industry in Texas. It involves a wide variety of firms, including hotels; motels; attractions such as amusement parks and sports facilities; restaurants; and gasoline stations. In addition, all of the other businesses that supply these businesses are part of the tourism industry.

inflation. Inflation is a general rise in the level of prices. Inflation occurs when the amount of money expands faster than the production of goods and services. Inflation always means that the value of money is depreciating or going down. For example, during the period of the Texas Republic the government issued a large amount of redbacks, which quickly lost their value and drove up prices, precipitating a financial crisis that ultimately led to Texas joining the Union. *See* redbacks.

infrastructure. The government facilities and projects that support an industry are known as infrastructure. Examples of infrastructure are roads and education. Without an adequate set of roads to transport goods and services, most Texas industries would not be successful. Without education, skilled workers would not be available to fill the jobs being created. Other examples of infrastructure are water and sewer facilities, and airports and other transportation terminals. *See* industry.

insatiable. In economics, this term refers to the fact that people always want more. They can never be satisfied. Even when one want is taken care of, another want emerges. Since people have unlimited wants, total demand is insatiable. *See* demand.

insolvent. Insolvent is another term for bankrupt. It means that the firm or an individual is no longer able to pay its bills. The expenses of the individual or the firm have exceeded its income and it has no way of paying the debts that it owes.

interest. Interest is what is paid for the use of another person's money. When an individual deposits money in a savings account he is paid interest because those savings are borrowed by someone else who uses them.

interest rate. The interest rate is the amount paid to an individual who allows others to use his or her money. Interest rates vary depending upon the length of time the money is borrowed and the risk associated with the borrower.

internationalization. Internationalization is the process by which Texas has become more and more dependent upon foreign countries as markets for the goods and services which are produced here. *See* globalization.

inventory.   Inventory is the supply of goods or products a business has available to sell to its customers. For example, the products one sees on the shelf in a grocery store are part of that store's inventory.

investor.   An investor is one who assists in financing a company by supplying it money. Investors may either buy shares in the company, in which case they are owners, or they may buy the company's bonds and loan it money. Investors expect not only to get their money back, but also to earn an income off their investment.

just and reasonable rates.   Utility rates in Texas are required to be just and reasonable. This means that regulatory agencies must allow the utilities to charge high enough rates to their customers to allow the utilities to stay in business. Just and reasonable rates include a fair rate of return to investors, which is the amount they could earn if they put their money into other investments. *See* public utility.

labor force.   Individuals between the ages of 16 and 65 who are willing and able to work are considered to be members of the labor force. Not all people are part of the labor force. Those who are too young, too old, sick, in prison, or unwilling to work are excluded.

labor-intensive service industry.   Labor-intensive service industries are those service trades that require a large amount of labor or workers in the production of the service. Examples of labor-intensive service industries are retail trade, health care, and education. *See* industry.

land speculator.   A land speculator is an individual who buys land in hopes that its price will increase and the land can be sold in the future at a profit. Many of the early settlers in Texas were lured to the state by cheap land which they hoped would increase in value and make them wealthy when they sold it.

legislation.   Legislation refers to the acts of lawmaking bodies. Bills, resolutions, and appropriations are all examples of legislation.

levy.   Levy is another term for a tax or a duty. It may also refer to the process of placing a tax or a duty on an individual or a product. When someone pays the state sales tax, the sales tax has been levied on the product. *See* sales tax; duty.

license.   A license is permission to do something. An example would be a driver's license. Fees are usually charged to people when licenses are granted to them.

line-item veto.   The line-item veto is the power that the governor has to veto or eliminate specific appropriations which the legislature has made. The President of the United States does not have the line-item veto power and must accept all of the items in an appropriations bill. The governor of the state of Texas may choose to accept most of the items in an appropriations bill, but the line-item veto allows him to strike those he does not agree with.

linkage.   Linkages are the relationships between businesses within a given industry. For example, there are obvious linkages between the individuals who drill for oil, the companies that transport oil, the firms that refine the oil, and those that distribute the final product to the customer. All industries are held together by these types of economic linkages. *See* industry.

livestock.   Livestock refers to the beef, dairy, lamb, poultry, pork, and goat production in the state of Texas. The production of livestock is a major component of the Texas economy. Texas leads the nation in the number of cattle and calves produced.

macroeconomics.   Macroeconomics is one of the two branches of study in economics. It focuses on the total performance of the economy rather than the performance of the parts of the economy. It is concerned with topics like economic growth, inflation, and unemployment. *See* microeconomics.

mandatory wheeling.   *See* wheeling.

maquiladora program.   Maquiladora is the Spanish term referring to the twin plant system. The term comes from the Spanish maquila which means flour mill. *See* twin plant system.

marginal analysis.   The word marginal refers to change or addition. Marginal analysis answers questions like: "What will happen to costs if we hire more workers? What will happen to sales if we raise prices by $10?" For example, if the cost to the firm of producing one additional automobile is $5,000, then the marginal cost of that automobile is $5,000. When one looks at changes one is doing marginal analysis.

market/marketplace.   A market or marketplace is where a buyer and a seller exchange goods and services. Markets may be very complex, such as the New York Stock Exchange, or very simple, like buying a hamburger at a fast food restaurant.

market area.   A market area is a geographic region which is economically tied together. A market area can generally be determined by where people buy certain goods or services. The market area of your town is the area from which people come to your town to purchase certain items. Market areas may vary in size. For example, the market area for groceries may be just a few miles or even a few blocks; while the market area for an airport may be 50 miles, 100 miles, or more.

market economic system.   Under the market system the economic decisions are made by consumers and producers interacting in the marketplace. A market economy is characterized by private ownership of property, self-interest motives (where people pursue what is best for them) and limited government involvement in economic decision making. Supply and demand determine market prices. The prices serve as signals to producers telling them what consumers want more of or less of. The prices also are signals to consumers causing them to change their consumption based on changes in prices. While not a pure market system, the United States comes the closest of any nation in the world.

market value.   The price at which a buyer and a seller exchange a good or service is its market value. A price is what a seller asks for something the seller places in the market. The price may have to be lowered in order to make a sale. The market value is the final price at which the trade is made.

market value of property.   What a piece of property such as a farm, house, factory, or retail building would sell for in the open market is said to be its market value. The market value of property is the basis for the property tax. The property tax base for a government, such as a city or school district, is the total market value of all property within the district minus some exemptions such as those for homesteads and the elderly. See property tax; assessed value.

marketing strategy.   A plan put into affect by a local government, chamber of commerce, or industrial development agency to sell a particular location's advantages and assets in order to attract new jobs and industries is called a marketing strategy. This strategy focuses upon bringing new plants into an area or region. Under this strategy new industries are picked and actively recruited. See economic development strategy.

marketplace.   See market.

Master Plan for Vocational Education.   The state Master Plan for Vocational Education was adopted in 1986. Its purpose is to redirect vocational education to provide vocational education students with a strong grounding in basic subjects in addition to preparing them with broad occupational skills.

maximize.   See economize.

mean.   Sometimes called the arithmetic mean, it is derived by adding all of the observations and dividing by the total number of observations. For example, to find the mean income in a community, add up the individual incomes and divide by the number of people. The mean is one measure of what statisticians call central tendency. (Other measures are the median and the mode.)

median.   The median is a measure of central tendency in statistics. It is the value at which half of the observations are above and half of the observations are below. For example, if you have 25 observations arranged from highest to lowest, the median will be the 13th observation on the list. (Other measures of central tendency are the mean and the mode.)

Medicare/Medicaid.   Medicare and Medicaid are governmental programs to assist certain groups of people in paying their medical bills. Medicare is a system of medical insurance for those people on Social Security. Medicaid is a program designed to assist low-income individuals with their medical bills.

medium of exchange.   Money serves a medium of exchange. A medium of exchange is anything accepted as a standard of value and used in market transactions.

merger.   A merger occurs when two firms become one. Firms often merge to improve their financial condition. Mergers may also take place in order to acquire a new product or to gain access to a new market. See acquisition.

metropolitan statistical area (MSA).   See urban area.

microeconomics.   Microeconomics is one of the two branches of the study of economics. It focuses on factors such as cost, productivity, supply, and demand. It deals with the parts of the economy such as a single consumer, business, or market. See macroeconomics.

migration.   Migration refers to the movement of people from one place to another. In recent years there has been a large migration of workers from Mexico, where wages and living conditions are lower, to Texas, where wages and living conditions are higher. Migrant groups have also included political refugees from Southeast Asia and Central America.

mission system.   During the period when Texas was a colony of Spain the mission system was established in Texas. The missions served three purposes—to convert the Indians to Christianity, to make them productive colonists, and to strengthen Spain's claim to the land. The mission economy was tightly controlled and highly restricted by the Spanish government. The Spanish government promised protection to the Indians and basic education. In return, the Indians were to supply crops to feed the mission and for export. Despite being successful in California, the mission system failed in Texas.

mode.   The mode is a measure of central tendency in statistics. It is the value which occurs most often. For example, if there are five observations, 10, 20, 20, 30, 40, then 20 is the mode. (Other measures of central tendency are the mean and the median.)

mohair.   Mohair is the wool of angora goats. It is an important product for Texas agriculture. It is very fine and highly valued for use in producing clothing. Texas produces 97 percent of all mohair in the United States.

monetary policy.   When the Federal Reserve wishes to change the amount of money in the economy it uses monetary policy. The discount rate, reserve requirements, and open market operations are the methods used by the Fed to control the money supply. See Federal Reserve System.

money supply.   Money supply refers to the total amount of money available to be spent in the economy. It consists of the coins and currency individuals have, plus the amounts of money they have in their checking accounts. Some economists would also add in savings accounts as part of the money supply.

monopoly.   A monopoly exists when there is only one supplier or source for a product. When monopoly exists there is no competition to insure low prices to consumers. The result of monopoly is often overcharging, as was the case with the railroad monopolies in Texas around the turn of the century. See competition.

motor fuel tax.   Motor fuel taxes are levied on the sale of gasoline. In Texas and most other states, motor fuel taxes are dedicated to pay for building and maintenance of roads and bridges. See dedicated revenue.

MSA (Metropolitan statistical area).   See urban area.

multiplier effect.   The multiplier effect is the respending that occurs when money introduced into a region's, state's, or nation's economy is spent again by the recipients. A new dollar of spending introduced into a region's economy may induce as much as $3 of income as it passes from hand to hand during the respending process. For example, when tourists from Iowa visit Texas they spend their money at hotels, motels, trailer parks, restaurants, and amusement facilities. These dollars are then respent throughout the economy as the owners and workers in those businesses spend the dollars again for the products they want. See spillover benefit.

Napoleonic Code.   The Napoleonic Code was the rules of law adopted by Mexico and applied to Texans during the period when Texas was a part of Mexico. The Napoleonic Code provided neither the civil nor the economic rights that were provided under the Anglo-Saxon system of justice.

National Industrial Recovery Administration (NIRA).   The National Industrial Recovery Administration was established in 1933 as part of the New Deal of President Roosevelt. It allowed industries to ignore antitrust legislation and to set prices for the products they sold. The idea was to insure businesses a profit through price setting. See New Deal.

National Labor Relations Act.   The National Labor Relations Act prohibited employers from discriminating against union members, allowed workers to join unions, and required management to engage in collective bargaining with unions. It was one of the acts passed by the Roosevelt Administration during the New Deal. See New Deal.

natural monopoly.   A natural monopoly results when one firm is more efficient in providing a good or service than many would be. This usually happens when there are large technical efficiencies or economies of scale involved in the production of the service. For example, one large electrical generating plant can produce electricity at a lower cost than many smaller less efficient plants could. See monopoly; efficiency; economy of scale.

natural resources.   The inputs that are found in the environment are called natural resources. Natural resources include oil, minerals, natural gas, and the fertility of the soil.

New Deal.   The New Deal was the legislation proposed by President Roosevelt and enacted by Congress during the early days of the Great Depression. It included such items as the Civilian Conservation Corps, the Public Works Administration, the Works Progress Administration, the

Federal Deposit Insurance Corporation, and the National Industrial Recovery Administration. *See* Great Depression.

nominal growth.   Nominal growth is the expansion of output without any adjustment being made for inflation. It measures both the increase in goods and services produced, and the increase in the prices of those goods and services. *See* economic growth; inflation; real growth.

nonprofit sector.   The nonprofit sector includes any business which is established for some other purpose than to earn a profit for its investors. Community service groups and clubs are examples. They may be motivated by a sense of achievement and the desire to see a community problem solved; their principal motivation is not to make money.

normative economics.   Normative economics is an approach to economics that makes use of values. Normative economics seeks to change economic conditions which do not agree with the commonly held values of society. For example, normative economics would consist of devising policies to reduce an unemployment rate that society felt was too high.

not-for-profit organization.   Any group or business which provides a good or service whose principal motive is not to make a profit. Not-for-profit organizations are often exempt from paying taxes. *See* nonprofit sector.

Obnoxious Acts.   The Obnoxious Acts were imposed by the federal government upon Texas and the other southern states after the Civil War. Among the Obnoxious Acts were those which excluded most white males from voting and gave the federally appointed governor the power to appoint local officials. *See* Reconstruction.

Occupational Safety and Health Administration (OSHA).   The Occupational Safety and Health Administration was established by Congress to enforce regulations protecting workers. Its responsibility is to make sure that the workplace is safe and that no hazardous conditions exist that might endanger the safety or health of the workers.

Office of the Comptroller of the Currency (OCC).   The Office of the Comptroller of the Currency is located within the U.S. Treasury Department and is responsible for seeing that all federal laws regarding national banks are adhered to. The Office of the Comptroller of the Currency also must approve new national banks before they can do business. *See* comptroller.

oil and natural gas production tax.   Oil and natural gas production taxes are levied on the market value of the oil and gas which is extracted in Texas. When the price of oil and natural gas is high, these taxes are good revenue producers, but in recent years when oil and natural gas prices have fallen, these taxes have become less productive revenue raisers.

oil boom/bust.   The oil boom/bust cycle which hit Texas during the 1970s and 1980s explains both the past prosperity of the state and its current financial dilemma. When the Organization of Petroleum Exporting Countries (OPEC) limited the amount of oil coming into the United States in the early 1970s, the price of oil boomed, creating great prosperity for Texas, the nation's leading oil-producing state. By the 1980s OPEC was no longer able to set the price for oil, and oil prices crashed. This led to an economic recession in Texas called the oil bust due to the state's overdependence on the oil industry. *See* Organization of Petroleum Exporting Countries; recession.

OPEC.   *See* Organization of Petroleum Exporting Countries.

open market operation.   The Federal Open Market Committee engages in what is called open market operations, which is the buying and selling of bonds in the open market. This is one way the Federal Reserve seeks to control the supply of money. By selling bonds to the general public and to the banks the amount of money in circulation is reduced. By buying bonds from the banks and the public the supply of money in the economy is increased. *See* Federal Reserve System.

opportunity cost.   In economics, opportunity cost is what has to be given up in order to get something else. It does not refer to the price of a product. The opportunity cost of going to a movie is what else could have been done in the time spent at the movie and what else could have been purchased with the money spent on the price of the ticket.

Organization of Petroleum Exporting Countries (OPEC).   OPEC is a cartel established by the governments of the oil producing countries, most of which are located in the Middle East. OPEC attempts to maintain a high price for oil by limiting the amount that each member country can produce. During the 1970s OPEC was very successful, but in recent years members have tended to cheat and overproduce. This has driven down the price of oil. *See* cartel.

original jurisdiction.   Original jurisdiction refers to which governmental body has the first responsibility to hear a request for a change in rates from a utility. In most instances, original jurisdiction for gas and electric companies rests with the cities that must pass upon the reasonability of the rate increase. The decisions of the cities can then be appealed by the utilities to either the Public Utility Commission (for electric utilities) or the Texas Railroad Commission (for gas utilities). *See* Public Utility Commission; Texas Railroad Commission.

outlay. Outlay is another term for expenditure. It is the amount that must be paid to obtain a good or service in the marketplace.

pay-as-you-go provision. The pay-as-you-go provision in the Texas constitution requires that revenues must equal expenditures for most state functions. This means that an expenditure cannot be made until provision has been made for the revenue to pay for it. *See* revenue.

per capita. Per capita, meaning "per head," is a statistical average or mean. It is found by taking all of the observations and dividing by the number of people. For example, if you want to know the per capita income in a nation, you add up all of the individual incomes and divide by the number of people. *See* mean.

Permanent School Fund (PSF). The Permanent School Fund has existed in Texas since the 1800s. Monies in the Permanent School Fund are dedicated to the support of education in the state. The public domain or state-owned lands are sold and the income from those land sales is invested in stocks and bonds. The income of those stocks and bonds is then used to support public education. *See* dedicated revenue.

Petri dish strategy. The Petri dish strategy of economic development borrows a term from laboratory science. Under this approach to economic development, a community or area attempts to create a total economic environment which will induce new firms to locate there. It holds that government should work to improve education, health care, streets, water, and other government services, and that these superior services will attract new industry. *See* economic development strategy.

positive economics. Positive economics is principally concerned with giving factual explanations about economic conditions as they exist. It makes no evaluation as to whether those conditions are good or bad, but merely seeks to discuss them and describe them as accurately as possible. *Compare* normative economics.

pricing distortion. Pricing distortion results from social pricing. Some people's rates are too high since what they must pay is in excess of the cost of providing them utility service. Other people pay too little since their rates do not cover the cost of providing the service to them. Long-distance telephone rates are usually set above cost so that local services can be provided below cost. *See* social pricing.

principle of diminishing returns. The principle of diminishing returns describes consumer behavior. It means that each additional unit provides less satisfaction than did the previous units. For example, on a hot day the first cool drink will provide a great deal of satisfaction. The second cool drink will provide less satisfaction, the third even less, and so on.

private property. Private property refers to individual ownership of the factors of production. It is an essential characteristic of a market economy. Individuals rather than the state own the means of production. For example, individuals own their own labor. Individual ownership of labor is then a private property right which people may exercise in a market system. *See* market economy.

production sharing. Production sharing exists when an item manufactured in the United States is assembled in Mexico. It is an essential feature of the twin plant (maquiladora) program. *See* twin plan program.

productivity. Productivity refers to the change in output for each worker. If each additional worker's output increases during each hour worked, then productivity has gone up. If the output for each hour worked goes down, then productivity has fallen.

professional liability. Professional liability is a legal term referring to the concept that providers of health care and other services are responsible for the results of their professional activities. For example, doctors are being held liable for mistakes they make in the diagnosis and treatment of their patients. When doctors make mistakes, they can be forced by the courts to pay for the harm they cause.

profit. This term can have two meanings. One way of defining profit is the difference between income and expenses for a business firm. Under this definition, profit is what is left over after the business has paid all of its expenses. High profits serve as an indicator to businesses to expand production, while low profits have a discouraging effect. Profit also may be viewed as the reward an entrepreneur receives for having taken the risks of bringing new products, services, or technologies to the marketplace. Without profit as an incentive, entrepreneurial activity would not be forthcoming. *See* entrepreneur.

profit margin. The difference between a firm's income and its expenses is called its profit margin. It is often expressed as a percentage of the gross income of a firm. For example, if a firm has $1 million in revenue and $900,000 in expenses, its profit margin is 10 percent.

profit motive.   The profit motive is the principal incentive in a market economic system. It explains most business behavior. Businesses seek to produce those items where they will make the greatest profit. Consumers reward with profits those producers that manufacture or supply what they want. *See* market economic system.

property tax.   The property tax is the basic source of support for cities and school districts in Texas. It is levied on all property in the area. The property tax rate is expressed in cents per $100 value. For example, a $2 tax rate would mean that the tax bill on a $100,000 house would be $2,000. *See* market value; assessed value.

prospective payment system.   Under the prospective payment system, hospital and medical providers are no longer paid by the federal government under Medicare and Medicaid on the basis of the cost of providing certain treatments. Instead, they receive a flat fee determined beforehand and based on the diagnosis of the patient's ailment. If the hospital's costs are greater than the payment, they profit. If the care costs more, the hospital loses money. Prospective payments are now usually less than the costs of providing medical treatment. As a result, many Texas hospitals currently find themselves in financial difficulties. *See* Medicare/Medicaid.

proven reserves.   The amount of oil or natural gas that is known to exist and that can be extracted using current technology is called proven reserves. Recent years have seen dramatic decreases in the amount of proven reserves of oil and natural gas in Texas. The lower the price of oil, the less incentive there is to go out and develop new proven reserves.

public assistance.   Public assistance refers to payments made by the government to individuals with low incomes or special problems. Sometimes this is called welfare spending. Examples are food stamps, Medicaid, and housing subsidies.

public utility.   Public utilities are natural monopolies which provide an essential service to individuals. Examples are electric and natural gas companies. As natural monopolies, utilities face no competitors and are therefore regulated by the government, as to the price they can charge and the service they must provide their customers. *See* natural monopoly; Public Utility Commission.

Public Utilities Regulatory Practices Act (PURPA). This law was passed in 1978. It encourages large industrial plants to generate electrical power as a by-product of their manufacturing process. *See* utility; by-product; cogeneration.

Public Utility Commission.   The Public Utility Commission was established in 1975 to regulate electric companies in Texas. It is responsible for setting rates and determining the quality of service that electric utilities must provide their customers. *See* public utility.

Public Works Administration.   The Public Works Administration was established to undertake certain public works projects in Texas and other states during the Great Depression. *See* Great Depression.

pure-public goods and services.   Certain goods and services such as national defense would not be provided by the market. We want national defense, but no one would be willing to pay for it because those who do not pay could not be excluded. Therefore, everyone would want someone else to pay the bill. Because everyone consumes the same amount of a public good at the same time, everyone would hope that someone else would pay for it.

PURPA.   *See* Public Utilities Regulatory Practices Act.

quota.   A quota is a limit or a restriction. For example, the United States places quotas on some products produced in foreign countries to be imported here. No more than what the quota allows can be brought into this country.

Radical Republicans.   The term Radical Republicans applies to the Senators and Representatives from the northern states who wanted to punish the south for having seceded from the Union. During Reconstruction the Radical Republicans gained control of Congress and passed legislation that severely restricted the ability of the south to govern itself. *See* Reconstruction; Obnoxious Acts.

raider.   A raider is a businessman who attempts to take over another company. Raiders are always looking for businesses that they feel are poorly managed so they can take them over and run them more efficiently and more profitably. One of the nation's best known raiders is T. Boone Pickens of Amarillo. *See* acquisition.

rain-fed states.   A rain-fed state is one where there is sufficient rainfall to support agriculture without irrigation. The eastern part of Texas is rain-fed. This is not true for west Texas.

range wars. The range wars occurred in the late 1870s in Texas. They happened because the farmers erected barbed-wire fences to keep the roaming herds of cattle off the land and out of their crops. Ranchers were opposed to this practice and often cut fences and in other ways harassed the farmers. Often this resulted in violent confrontation between the farmers and the ranchers.

rate making. Regulatory bodies that oversee public utilities are responsible for rate making. Rate making occurs when a utility wishes to change a rate currently being charged customers. The utility must demonstrate to the satisfaction of the regulatory body that there is a justification for that change. Regulatory agencies are to set rates that allow utilities to earn rates of return or profits which are at least equal to those which could be earned by utility investors if they put their money in other industries. See public utility; Public Utility Commission.

rational. In economics, rational means that people behave as they are expected to. For example, when consumers decide to purchase or not to purchase a product, they consider all factors which will give them satisfaction, not just the product price. This is rational behavior.

real growth. The expansion of output in the economy adjusted for the impact of inflation. If nominal GNP (in current prices) goes up by 6 percent, but prices have gone up by 3 percent, real growth has been only 3 percent. See economic growth; nominal growth; inflation; Gross National Product.

recession. A recession is a general downturn in the level of economic activity. Recessions are usually characterized by falling incomes and rising unemployment. See unemployment.

Reconstruction. Reconstruction was the period of time following the Civil War. The purpose of Reconstruction was to reintegrate the southern states back into the Union. In Texas, Reconstruction ended in 1874 when local elected officials regained control of the state government from the Radical Republicans. See Radical Republicans.

Reconstruction Finance Corporation. The Reconstruction Finance Corporation was established by President Hoover in 1932 to provide loans to banks, insurance companies, and other businesses. The purpose of these loans was to help these firms deal with the financial problems created by the Great Depression. See Great Depression.

redbacks. Redbacks were money issued by the Texas Congress in 1840. These were noninterest-bearing notes and were issued in unlimited amounts. As a result, they very quickly devalued. They were called "redbacks" because the backs of the notes were printed in red ink. See devaluation.

relative scarcity. The term applies to goods and services which are scarce relative to the demand by consumers for them. Some things may be scarce, but no one wants them. Other things, while abundant, may be relatively scarce because there is a tremendous demand for them. Everything is scarce, but not all things are relatively scarce. See demand; supply.

research and development (R&D). Research and development refers to the discovery of new technologies and their applications to the production of goods and services. R&D is a major activity which is critical to the economic future of Texas. Devising new technologies and implementing them is what will make the Texas economy and the United States economy prosperous in the years to come.

reserve requirement. Reserve requirement refers to the amount of money that must be held by a bank as backing for its deposits. This is usually expressed as a fraction. A 15 percent reserve requirement means a bank must keep 15 percent of its deposits as reserves. The rest of its deposits can be loaned.

reservoirs. When a river is dammed and water stored behind it, a reservoir has been created. Sometimes called surface water, reservoirs are becoming an increasingly important source of water for Texans.

resource. A resource is anything that can be used to create value. It may refer to natural resources such as minerals and the fertility of the land. People are also resources since they create value. Anything that can be used to create a product or a service is a resource.

retail. Retail is the final step in the production process where customers buy the product for their own individual use. When a product is bought at retail it is not being purchased to be sold again. Compare wholesale.

retail sales tax. The retail sales tax is levied on every sale of goods in states that impose the tax. In Texas, some items such as food and prescription drugs have been exempted from the retail sales tax to make it fairer to low income and ill people. The sales tax is paid by the retailer to the state government, but the retailer passes it on to customers who find it added to the price of the product. *See* tax revenue.

revenue.   The amount of money received by a firm or by a government is called its revenue. Governments receive revenue from taxes, fees, and borrowing. Businesses receive revenues when they sell their goods or services in the marketplace.

revenue shortfall.   A revenue shortfall occurs anytime a government's revenue is not equal to its expenditures. In Texas, according to the Texas Constitution, this is not supposed to happen in the state. The legislature is to pass a balanced budget .

right-to-work state.   States which do not require that workers join unions in order to keep their jobs are known as right-to-work states. Under federal law unless a state passes legislation to the contrary, what is known as the union shop prevails. Under the union shop arrangement if a union has been voted in by the workers, then a person must join the union in order to keep the job. In a right-to-work state, even if a union has been voted in, the open shop prevails and workers do not have to join the existing union. A third shop, the closed shop, is generally illegal in the United States. Under the closed shop arrangement a person must join the union before he can be considered for a job.

rollback election.   A rollback election is provided for by Texas law whenever property taxes rise by more than 8 percent. If a city or a school district raises property taxes in excess of this percentage, then the voters by petition may call for an election. If the majority of voters favor the rollback, then the property taxes the next year must be reduced. *See* property tax.

S&L.   *See* savings and loan association.

savings and loan association (S&L).   Savings and loan associations specialize in providing funds to individuals wanting to buy their own homes. Under recent legislation, savings and loan associations have been allowed to make loans to businesses and industries. Currently, many Texas savings and loans are in trouble and have been forced either to go out of business or to be sold to other financial institutions. *Compare* commercial banks.

secession.   Secession occurs when one part of a nation leaves the rest of that nation to form an independent country or state. Immediately preceding the Civil War, the southern states, including Texas, seceded from the Union and formed their own nation called the Confederate States of America.

selective breeding.   Selective breeding occurs when farmers and ranchers select the best animals and breed them to produce offspring which possess certain desirable characteristics. For example, the selective breeding of cattle has allowed for animals that produce meat with less fat and that gain weight much more rapidly. Selective breeding is part of the genetic revolution which is sweeping the livestock industry.

service area.   The territory that a public utility is required to furnish power in is called its service area. Within that service area the public utility may not decline to furnish electrical service to anyone who requests it. *See* public utility.

service-driven economy.   A service-driven economy is one that is more dependent upon firms producing services for income and jobs than it is on manufacturing. Both the United States and Texas are becoming more and more service-driven economies. This is not because manufacturing is declining, but because the service industries are growing faster. *See* service industry.

service industry.   Service industries are those that are not involved in producing manufactured goods. The service sector includes firms that operate in health, transportation, communications, public utilities, retail trade, wholesale distribution, finance, real estate, and government. In recent years, services have grown faster as part of the American economy than has the production of goods. This has also been true in Texas.

service sector.   The service sector refers to firms which produce services rather than manufactured goods. *See* service industry.

services.   Services are those things that consumers desire, other than tangible products. Examples of services are health care, education, retail sales, wholesale trade, government, finance, communication, entertainment, and real estate.

shareholder.   A shareholder is one who has bought shares or stock in a corporation. Shareholders own the corporation, but as owners they are not responsible for the debts of the corporation. Shareholders buy shares with the expectation that they will earn an income (called dividends) on their shares. *See* dividends.

social pricing.   Social pricing is what happens when regulatory agencies set prices so as to benefit one group at the expense of the other. For example, in the telephone industry rates are set high for some customers so that rates can be set low for other customers. Social pricing has little to do with economics, but it reflects the values of the regulatory bodies which feel that some people should receive a utility service at a reduced rate. *See* public utility; Public Utility Commission.

Southwest Plan.   During the late 1980s many Texas banks were failing. The Southwest Plan was a method devised by the federal government to merge weak and failing savings and loans with stronger ones. Over 100 insolvent savings and loans were merged under this plan in 1987. *See* savings and loan.

Spanish colonial system.   When Texas was a Spanish colony, Spain attempted to impose a command economy. The Spanish colonial system was based on the establishment of missions and the restricting of trade to keep the Texas colonists dependent upon Spain and Mexico. *See* command economy; mission system.

specializing.   When an individual or a firm produces only one good or service they are said to be specializing. Most producers specialize in a single product or service or a group of products or services which are closely related. By specializing in what they do best they are able to be more productive and to increase their income. Regions also engage in specialization, producing products in which they have an advantage over other regions. There is specialization of fruit and vegetable farming in the Texas Valley because of its excellent year-round climate.

spending by object.   Spending by object refers to one of the ways by which a government accounts for its spending. Rather than accounting for its spending by functions such as highways, defense, or education, it classifies them by object, such as salaries, supplies, and operating expenses.

spending dedications.   *See* dedicated revenue.

spillover benefit.   A spillover benefit results when individuals or industries which are not directly involved in the production of a product benefit from that product's production. For example, all Texans benefit from the tourism industry. While the primary beneficiaries are the hotels, motels, restaurants, and attractions where the tourists spend their dollars, the benefits spill over to other Texans when those who work at the hotels, motels, restaurants, and attractions spend their incomes at other businesses. *See* multiplier effect.

stability.   Stability refers to the equilibrium condition in a marketplace when supply and demand are equal to each other. *See* supply; demand; equilibrium.

standard of living.   How many goods and services people are able to consume is their standard of living. The standard of living is related directly to people's incomes. The higher a person's income is, the more goods and services they can purchase and the higher their standard of living will be.

star money.   Star money was issued by the Republic of Texas during the administration of Sam Houston. These were interest-bearing notes issued by the Republic of Texas which served as money. Because they were issued in limited amounts and redeemed by the Republic at face value they did not devalue. They were called "star money" because the Texas lone star was printed on the notes. *See* devaluation.

stock exchange.   A stock exchange is where the shares or stock of corporations are traded. The largest stock exchange is the New York Stock Exchange where hundreds of millions of shares of American businesses are bought and sold each business day.

superconductivity.   Superconductivity occurs when various materials are put under pressure to reduce electrical resistance. Research in superconductivity is currently in its infancy, but it promises to be a growth industry in Texas and across the United States in years to come.

supply.   Supply is the total amount that producers will put on the market at all possible prices. As a general rule, if price goes up producers are willing to put more on the market than they were at lower prices. *Compare* demand.

supply-side economics.   Supply-side economics seeks to expand the level of economic activity by increasing the supply of goods and services produced in the economy. Supply-side economics consists of tax cuts and other legislation favorable to businesses, which will hopefully induce them to produce more at a lower cost. *See* supply.

tariff.   A tariff is a tax or duty placed upon products imported into a country.

tax revenue.   The amount that is collected each year from a tax on a specific product or economic activity. For example, the money collected from the tax levied on oil and natural gas production in Texas is tax revenue for the state.

technical efficiency.   *See* efficiency.

technological competitive advantage.   The term technological competitive advantage refers to an edge that one city or area would have over another in attracting industry. An area with a major research university and an abundant supply of highly educated, technically trained people would have a technologically competitive advantage over other possible sites that a high-tech firm would be considering for its location. *See* competitive position; *compare* cost competitive advantage.

technology-based industry.   A technology-based industry depends upon the use of high technology to produce either its goods or services. Computer manufacture is an example of a technology-based industry.

telecommunications.   Many of the firms in the information industry are said to be in telecommunications. Telecommunications involves the transmission of data from one point to another. Television is one form of telecommunications, as are automatic teller machines, computer linkages, and fax machines (which allow us to send copies over long distances). When most of us think of telecommunications we think of the phone company.

tenant farmer system.   Under the tenant farmer system a farmer works the land owned by another individual. Since the farmer does not own the land he is a tenant. Usually the tenant farmer pays the landowner by sharing with the landowner a certain proportion or percentage of the crop grown on the land.

Texas Railroad Commission.   The Texas Railroad Commission was established in 1891 to regulate Texas railroads. Since then it has assumed the responsibility for regulating not only the railroads and other transportation companies, but gas utilities, as well. It shares these responsibilities with the cities in the state of Texas. *See* original jurisdiction; *compare* Public Utility Commission.

think tank.   A think tank is a group of scientists and researchers brought together to investigate a specific problem or to develop new technologies. Think tanks sell the results of their studies to firms and government agencies that make use of them. One very important think tank is the Microcomputer Technology Corporation located in Austin.

thrift institutions.   *See* savings and loan associations.

tidelands.   Tidelands refers to the 12-mile area off the coast of a particular state. The question arose in the 1950s as to who owned the Texas tidelands—the federal government or the state of Texas. The reason why ownership was important was that the owner would receive the benefit of the vast amounts of offshore oil found in these tidelands. After a long dispute, Texas was finally able to gain control of the Texas tidelands and the oil under them.

tight job market.   A tight job market is a situation where the demand for workers exceeds the supply. In a tight job market wages rise, reflecting the scarcity of workers. In Texas, a tight job market is

continuing to develop for highly trained and skilled workers. *See* demand; supply.

trade deficit.   The amount by which a nation's imports exceed its exports is called its trade deficit. Imports are what we buy from businesses located in other countries. Exports are what our businesses sell to people located elsewhere in the world. When we sell to foreigners, money flows into the United States. When we buy from foreigners, money flows out from the United States. Recently, the United States has been running a significant trade deficit.

trade restrictions.   Any legislation which limits the flow of goods and services across the political boundary is a trade restriction. Tariffs and import quotas are frequently used as a way of controlling trade between governments. For example, when Texas was a Spanish colony, Spain allowed Texans to trade only with Mexico and not with the United States, even though trade with the United States would have been more profitable.

traditional economic system.   Rules and beliefs handed down from the past form the basis for a traditional economic system. All economic decisions are made according to the rules and traditions established by society. What is produced, how it is produced, and who gets it, are determined by the rules of the family, clan, or tribe. There is very little use of money or exchange. Traditional economies are generally associated with backward economic societies, although all economies will contain some traditional elements.

transaction.   A transaction is when a buyer and a seller exchange a good or service for money. Transactions happen in a marketplace when one individual buys something from another individual.

twin plant system.   The twin plant system refers to when a company operates on both sides of the United States/Mexican border. The product is often designed and distributed from the U.S. side, while being manufactured and assembled in Mexico where labor is cheaper.

tycoon.   Tycoon is a slang word used to refer to a successful business entrepreneur. The image of a tycoon is one who has achieved great monetary success and controls a large business empire. *See* entrepreneur.

unemployment.   Unemployment exists when people in the labor force who are looking for jobs are unable to find them. *See* labor force.

unemployment rate.   The unemployment rate measures how many people are out of work. More precisely, it refers to the percentage of the labor force that cannot find jobs. An individual is not considered to be unemployed unless he or she is actively looking for a job. *See* labor force.

union. A union is an organization of workers that bargains or negotiates with the managers of a business over wages, hours or other conditions in the workplace. When the majority of workers vote to have a union, then the union speaks for the workers in that business. The union negotiates with management for all the employees of the firm.

urban area. An urban area is a single city or a group of cities which are near to each other. The federal government designates certain urban areas as metropolitan statistical areas (MSAs) and keeps statistics on economic activity within these areas. An urban area may be quite extensive, as is the Dallas/Fort Worth Metroplex, or it may be relatively small, as is San Angelo. *Compare* market area.

utility. *See* public utility.

value added. When a manufacturer takes raw material and makes a finished product out of it, the manufacturer has added value to that raw material. Value added is the amount by which the worth of an item is increased by having additional processing done to it. The price of any product is the sum of the value added at each step in the production process.

venture capital. When a firm is getting established it needs money to go into business or to begin the venture. The funds that are raised to start the business are called venture capital. Oftentimes, venture capital comes from a group of investors who are willing to take an ownership position in a new firm supplying it with the needed start-up money in the hopes that it will later become successful. *See* capital.

water mining. Water mining occurs when water is taken from the aquifer in a greater amount than the

aquifer can replace. Water is taken out of an aquifer by wells for municipal use or farm irrigation. Water is returned to an aquifer by rainfall seeping through the ground into the underground river or lake. When the amount extracted is greater than the amount returned then water mining or depletion has taken place. *See* aquifer.

weighted average. A weighted average is a way of adjusting the mean to reflect the importance of some of the items used in the calculation. For example, the Consumer Price Index consists of 400 different items, but since food products constitute 30 percent of the expenditures of an average household, those items are "weighted" so as to make up 30 percent of the Consumer Price Index. *See* mean; Consumer Price Index.

wheeling/mandatory wheeling. Wheeling occurs when an electric utility company transports power generated by another company along its electrical lines to serve the other company's customer. When a utility does this voluntarily, charging the other company for the use of its lines, it is called voluntary wheeling. When the government forces a utility to transmit another company's power at a predetermined price, this is called mandatory wheeling.

wholesale. Wholesale is the level in the productive process where goods and services are sold to retailers who will later sell them to their customers. Those engaged in wholesale trade buy products from manufacturers and then sell them to retail stores. *Compare* retail.

workforce. *See* labor force.

Works Progress Administration. The Works Progress Administration was responsible for many thousands of projects in Texas and other states during the Great Depression. Its activities focused on the building of streets and highways, public buildings, parks, and airports. It was designed to put people to work improving their communities. *See* Great Depression.

INDEX